COLLECTING AMERICAN 19TH CENTURY SILVER

COLLECTING AMERICAN 19TH CENTURY SILVER

by Katharine Morrison McClinton

AUTHOR OF *COLLECTING AMERICAN VICTORIAN ANTIQUES*

BONANZA BOOKS • NEW YORK

FRONTIS. One of a pair of urns presented to Governor DeWitt Clinton, 1825, showing a view of the Erie Canal. Fletcher and Gardiner. *Courtesy of the Chamber of Commerce of the State of New York.*

ACKNOWLEDGMENTS

A NUMBER of collectors, colleagues in libraries and museums, and officials of silver companies have helped in locating material and photographs used in this book. The list is long and I am grateful for the help of each and every one.

Special thanks go to the well-known collector of American silver, Philip H. Hammerslough, for the pleasure of studying his collection, for photographs, and for his reading of chapters I and II. Also to J. Herbert Gebelein for many excellent photographs and notes and reading part of the manuscript. E. P. Hogan, Historical Research Librarian for The International Silver Company, has also supplied information and photographs.

A special note of gratitude is due to Russell Price, Director of the Design Department of The Gorham Company, for the use of the library, catalogues and photograph files, and for many photographs. Also a thank-you to Russell Woodward, Ann Holbrook and W. Dan Lemeshka of The Gorham Company. S. Kirk Millspaugh, Vice President, and Emanuel Levine of Samuel Kirk & Son were most generous in supplying photographs, as were Stafford P. Osborn of Reed & Barton; T. H. Hoffman of Shreve & Co., and Arthur L. Roy of Towle Silversmiths.

A thank-you to the curators of various museums, including George O. Bird, The Henry Ford Museum; Harriet R. Cabot, The Bostonian Society; Louisa Dresser, Worcester Art Museum; Judith Conrad, The Cleveland Museum; Calvin S. Hathaway, Philadelphia Museum of Art; Carol Macht, Cincinnati Art Museum; Nancy O. Merrill, The Chrysler Museum of Provincetown; Norman S. Rice, Albany Institute of History and Art; Marvin Schwartz, The Brooklyn Museum; Carolyn Scoon, The New-York Historical Society; J. Stewart Johnson, The Newark Museum; John D. Kilbourne, The Historical Society of Pennsylvania; Charles A. Wood, Marine Corps Museum; Dale Mayberry, Capt. U. S. N. (Ret.), United States Naval Academy Museum. A special thanks to Jay P. Altmayer for notes and photographs of swords from his collection. Also special thanks to Grace R. Curtis, Reference Librarian, Grand Lodge, F. & A. Masons of The State of New York, for reading the chapter on Masonic jewels. Also to the following: Earl W. Taylor, Grand Secretary, The Most Worshipful Grand

Lodge A.F. & A.M., of the Commonwealth of Massachusetts; Charles S. Baker, Jr., Assistant Librarian, Masonic Temple, Philadelphia; Oliver Lloyd Onion, Chairman, Archives Committee, Alexandria-Washington Lodge No. 22. A.F. & A.M. Edward Buchmaster, Curator, The George Washington Masonic National Memorial Association; Arthur Gay, Grand Secretary, The Most Worshipful Grand Lodge, A.F. & A.M., of The Commonwealth of Virginia; George G. Walker, Secretary, King Solomon's Lodge A.F. & A.M., Somerville, Massachusetts; William C. Murray, Past Master, Historian, St. John's Lodge No. 2, A.F. & A.M., Middletown, Connecticut; Raymond W. Morse, Secretary, Washington Lodge A.F. & A.M., Lexington, Massachusetts; and finally to Carl Uddo Zachrisson, Past Master, Oriental Lodge, A.F. & A.M., San Francisco, California, who gave me instruction in Masonic symbolism. S. Victor Constant, Colonel U.S.A., Governor of the Society of Colonial Wars, provided the photograph of the Society's bowl.

Helen Rose Cline made the silver at Trinity Church, New York City, available for study and photographing, and The Reverend Edward N. West, Canon, Cathedral of St. John the Divine, New York City, furnished photographs of the silver in the collection of the Cathedral.

For assistance and photographs of San Francisco silver: Mrs. H. W. E. Erskine, Curator of Art, and James deT. Abajian, Librarian, California Historical Society; Dr. Elliot Evans, Curator, Society of California Pioneers; Paul F. Evans, Editor, Western Collector; and Mr. and Mrs. Carl Uddo Zachrisson.

TABLE OF CONTENTS

COLLECTING
AMERICAN
19TH CENTURY
SILVER

I *Collecting American Nineteenth Century Silver*

Now that the silver of the nineteenth century is of serious interest to collectors, many articles of grandmother's day which have been in drawers or back shelves of the china closet are being brought out for display on the sideboard. However, much of this silver, like that of earlier centuries, has been destroyed or re-shaped into newer-styled pieces, for the housewife was always interested in the latest styles. In *Pintard's Diary,* 1831 (Vol. 3, p. 243), Mrs. Pintard expresses dislike for the "antiquated teapot, old tankards and mugs," which she considers "quite a bore" and would like to "exchange for something modern."

Not all of the products of the nineteenth century silversmiths are attractive but the pieces bear the distinguishing characteristics of the era, and although they may not have the touch of a well-known silversmith or trade-mark of a silver manufacturer, the mark which they bear may lead to the discovery of a yet unknown local craftsman and thus give added information about nineteenth century silver and silversmiths.

Collecting nineteenth century American silver can be as interesting and as rewarding as collecting that of the earlier periods. However, your sights and goals are different and your taste must be readjusted to that of the era. First we learned that silver before 1800 was good design and any silver after that date was bad taste. Then the criterion of good taste was moved to the 1830's. Now with a reappraisal of the taste and times of Queen Victoria the canons of good taste include the decorative arts of the middle and late nineteenth century and we find that there were not only good furniture designers but also silversmiths of taste and ability working in nineteenth century America. However, we are in disputable territory and when a piece is labeled rare or fine it must be judged in relation to its period, since most of the silver of the nineteenth century does not fit the aesthetic standards of earlier periods. In many instances the designs were not only bad but there was a misuse of materials by the silversmiths who, in order to produce sensational effects, imitated the literary approach to the arts as seen in the works of sculpture and painting of the period.

As silversmithing was one of the finest crafts practiced in Colonial America, so it was also one of the earliest. The seventeenth and eighteenth centuries were the great periods in American silver. Early American silver collecting is now in the realm of the museum or advanced collector of unlimited means. It is not territory for the beginning collector. Also, the scarcity of important early pieces creates a situation that puts such silver practically out of reach of the beginning collector, for when a dealer has a piece of early silver he usually contacts a museum or one of his important collectors who are always waiting to buy valuable pieces. Thus, unless the amateur has considerable money to invest he should skip the silver of the early periods and look to the nineteenth century.

Until recently, nineteenth century American silver was scorned and considered heavy, cumbersome and lacking in artistic merit. However, the present-day interest in nineteenth century American architecture, art and decorative arts including silver has brought about a revaluation and kindled an interest in the later silver, and this, together with the scarcity of earlier pieces, has created a demand for nineteenth century silver. For many years nineteenth century silver, particularly of the Victorian Era, (1837–1901), was only to be found in historical societies and local museums, where it was acceptable because of its association with an important personage or events of national or local interest. Now this silver, especially that of the first quarter of the nineteenth century, is collected by major museums and important advanced collectors. Because of this interest prices have increased and not too many pieces reach the general market.

Much has been written about Early American silver and its makers. In addition to several general books, there are books on regional silver, books on individual silversmiths, and specialized books on marks as well as catalogues of museum exhibitions, and private collections. However, the major part of this literature relates to the early period of the seventeenth and eighteenth centuries or at most covers only the first quarter of the nineteenth century. The first museum exhibition of nineteenth century American silver was that included in the exhibition "Classical America 1815–1845" held at the Newark Museum in 1963. Studies of regional silversmiths of St. Louis, Missouri; Charleston, South Carolina; Vermont, Ohio, Kentucky, and other localities have been made and local exhibitions have collected and exhibited their works, but this material has never been gathered together and for collectors of later American silver there is no general guide. In fact, little is known about the silversmiths and silver manufacturers of the last three quarters of the nineteenth century. Many companies which came into being in the era and which are still in existence have lost the records of their early years. Others do not consider it worthwhile to search out the old records in their storerooms. Thus, any study of their output is deprived of such valuable sources as old day books, bills or other business details, and must rely for the most part on literature such as newspapers, magazines and the occasional mention in diaries of the period.

This book is written to help fill the gap. I have endeavored to search out and gather together information about the silver of the later periods of American silversmithing and also to record data not hitherto available. This is a general book designed to give the beginning collector a survey of the period. Many silver experts have been studying the early periods and the list of Early American silversmiths is now almost complete, but since there has been little interest in nineteenth century silver until recently the field is still open and the research just beginning, so that there is room for discovery. Records of many localities such as California, Nevada and Colorado are not complete. Names of silversmiths unknown up to now are constantly being added to the list of nineteenth century American silversmiths. There is no limit to the possibilities of the subject. Only a thorough search of city directories, histories, newspapers and legal documents of each locality would make possible a history of all of the companies making silver in America in the nineteenth century. But one cannot go on forever. This book is a beginning. It is hoped that it will create interest and stimulate others to continue the research.

To supply the collector with a comprehensive knowledge of the silver made and available, the material is divided into chronological periods, illustrating the styles and dominant characteristics of each period and listing the articles made in each period. A general survey such as this does not call for intensive specialization such as lists of silversmiths or reproductions of their marks. There are a number of volumes already in print which give this data. Also, for the advanced collector there is information dealing with the characteristic differences of the silver of various geographical locations in exhibit catalogues of museums. Since this book is for the beginning collector such detailed information is not given here but the various sources are listed in the bibliography.

The American silversmith was at the height of his achievement in the seventeenth and eighteenth centuries. Purity of form and perfection of line based on geometrical shapes were preferred to elaborate design. The articles were simple in shape, solid in weight, and relied on the beauty of the metal itself and the structural design rather than the skill of the worker to produce added surface decoration. Articles made by Early American silversmiths reflect the customs of Colonial days. Our early ancestors drank from beakers, caudle cups, canns, tankards, and standing cups. These articles were used in the church as well as in the Colonial household. Porringers, pepper boxes, braziers, brandy warmers and pipe lighters were also necessary early pieces. Early articles of personal use included waistcoat buttons, shoe and knee buckles, sword hilts, spectacles and cases, thimbles, bobbins and bodkins. Nutmeg boxes, snuff and patch boxes were also required items in the eighteenth century. Also, the punch bowl was popular and punch strainers, wine siphons, and punch ladles were much in use.

In the late eighteenth and early nineteenth centuries, when living became more ceremonious, the custom of tea drinking increased and tea was a household necessity. The tea and coffee service became popular and took the place of the earlier single teapot, coffee pot or chocolate pot. Tea caddies, caddy spoons, and sugar tongs were in great demand. With more luxurious living, other specialized articles of silver such as coasters, caster sets, dish rings, fish slices, grape scissors, and asparagus tongs were required. Many of these pieces remained in popular usage down through the nineteenth century, but some articles such as nutmeg graters, patch boxes, punch strainers, and tea caddies, when no longer used because of changing customs, were discontinued. In their place many new articles were demanded by later customs and the increased prosperity and wealth of the average nineteenth century American citizen. New pieces seen on the nineteenth century table included tête-à-tête sets, knife rests, napkin rings, and spoons and forks for serving various foods such as orange spoons, berry forks, cake knives, jelly spoons, carving sets, oyster forks, small after-dinner coffee spoons, and individual forks for different courses.

The spirit of the age and the political and social events of each era are reflected in the subject matter of silver design. The Federal Style makes use of the eagle and star and other patriotic symbols and the age of agricultural expansion incorporates agrarian motifs such as wheat sheaves, plow and scythe and baskets of fruit and flowers. Even the literature and poetry of an era are reflected in silver design. The evolution and gradual change from the simple to the more elaborate forms and greater variety of articles made in the later periods is interesting in that it reflects the growing luxury and more complex life of the early and late Victorian period in America. The nineteenth century gentleman no longer wore knee and shoe buckles, but he continued to require his snuff box, a sword with silver hilt, and a cane with silver head. Silver cigar holders, a silver liquor flask and silver-trimmed razor strops were popular at the end of the nineteenth century. Silver for the dressing table also came into vogue at this time and there were silver perfume bottles, powder boxes, brush and comb sets, buttonhooks, shoehorns, and even curling irons and glove stretchers and fasteners.

Articles of nineteenth century American silver for collectors may be classified as follows: (1) Silver for eating and drinking, including small table accessories; (2) Silver for miscellaneous household and personal uses; (3) Silver with social and historical significance; (4) Ecclesiastical silver.

Silver for eating and drinking includes spoons of all kinds and sizes, knives and forks, porringers, salts, pepper boxes or shakers, sugar tongs, trays, casters, cruet stands, cups, canns, mugs, tankards and goblets; teapots, coffee pots, creamers, sugar bowls and cake baskets. Silver for household and personal use includes centerpieces, plateaux, vases, candlesticks, snuffers, and trays and boxes of all sizes. Gentlemen's articles include snuff and tobacco boxes, spectacles and cases; sword hilts, spurs, silver-mounted pipes and waistcoat buttons. For ladies' personal use, there were patch boxes, combs, chatelaines, posy holders, thimbles, scissors and bobbins. Silver with social or historical significance would include articles with inscriptions referring to historic events or mentioning well-known persons; prize or premium cups with inscriptions of agriculture or sports accomplishments, or even small tokens for best in spelling or arithmetic, Masonic jewels and other medals. Ecclesiastical silver includes flagons, chalices, patens, beakers, cups, alms basins, baptismal bowls, crosses and candlesticks.

At the beginning of the nineteenth century silversmithing was still practiced as a handicraft and the silversmith learned his craft with years of apprenticeship. The early silversmith was a many-sided man. He was designer, die-sinker, solderer, burnisher, chaser, and engraver. These processes included melting and refining the bullion, hammering it into sheets and raising the shapes, casting, soldering, annealing, embossing, chasing, engraving, and polishing. The body of a piece was formed by hammering the flat silver into shape. Spouts, handles and covers were made separately and applied to the body. Such pieces as finials, thumb pieces and hinges were cast. There is a difference in the appearance of antique and modern machine-made silver. This is mainly due to a contrast in methods of workmanship between the craftsman and the machine. Early straight-sided silver forms such as teapots were simple to produce; they were made by cutting a thin piece of sheet silver of the proper size and bending it around a circular or oval form and soldering the seam. A disc of the proper shape served as the base and another disc was cut and shaped to form the lid. The spout was made of a piece of flat silver bent into the desired shape and seamed. The process had to be repeated for each piece. With the development of machinery in the mid-nineteenth century different methods of producing hollow ware came into use. Today, once the patterns are made, many similar pieces can be reproduced. The simpler forms are made under the weight of a drop-press or by spinning. The piece is finished by buffing with rouge and emery to remove the tool marks. This modern method results in uniformity of shape and surface and mechanical perfection.

By the old methods of raising and burnishing the silver had variation in form and surface and a character and charm in contrast to the hard impersonal appearance of the machine-made article. The early craftsman was more interested in fine line and proportion than in mechanical perfection. He left tiny hammer marks and these gave the surface of old silver a mellow quality as contrasted with the hard brilliant surface of machine-made silver. Also, the early craftsman completed his article, but today the workman is trained to do one small task such as cutting the same design on dozens of pieces of silver for an article which he has never been trained to make. Such procedures as this have led to the production of designs unsuited to the shapes which they are made to ornament and forms unadapted to the materials in which they are made.

The decorative processes used for the embellishment of American silver included engraving, chasing, moulding, embossing, stamping, and gadrooning. *Engraving* was the decorative process most often used. Engraving is peculiarly adapted to metal and with the ordinary graving tools the silversmith could engrave lettering such as monograms and inscriptions. Armorial and other symbolic devices were also engraved on silver and each period had its own characteristic decorative motifs. Bright-cut engraving used in the classic Federal Period of American silversmithing consisted of shallow side cuts or gouges which produced small facets at a side angle. *Chasing* differed from engraving in that the design was made with punches and none of the metal was removed. Thus chasing lasts, while engraving or etching wears smooth. Borders of *fluting* and *gadrooning,* vertical or spiral, were an effective way of emphasizing the base or side of a bowl or tea or coffee pot and giving variety to the surface. *Embossing* or *repoussé* was made by working on the interior of a piece with a hammer. The design itself is traced into the outer side with defining tracers or punches, the body of the vessel having been filled with pitch. Thus the design stands out in relief on the exterior surface. Embossing is like flat-chasing but with heavier pressure than delicate chasing. Embossing was enriched by flat-chasing with a blunt-edged tool. Embossing and repoussé were used principally on silver of rococo design. *Moulding* is a word that has been used ambiguously in the describing of much old silver. The writers relate the word to its architectural meaning rather than a foundry process. They say a tankard has a moulded rim or base, meaning that it has a banding application that has been grooved or stepped as by turning on a lathe or by squeezing through turned steel rollers or by casting in a strip, then rounded up to the circumference to be fitted. The wire or rim may be applied (soldered) to the round body in the plain state, then the entire vessel chucked on the lathe, to have the moulding effect turned into it with cutting tools. *Casting* was used particularly for porringer handles, scrolled handles of teapots, coffee pots and urns. Lion and eagle ornaments, feet and finials were also cast. Cast parts on silverware include those done solid and those done in halves or more divisions and soldered together. *Stamping* was used to make decorative borders and repeats. When stamped by dies in a strip the decorations were then soldered in place.

As has been stated, Early American silver collecting is an expensive hobby and only to be undertaken by the advanced collector. Silver of the first quarter of the nineteenth century is also expensive. Tea sets which sold for a few hundred dollars five years ago are now priced in the thousands. If the collector's eye is sighted toward the early nineteenth century, unless he has a large pocketbook, he would do well to collect such articles as spoons, sugar tongs, and tea bells, or articles of personal use like buttons, silver-headed canes, spectacles and spectacle cases. Sewing accessories such as thimbles, bobbins, bodkins, and scissors are also available and some of these are marked with the names of known silversmiths. Although shoe and knee buckles were seldom made or worn after the first quarter of the nineteenth century, there was a vogue for ladies' belt buckles. Also for collectors of Victorian silver there are bud vases, knife holders, napkin rings, various later serving pieces such as asparagus forks, fish forks, butter knives, butter pats, sugar spoons and sardine forks. Silver-mounted pincushions, desk sets, tiny boxes of all shapes including match safes, card cases, silver bookmarks, and even silver-headed hatpins are available. The late nineteenth century craze for silver souvenir spoons produced many interesting designs and this is one of the biggest fields of silver collecting today. Good values are also still to be found in earlier nineteenth century spoons and it is possible to collect spoons marked with the names of well-known silversmiths as well as many lesser known regional craftsmen.

Your silver collection will only be as good as your knowledge of the subject. Books give important information, but visits to museums, shops and antique shows where the actual pieces can be seen will acquaint the collector with the best craftsmanship and thus cultivate a taste for the finest in design and workmanship. A mark is only a signature and can be copied.

One must learn to recognize pieces by their shape and construction. Sizes and shapes indicate the age of a piece and the style of decoration is an aid in determining the date. The earliest teapots were small because tea was expensive. When tea became cheaper, the size of the teapot increased. Silver shapes followed the general decorative styles of furniture and other decorative arts. Thus a knowledge of period styles and decorative ornament is an aid to the collector. The dating of such articles as spoons is simple because the shapes and methods of construction made more definite changes. Early handles were straight, then up-curved, but in the second quarter of the eighteenth century the tip began to turn down and the bowl became a narrow oval shape. In the nineteenth century fiddle-back spoons mostly turned back, but by mid-century the up-turning effect became more in evidence. In the nineteenth century spoons were usually made from one piece of silver.

Hand-wrought silver has a touch or feeling and much can be learned by handling. Working by hand also gives a texture and the metal has a mellow beauty superior to the modern metal which is rolled out under heavy machine pressure and has a hardness of texture. Today there are many reliable dealers who will advise and help the beginning collector. The beginning collector would be wise to start his collection by buying from a reputable dealer. Here he may examine and handle an article and ask questions that will increase his knowledge. The answers which he gets from a knowledgeable dealer will be correct and instructive. This will also add zest to his collecting, for collecting is always more fun when you know the how, where, and when.

1. MARKS

ANY collector of silver must necessarily understand the system of marking. Although not all American silver is marked, much of it is. The American silversmith usually stamped his piece when he completed it. Thus he followed European custom. However, no official stamps or date letters were used by American silversmiths and, except for the Maryland law passed in 1814, there was no government regulation. Between 1814 and 1830 Maryland regulated the amount of silver required and Baltimore silver between these dates usually bore stamps with the arms of Baltimore, the mark of the assayer, the maker, and the date letter.

The usual marks which are stamped on Early American silver are composed of the maker's initials or name, generally enclosed within a shape such as a heart, shield, trefoil, star, square, circle, oval or rectangle. Frequently, a personal device such as a bird, star, hand or leaf was added. The Early American silversmith, John Coney, used the device of a figure of a coney below his initials. Some early silversmiths, following the English tradition, placed a crown above their initials which were enclosed within a device such as a heart or shaped shield. Later the initials or name were more generally enclosed within a simple rectangle. When the number of silversmiths increased there was often confusion from the similarity of initials. To remedy this the last name with or without the initial of the given name was often used. Silversmiths sometimes further distinguished their work by adding the city or town of manufacture. The use of the punch with name is seen more frequently from the beginning of the nineteenth century, but initials only may be found on smaller pieces. While some silversmiths used only one mark others had several marks. The exact date of a piece of silver cannot be set unless there are documental records. However, the dates of the working period of a silversmith and the style and form of the piece are important in determining the relative date.

Some later American silver is marked by the jeweler or other company that sold the silver rather than by the name of the silversmith or in addition to the name of the silversmith or manufacturer. By 1837 the words Coin, Pure Coin, Dollar, Standard, and Premium, or the letters "C" or "D" were placed on the silver to indicate that it was 900 parts silver. However, the word Sterling was not generally used until about 1860 and this meant that the silver was 925 parts fine. Early silver was sold on the basis of weight, plus charges for "making" and an extra charge for engraving. This custom continued down into the 1890's as evidenced in some of the old catalogues of silver companies.

The manufacture of silver by large companies began in the 1840's although there were also many individual silversmiths who continued to work. After the Civil War the majority of the silver articles made in America were made by the large manufacturing companies, such as Gorham, Tiffany, Samuel Kirk & Son, Whiting Manufacturing Company and others. With the rise of manufactured silverware, the trademark began to be used by the manufacturer, but the wholesaler and retailer often added their marks to the marks of the manufacturer. Thus it is sometimes difficult to determine the actual maker of much of American nineteenth century silver. Many companies such as Tiffany and Gorham changed their official names several times. This can be a help in establishing the date of an article when the dates of the change in trade name or trademark are known.

The Gorham familiar trademark, the lion, anchor, and old English capital "G," had been in use before 1868 when the sterling standard was adopted. Tiffany did not actually manufacture silver until 1868 when they acquired the silverware factory of Edward C. Moore. Until Mr. Moore's death Tiffany silver bore the block or old English letter "M" in addition to variations of the mark, Tiffany & Co., and a system of dating the work. William Gale & Sons always dated their work, and the silver of Samuel Kirk & Son can be dated through the changes in the mark and the use of the Baltimore Assay Office stamps which were used between 1814 and 1830.

There are many different and conflicting influences in the design of American nineteenth century silver. Not only do the styles and periods overlap but many different style motifs are seen on one piece of silver, making it difficult to record the definite characteristics of a style. Through the century there is a constant swing of the pendulum between classic and romantic influences with no set dates possible for either element, thus the dates given for the various styles are only approximate.

Sauce boat. Classic borders, animal-head spout, snake handle and winged-owl feet. A. Rasch & Co., Philadelphia, c. 1810. (*The Metropolitan Museum of Art, Sansbury Mills Fund, 1959*)

II *The Classic Federal and Empire · 1800–1840*

THE nineteenth century opens with the refined Adam classicism of the Federal Period. Though English influence persisted in the forms of silver throughout the period, the detail and shapes gradually became identified with the French, which more nearly represented the developing spirit of Empire of our national independence. An increased heaviness and largeness of scale and an emulation of Greek and Roman models characterized the more important pieces of the period and even the smaller pieces of domestic plate were decorated with Greek frets, and oak leaves and Greek acanthus leaves were applied to the stems and bodies of tea sets. Bases were supported on winged feet, and handles and finials were in the forms of eagles' heads, dogs, dolphins or clusters of fruit and flowers. The round bulbous vase and helmet shapes changed to pyriform. These elements continued into the 1830's and 1840's.

1. FEDERAL

THE classic revival in silver styles began in Europe about 1765 as a result of the excavations in Herculaneum and Pompeii. The leading exponents of the classic in England were the brothers Adam who designed architecture and furniture, but the influence also soon spread to silver. Classic shapes, including the urn and helmet, and columnar candlesticks re-

TOP. Spoon with faceted feathered edge and bright-cut swag, pointed down-curved handle. Paul Revere, 1735–1818. CENTER. Salt spoon with down-curved handle and bright-cut engraving. Paul Revere. BOTTOM LEFT. Sugar shovel, fiddle handle with shouldered stem. H. M. Nichols, 1810–1840. BOTTOM RIGHT. Spoon with rounded down-curved handle and bright-cut engraving. Ebenezer Moulton, 1768–1824. (*All, The Metropolitan Museum of Art, bequest of A. T. Clearwater, 1933*)

placed the bulbous rococo forms of the period before. Instead of heavy asymmetrical shapes with exuberant ornament, straight structural lines, symmetrically balanced, and delicate and slender forms became the vogue. Motifs included laurel leaves, delicate swags, pendent husks, and zigzag or feather edging. These designs were lightly cut into the surface of the silver in a style of engraving known as bright-cutting. Other decoration included acanthus foliage, egg and dart and beaded borders which were rolled and applied or knurled in or chased, and slender columns which were impressed or embossed or hand-fluted as on vessels like teapots.

In America comparatively little silver was produced during the Revolution and when the industry was started again after the war it was no longer centered in New York, Philadelphia and Boston. There were also now many silversmiths in cities such as Albany, New York; Norwich and New Haven, Connecticut; Providence, Rhode Island; Baltimore, Maryland; and Charleston, South Carolina, as well as many smaller cities, so that the collector of nineteenth century American silver has the work of many more silversmiths from which to choose than the collector of Early American silver. The classic designs which were in full blossom in Europe were adopted by the new republic. The classical style in America received its foremost influences from England and secondary ones from France. American silver of the Federal period reflected various phases of the neoclassic revival. The early influences were restricted to ornament, later they spread to form. Although based on the English models, American silver of the late eighteenth and early nineteenth century shows a marked individuality. Delicate formal pieces with emphasis on straight structural lines of the classic column had wide shallow concave flutes and bright-cutting lent brilliance and elegance.

Tea-drinking became more popular than ever before and many tea services were made in the classic spirit. Cylindrical or drum-shaped teapots were the popular shape. These had straight sides and spouts and

TOP. Tablespoon, coffin handle. W. G. Forbes, 1773–1830. (*The Metropolitan Museum of Art, gift of Mr. and Mrs. William A. Moore, 1923*) CENTER. Teaspoon, sheaf-of-wheat design. Patrick Martin, Philadelphia, 1820–1850. (*The Metropolitan Museum of Art*) BOTTOM LEFT. Teaspoon, shouldered stem with monogram and bright-cut design. James D. Stout, c. 1825. (*The Metropolitan Museum of Art*) BOTTOM RIGHT. Ladle, fiddle handle, shell design. James D. Stout, New York, c. 1820–1930. (*The Metropolitan Museum of Art*)

TOP. Hartt tea set. Oval teapot, straight sides and spout, engraved bright-cut band, stand with claw feet. Urn-shaped sugar, helmet creamer. Paul Revere, late 18th century. (*Courtesy, Museum of Fine Arts, Boston, gift of James Longley.* BELOW. Drum-shaped teapot, straight sides and spout, beading, pierced gallery and pineapple finial. Abraham Dubois, Philadelphia, 1777–1807. (*The Metropolitan Museum of Art, bequest of A. T. Clearwater, 1933*)

were plain except for an engraved bright-cut design on the shoulder and a beaded band on the edge of the shoulder and at the base. These were the forerunners of the straight-sided octagonal or oval fluted teapots which were used with the vase-shaped sugar bowl and helmet-shaped cream jug. These teapots had flat bottoms and were sometimes fitted to a tray. Straight-sided teapots and helmet and urn-shaped cream jugs and sugar bowls were the popular styles into the first quarter of the nineteenth century. However, silver designs change slowly and old patterns continued in vogue for many years. Thus the tall inverted pear-shaped coffee pot of

ABOVE. Tea set. Oval-shaped teapot with straight sides and spout, bright-cut engraved borders, beaded edge and pineapple finials. Urn-shaped sugar, helmet creamer and oval tea caddy. Daniel Van Voorhis, New York, 1751–1824. (*Courtesy of The Art Institute of Chicago*) BELOW. Oval teapot. Daniel Van Voorhis. (*The Metropolitan Museum of Art, bequest of Charles Allen Munn, 1924*)

the earlier rococo period was made by Revere and others well into the first quarter of the nineteenth century. Also, the idea of the tea set designed "en suite" did not prevail at once. As a result, some pieces of a set may have earlier shapes than others, and creamers and sugar bowls may perpetuate the inverted pear-shape while the teapot may be a new fashioned straight-sided form and only the ornamental details may unite pieces of a set. Also, some of the pieces may have been made by a later silversmith.

Such silversmiths as Paul Revere and Hugh Wishart bridge the gap between the early rococo and the classic period. Paul Revere was the most famous silversmith of the period just before and after the Revolution. His designs include not only the pear-shaped coffee pots and globular teapots with engraved coats of arms similar in shape to the one shown in his portrait by Copley, but after the war, when fashions were changing from rococo to classical, Revere too changed his designs. His later classical straight-sided oval teapots with straight spouts, urn-shaped sugar bowls and helmet creamers decorated with floral borders and swags of bright-cut engraving set the style of the Federal period. Revere was influenced by the shapes of pottery, particularly by the Chinese bowls whose form he exemplified in his handsome punch bowls. He also translated the forms of Liverpool creamware pitchers, which were at the height of their popularity in 1800, into silver. Other well-known silversmiths who made silver of classic design that straddled the century were Hugh Wishart, Edward Rockwell, John and Joel Sayre, and William G. Forbes of New York; Isaac and George Hutton of Albany; Joseph Lownes, Simon Chaudron and Christian Wiltberger of Philadelphia, and Thomas Warner and Charles Louis Boehme of Baltimore. These men began work in the late eighteenth century but continued working into the first quarter of the nineteenth century and influenced the design of silver made by the lesser silversmiths of the Federal period.

RIGHT. Porringer. Ebenezer Moulton, early 19th century. (*The Metropolitan Museum of Art, bequest of A. T. Clearwater, 1933*) BELOW. Inverted pear-shaped coffee pot. Ephraim Brasher. (*The Metropolitan Museum of Art, bequest of A. T. Clearwater, 1933*) BELOW. Waiter, mahogany with silver rail. Louis Boehme, Baltimore, c. 1800–1810 (*The Metropolitan Museum of Art, Rogers Fund, 1943*)

BELOW. Waiter, mahogany with silver rail. Charles Louis Boehme, Baltimore, c. 1800–1810. (*The Metropolitan Museum of Art, Rogers Fund, 1943*)

The most popular silver shape introduced in the Federal period was that inspired by the funerary urn of classic Rome. It had an ovoid body, plain or fluted, and was decorated with bright-cut engraving in the Adam manner. Tureens of plain boat-shape rested on an oval base and had strap handles. Although possessing characteristics of the general style, the silver made in different geographical sections of the country showed variations. Philadelphia silver of this period is recognized by the simplicity of the ovoid body and by details such as the pineapple or vase-shaped finial, beaded mouldings, and the pierced gallery around the top of sugar urns and waste bowls and less often about the tops of tea and coffee pots. Philadelphia silversmiths who are known to have made silver with these characteristics include John Letelier, Joseph and Nathaniel Richardson, Joseph Anthony, Jr., Joseph Lownes and many lesser known silversmiths. The monogram on Philadelphia silver of this period is also a characteristic detail. It was usually put in an ornamental framework with flowers and leaves, a bowknot, and sprays of wheat ears. Similar tea set designs were made by silversmiths in Wilmington, Delaware; Burlington, New Jersey; and Baltimore, Maryland, where George Aiken, Louis Buichle, Littleton Holland, Charles Louis Boehme and John Lynch were some of the important silversmiths at this time. The Philadelphia design influence also spread as far south as Virginia and the Carolinas, and a teapot with pineapple finial and pierced gallery was made by the Bermuda silversmith Peter Pallais.

In the second decade of the nineteenth century the popularity of the refined Adam forms with helmet bodies diminished. The neck of the teapot became curved and the helmet cream pitcher and urn sugar bowl which accompanied these early classic design teapots gradually changed

TOP. Tea set. Horizontal-swelling sides, honeysuckle and star borders, heavy eagle handles. Farnam & Ward, Boston, c. 1816. (*Gebelein Silversmiths*) BOTTOM. Tea set with gadroon and shell borders, Greek Key bands, ball feet and dolphin finials. James Ward, Hartford, c. 1815. (*Collection of Philip H. Hammerslough*)

to an oval shape with flat base which matched the base of the swelling oval boat-shape teapot with high domed lid and finial in the shape of a classic urn. Tea sets of this type were made by Hugh Wishart, John and Peter Targee, and Edward Rockwell in New York; Saunders Pitman in Providence, Rhode Island; Shepherd and Boyd in Albany, New York; and many other silversmiths throughout the eastern states. A little later the teapot and cream and sugar were set on a small platform upheld by four ball feet.

An interesting feature of many of the tea sets of the early nineteenth century is the patriotic star-spangled border. A tea set by Joel Sayre (1778–1819) in the New-York Historical Society has narrow star borders both at rims and bases of the various pieces. The teapot and sugar bowl have vase finials and the three pieces sit on ball feet. A similar tea set with swelling

TOP. Tea set with horizontal-swelling sides, ball feet and patriotic star-spangled borders. Edward Rockwell, 1807–1825. (*Gebelein Silversmiths*) BOTTOM. Tea set. Boat-shaped bodies, gadroon borders and cast lion finials. William Thompson, New York, c. 1810. (*Collection of Philip H. Hammerslough*)

sides and ball feet has star borders on the body of the pieces, on the finials, the silver handles and the socket of the ebony handle of the teapot. The set was made by Edward Rockwell. Heavy eagle handles are the feature of the tea set made by Farnam & Ward of Boston, c. 1816, and a small star border outlines the rims of the three pieces and the edge of the finials. But the most effective use of these patriotic symbols was made by Simon Chaudron of Philadelphia in the embossed eagle and oak bands on the tea set made for Snowden Henry of Philadelphia and the set with the beautiful broad star and ribbon bands which now belongs to the Society of Colonial Dames, Condé-Charlotte House, Mobile, Alabama. This set is marked Chaudron & Rasch. Chaudron became coupled with Anthony Rasch in 1812.

RIGHT. Basket, cut-work handle and border of acanthus leaves. Charles L. Boehme, Baltimore, c. 1815. (*Lent by the Baltimore Museum of Art to the exhibition, "Classical America" at the Newark Museum*) BELOW. Creamer and sugar bowl, Federal style with bands of ribbon and stars. Chaudron & Rasch, 1812–1820. (*Collection of the Colonial Dames Society of America, Condé-Charlotte House, Mobile*)

Other silver articles, while they followed the general classic style, showed less change than that evidenced in the tea and coffee service. Tall standing cups took on the vase shape, but these were used mainly as chalices in churches since silver drinking cups had by this time been superseded by glasses to a certain extent. Two-handled cups and flagons with covers were made in vase shape, but fewer flagons were made than in preceding years. However, tankards, mugs, canns, and large pitchers for beer or punch continued in use. Canns and mugs of this period have a moulded base and a swelling bulbous lower part with a shaped outward curving upper part and a plain "S" curved handle; later, some were made on a pedestal base.

The tankard which was the popular drinking vessel of the seventeenth and eighteenth centuries was based on English models and there are many interesting variations in form and decoration according to locality. However, a discussion of these belongs to a more specialized book. Also, the tankard, although it continued to be made throughout the nineteenth century, did not hold the place of importance that it had in the earlier centuries. In the early nineteenth century the flat-top tankard gradually gave place to the tankard with domed lid, pear-shaped body, and scrolled handle and thumbpiece. This style was especially favored in Philadelphia from 1800 to 1815. Small straight-sided tankards with bar-

RIGHT TOP. Flagon. William Moulton, 1772–1861. (*Towle Silversmiths*) BOTTOM. Tankard. Joseph Anthony, 1762–1814. (*Philadelphia Museum of Art, Photograph by A. J. Wyatt, Staff Photographer*)

BOTTOM, LEFT TO RIGHT. Mug. John Sayre & Thomas Richards, New York, c. 1802–1811. (*Newark Museum*) Silver cann. Fletcher & Gardiner, Philadelphia, c. 1810. (*Philadelphia Museum of Art, Photograph by A. J. Wyatt, Staff Photographer*) Mug. Gregg & Veal, Columbia, South Carolina, c. 1830. (*Columbia Museum of Art*) Mug inscribed "4th Church of Newburyport." William Moulton IV. (*Towle Silversmiths*)

rel-hooped sides and a flat lid were also made in various localities at this time.

Beakers continued to be made in the nineteenth century and a pair of beakers was a popular gift. A pair by Samuel Kirk made in 1825 is in the duPont Winterthur Museum and a set of eight beakers made by Scovil, Willey & Co. (c. 1818) of Cincinnati, Ohio, was recently offered for sale by a well-known dealer. In Kentucky beakers were given as premiums by the Kentucky Agricultural Society as early as 1814. Today these are collected and used as julep cups.

Early beakers which were low and wide in New England, and tall, following the Dutch style, in New York, became small squat cups in the early nineteenth century. They had flat bottoms, curved barrel or bell-shaped sides, moulded or reeded bands, and many had bright-cut classic engraved designs. Thomas Carson of Albany, New York, made a round-bodied beaker with flaring lips and moulded engraved base which was given as a prize by the Berkshire Agricultural Society in 1823.

Small camp cups with round body are similar to the camp cups made for George Washington by Edmund Milne in 1777. A pair in the United States Naval Museum made by Charles Burnett of Alexandria, Virginia, was probably copied from the earlier cups. At Monticello there are two small round-bottomed cups made for Thomas Jefferson by John Letelier. A letter dated March 27, 1810, to Letelier from Jefferson, placing the order for the cups is in the Bixby Papers, Missouri Historical Society.

The porringer was another article of American silver which was made in great numbers in the early centuries, but although it continued to be made in the nineteenth century it was less popular. The porringer is a circular shallow bowl with a decorative pierced handle. Late porringers with the keyhole type handle were made by Elijah Lincoln of Hingham, Massachusetts, Joseph Moulton, John Vernon and others, and are to be seen in museum collections and are also found in antique shops today.

The early nineteenth century dining table of families of means had many small silver articles which are of interest to the present-day collector. Spoons had become plentiful and, in addition to those made by well-known silversmiths in large cities, almost every small town had its spoon-maker, as is evidenced by newspaper advertisements.

The form of American spoons has changed through the years. The early spoons made in America followed simple English styles and were copies of the English spoons brought over by the first settlers. The bowl

TOP. Water pitcher and salver with classic leaf borders. Gerardus Boyce, 1824–1841. (*The New-York Historical Society*) BOTTOM LEFT. Water pitcher. Classic gadroon borders and double scroll handle with acanthus-leaf decoration. William Thompson, 1810–1834. (*Collection of Philip H. Hammerslough*) RIGHT. Cream pitcher, classic style with hand-beaten fluted body and Greek key and anthemion borders. Samuel Kirk, 1818. (*Samuel Kirk & Son*)

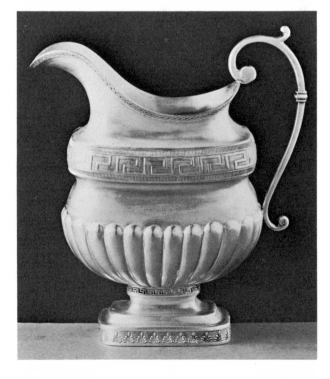

was wide and the spoons were heavy. The handle was thin and had little importance. As the spoon developed it became lighter in weight and took on a form more convenient to handle and use. In the mid-eighteenth century the handle began to turn down and the bowl became more pointed and oval. The decoration and monogram which had at first been on the backs of spoon handles was moved to the front in the late eighteenth century. The handles were slender and tapering, rounded or pointed at the ends. These spoons were usually decorated with bright-cut engraving of delicate flowers or ribbons, with an oval space for a monogram. Other spoons had a decoration of a zigzag line border called feather cutting. Spoons of these types were made by Paul Revere, Joseph Moulton, Joseph Richardson, Jr., Joseph Loring, William Homes, Jr., and many others. Spoons with a feathered edge and Washington's crest were made a few years earlier by Richard Humphreys and are now in Mount Vernon.

The top and sides of spoon handles were sometimes clipped off in a form resembling an old-fashioned coffin. This design may have been introduced to exemplify a funeral spoon. These "coffin-handled" spoons are usually plain, but occasionally they are decorated with bright-cut engraving. The "fiddle-shape" handle made its appearance early in the nineteenth century. The handle widened and the shoulder above the bowl was right-angled. The bowl remained thin and pointed. The end of the spoon handle was sometimes plain, and sometimes had a tip and was called "plain tipt." Fiddle-shaped spoons were often decorated with an embossed shell, sheaf-of-wheat, or basket-of-flowers from about 1810 to 1830. All of these teaspoons are smaller than teaspoons today.

Porringer spoons and tablespoons were larger than present-day spoons of the same type. There were also tiny salt spoons and larger basting spoons and ladles. Matching sugar tongs in bright-cut and plain fiddle patterns are also available. Sugar tongs of the eighteenth century were of scissors type with scroll arms and shell grips. The plain side of the circular spring box which held the two arms together usually had the owner's monogram or initials. Tongs of this type were made by Paul Revere and other American silversmiths in the first four years of the nineteenth cen-

TOP. Ladle, Onslow pattern. Joseph and Nathaniel Richardson, c. 1800. (*The Metropolitan Museum of Art, bequest of A. T. Clearwater, 1933*) CENTER. Salt spoon, fiddle shell. Early 19th century. (*The Metropolitan Museum of Art, gift of Mrs. William E. Goff, 1919*) BOTTOM. Sugar tongs with bright-cut design. Maker "I.C.," early 19th century. (*The Metropolitan Museum of Art, bequest of A. T. Clearwater, 1919*)

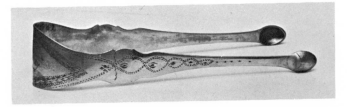

tury. The scissor-type sugar tongs was followed by the spring-type U-shaped tongs late in the eighteenth century and these continued to be the popular style made in the nineteenth centry. At first the arms were of openwork designs with bright-cut ornament and the owner's monogram on the arched section. Later the arms were made in one piece of thin silver, but might have shell-shaped grips soldered to the end of the arms. The tongs were ornamented with simple chasing or bright-cut engraving and the spoon-shaped grips might be plain, shell-shaped, acorn-shaped or stamped in the form of tea leaves. The feathered edges or bright-cut engraving gave way to threaded edges and arms that had fiddle-shaped ends. Later, the arms matched the various spoon patterns such as Shell, Kings, Queens, Beaded, and all the successive designs of the hundreds of flatware patterns of the late nineteenth century. The collector can assemble an interesting and valuable group of sugar tongs made before 1850, including those made by many well-known American silversmiths.

A set of unusual spoons and forks of fiddle-shape with a bust of Washington and a wheat border and anthemion motif was made by Thomas Harland (1735–1807) and is now in Winterthur Museum. The various thread designs—French Thread, Plain Thread, and Thread and Shell, were first made at the beginning of the nineteenth century. These patterns had a double-threaded outline on a fiddle shape. The Pointed Thread pattern was initiated a little later. Knives of Thread pattern were made by Baldwin Gardiner in 1814 and forks and spoons of various sizes including tablespoons, mustard spoons and sauce ladles in Thread and Shell pattern were made by Andrew E. Warner of Baltimore and by Thomas Fletcher of Philadelphia, c. 1813. These designs were also made by William Gale, William Forbes and others in New York and elsewhere. Pistol-handled knives and forks were also made at this time. Other patterns included Threaded Fiddle, Fiddle Shell, Old Olive Tipt, Queens, and Kings patterns. The Kings and Queens patterns which were variations on the fiddle-shape form were developed in the 1820's. These designs were stamped or cast, the pattern being die-embossed instead of being chased or engraved. Samuel Kirk made Kings pattern flatware in 1824

TOP. Teaspoon. Basket-of-Flowers, fiddle handle. William I. Tenney, New York, c. 1840. (*The New-York Historical Society*) CENTER. Spoon with fiddle handle. Fletcher & Gardiner, Boston, c. 1810. (*Worcester Art Museum*) BOTTOM. Sugar tongs with bright-cut designs. Phinney & Mead, c. 1825. (*The Metropolitan Museum of Art, bequest of A. T. Clearwater, 1933*)

and he made the first flatware pattern of repoussé in 1828. The fiddle-handled spoon with straight stem remained in style until the 1830's when it was superseded by a spatulate up-curved handle thickened at the thumb piece and outlined with a thread moulding.

Until about 1820 flatware consisted mainly of spoons made in silver coin. These were made in two sizes—teaspoons, four to five inches long, and tablespoons, six to seven inches and longer. After 1820 spoons were made in three sizes—teaspoons, dessert spoons and tablespoons. A few serving spoons, ladles and salt spoons were made. Forks were made in two sizes but there was no uniformity controlling the size. Forks and knives with silver handles were rare. Few silver forks or knives were made in the early years of the nineteenth century. A few were made to match spoons but they were not generally made until 1850. Sheffield steel blades with wood, ivory, bone, or china handles were commonly used until the latter half of the century. In 1840 the designs of handles began to multiply. From now on until the middle of the century the patterns had few important points of variation from established forms, and innovations were chiefly in the designs that covered the handles and not in the form. Some of the patterns made by Gorham between 1855 and 1865 were Beaded, Cottage, Josephine, and Saxon Stag. After the turn to sterling, in general after 1865, there were patterns with matching knives. However, because

LEFT. Caster set with beaded edges and paw feet. John McMullin, Philadelphia, 1765–1843. (*Philadelphia Museum of Art*) BOTTOM. Tray with engraving and gadroon edge. Samuel Kirk, c. 1815. (*The Metropolitan Museum of Art, gift of Samuel Kirk and Son, Inc., 1926*)

of hollow handles and wear and erosion of the blades the knives were not as durable as spoons and forks and require replacement for use today.

Silver skewers for meat, and marrow and cheese scoops also continued to be made into the second quarter of the nineteenth century. Other table articles at this time included pepper boxes and vase-shaped casters which had pierced geometric designs in their high-domed covers and cast button finials. The small round salt cellar on three curved legs with hoof feet and shells at the top of the legs remained the popular type although classic boat-shaped salt cellars were also made. There are round open salts by such silversmiths as Andrew Billings of Poughkeepsie, New York (1784–1810) and other provincial silversmiths and those manufactured by Gorham in the 1860's with ram's head and hoof feet are often on the market.

Rare braziers, saucepans, brandy warmers and pipe lighters of the period are available for the advanced collector. Cake baskets and sauce boats were other items made. Trays conform to the prevailing fashions. Large oval tea trays were seldom made in America and are rare. The round

RIGHT. Detail of White House plateau. Openwork border of an Urn, winged lions and leaf and flower motifs. Paw-foot pedestals with figures of Flora and Pomona surmounted by a spread eagle. BELOW. Plateau in three sections. Made for the White House in 1824 by John W. Forbes (*Collection of the White House*)

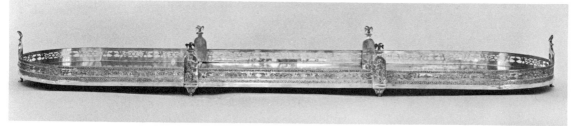

trays or salvers of this period usually follow the rococo style with scroll and shell borders rather than the classic, although many, particularly those made in Philadelphia and Baltimore, have a classic bead or reed border. Thomas and Andrew Warner of Baltimore made a set of three salvers for Charles Ridgely. These have a knurled rim and claw and ball feet, a border of elaborate floral engraving and an engraved coat of arms. They are in the collection of Philip H. Hammerslough. An oval tray with heavy gadrooned border and classic floral engraving made by Samuel Kirk in 1828 was recently on the market as was a round tray by Taylor & Hinsdale of New York (c. 1805) which had a heavy rococo rim and floral engraving of similar design.

Punch brewing and drinking was an important social function in seventeenth and eighteenth century America and the custom continued into the nineteenth century. Besides the punch bowl, of which few exist and these probably are all in museums, there were punch ladles, strainers, and siphons. These too are rare, but enough strainers and siphons of the early nineteenth century have come into the market lately to recommend them to the collector. However, they are expensive.

Candlesticks of the Federal era followed the classic Adam influence. The shafts were columnar-shaped, based on the classic Greek orders, and some were ornamented with festoons of flowers or drapery, urns, masks, and other classical motifs in engraving or low relief. The fluted column rested on a stepped foot decorated with beading or gadrooning. Some columnar shafts had a capital of Corinthian style, but more often they were of simpler design such as the candlesticks with shafts of simple Doric columns made by Isaac Hutton of Albany which are in the Metropolitan Museum of Art. Other candlesticks had square shafts with concave sides tapering to a square base and were ornamented with swags and other classic decoration. Another type of candlestick had a shaft in the form of an inverted cone with a helmet-shaped candle cup. It stood on a circular base and had fluted decoration and beaded borders. Candlesticks of this type were made by Joel Sayre of New York in the first quarter of the nineteenth century. In the second quarter of the century there was a debasement in the designs and candlesticks with heavy cast rococo ornament on

TOP. Candlestick, classic columns. Isaac Hutton, Albany, 1767–1855. (*Metropolitan Museum of Art, bequest of A. T. Clearwater, 1933*) CENTER. Candlestick, rococo style, William Thompson, New York, 1812–1830. (*The Metropolitan Museum of Art, gift of Frederic Ashton de Peyster, 1946*) BOTTOM. One of a pair of candlesticks with snuffers. Shepherd & Boyd, Albany, 1814. (*Museum of the City of New York*)

LEFT. Teapot, urn-shaped body with gadrooned lobes and pine-cone finials. Scroll handle ending in griffin's head, curved spout with grotesque bird's head, latticework decoration on body and base. Charles A. Burnett, 1785–1849. (*Collection of Philip H. Hammerslough*) RIGHT. Coffee pot with swelling body, acanthus-leaf decoration ending in ball feet, gadrooned lobes, acorn finial and animal-head spot. Garret Eoff, mid-19th century. (*The Metropolitan Museum of Art, bequest of A. T. Clearwater, 1933*)

their shafts became the style. Also rococo and classic designs were combined on the same candlestick. Obadiah Rich (1830–1850) made a candlestick with a socket of classic design supported by a tripod of scrolls and hounds' heads. This was a combination candlestick and inkwell. Can-

BELOW LEFT. Teapot. Oak leaf and acorn, early repoussé. Samuel Kirk, 1826. (*Samuel Kirk & Son*) RIGHT. Covered urn, repoussé landscape and scroll design, ram's head handle. Samuel Kirk, 1822. (*Samuel Kirk & Son*)

delabra followed the same designs as single candlesticks, but there were few made.

Chamber candlesticks composed of a shallow saucer with a short central shaft supporting a socket and accompanied by a conical extinguisher were designed for carrying from room to room. They were generally made in pairs. The base was usually round and was decorated with a band of beading or gadrooning about its rim. A pair of chamber candlesticks made by Samuel Kirk in 1828 had a finely chased repoussé design in Oriental style. Later, borders of elaborate foliage decorated the rims of the base and the socket might be supported by lion feet or Egyptian motifs. Matching snuffers and trays were also made.

2. EMPIRE

THE next style development in American silver which began with Chaudron & Rasch, Thomas Whartenby, and Harvey Lewis in about 1810 was in full swing by 1830. It was taken from the French Empire, a decorative style adopted in the time of Napoleon I. In France, the style was pompous, severe of line, and formal. For design motifs it drew from Rome, Greece, and Egypt. These motifs included acanthus and laurel leaves, lotus flowers, cornucopias, wreaths, quivers of arrows, stars, antique heads, masks, caryatid figures, sphinx and other winged busts, cloven and lion feet, and borders of Greek fret, beading, fluting; and swan, dolphin, tree and bud finials were seen on covered pieces. Candlesticks

Sugar, creamer and waste bowl with anthemion and latticework engraved borders, square bases with winged-owl feet. Ram's head handles and rose finial on sugar bowl. William Mannerback, Reading, Pennsylvania, 1820–1825. (*Collection of Philip H. Hammerslough*)

ABOVE. Pieces of silver dinner service, High Empire style, eagle's head handles, winged-paw feet and applied cast borders. Fletcher & Gardiner, 1814–1838. Lent by The Maryland Historical Society to the exhibition, "Classical America." (*Newark Museum*)
BELOW. Pair of tankards, rose and anthemion borders and S-scroll handles. Teapot, round pedestal, grapevine border and urn finial. Fletcher & Gardiner. Empire bowl and sauce boat with winged-owl feet, acanthus-leaf chasing and rose border. Caryatid handles. Thomas Whartenby, 1811–1850. (*Gebelein Silversmiths*)

ABOVE. Tea set with swelling bowls, rose borders and finials. Thomas Richards, New York, c. 1815. (*The New-York Historical Society*) BELOW. Tea set with gadrooned bowls, rose borders and finials. Boyce & Jones, New York, c. 1830. (*The Metropolitan Museum of Art, gift of William Sneckner, 1894*)

ABOVE. Tea set. Oval-pedestaled fluted teapot, creamer and sugar. J. & I. Cox, New York, c. 1833. Round waste bowl, J. H. Connor and G. Eoff. (*Gebelein Silversmiths*)
BELOW. Teapot, creamer and sugar bowl with swelling bowls and gadroon borders. Garret Eoff. (*Metropolitan Museum of Art, bequest of A. T. Clearwater, 1933*)

had stems in the form of Egyptian mummies and Roman soldiers. The style was modified in England by the designs of Flaxman so that although articles were still somewhat formal and bizarre they were simplified. Antique heads, musical instruments, stiff flat acanthus leaves and stars are characteristic of this style which was called Regency in England, Empire in America.

The Empire style in furniture had become popular in America in about 1810 and this helped to bring about the change in the design of silver. Swelling curves dominate the forms. In the beginning of the period the sides of the oblong teapot, sugar and creamer are broken into heavy horizontal molded curves. The pieces often stand on ball feet and the

TOP. Late Empire coffee set with caryatid supports ending in claw feet. Tiffany, c. 1853. (*Gebelein Silversmiths*) BOTTOM. High Empire tea set. Teapot and sugar bowl cylix form with classic repoussé borders. Teapot has swan finial and sugar bowl has wreath handles. Samuel Kirk, 1828. (*Samuel Kirk & Son*)

ABOVE. Tea set, French Empire style with bands of spread eagles and leaves, beaded ball finials and animal-head spouts. Simon Chaudron, Philadelphia, c. 1812 (*Newark Museum*) BELOW. Tea and coffee service, acanthus-leaf decoration and borders with baskets of fruit. Andrew E. Warner, c. 1830. (*Gebelein Silversmiths*)

finials are moulded flower forms. Some of these pieces were decorated with body fluting and bands of heavy gadrooning which are characteristic decorative devices of the period. Although the American Empire style in silver was influenced by the pompous French style it has more restraint. The typical American Empire piece is heavy. It has C-shaped and scrolled handles sometimes in the form of a serpent, dragon, griffin, or ram's head. The curved spouts end in grotesque birds' heads. Rams' heads or lions' heads with rings in their mouths form the handles. Finials were in the form of dogs, dolphins, lions, roses, or sheaves of wheat and there were also large floral finials which seem to have been inspired by Empire cornucopias. Acanthus leaves or Greek water leaves are often applied around the rims and shoulders of pieces and legs and handles are sometimes foliated scrolls. Plinths were raised on animal paw, eagle or spread-winged owl feet while some pieces were set on heavy round bases. A tea set made by Samuel Kirk in 1824 is decorated with acanthus leaves and grapes. Sculptured leaves and grapes also decorate a pear-form wine ewer, and oak leaves and acorn decoration form an early repoussé pattern. A tea service in Empire design made in 1830 has classical repoussé decora-

LEFT. Pair of goblets with gadroon rim and chased design of acanthus and eagle. c. 1835. (*Gebelein Silversmiths*) BELOW. Gravy boat and tray, acanthus-chased body with grape and acanthus and shell borders. Thomas Fletcher. (*Gebelein Silversmiths*)

ABOVE LEFT. Pitcher with concave flutes and applied leaf borders. Coin silver. N. Harding, Boston, 1799–1862. (*Gebelein Silversmiths*) RIGHT. Silver pitcher. F. Marquand, Savannah, 1824. (*Collection of James A. Williams*) BELOW LEFT. Pitcher with acanthus chasing on body latticework and rose borders, winged-owl feet and grotesque animal-head handle. Ward & Bartholomew, Hartford, 1804–1809. (*The New-York Historical Society*) RIGHT. Urn-shaped pitcher, beaded rims and acorn finial. Hutton, Albany, early 19th century. (*Albany Institute of History and Art*)

tion on the bodies and foliated pedestals. The teapot and sugar are cylix form. The teapot has an animal figure on the spout and a swan finial on the cover, and the sugar bowl has wreath handles. Silver made by John & Peter Targee, Thomas Richards, and William B. Heyer, in New York, and Barzillai Benjamin and John Proctor Trott, in Connecticut, was heavy and bulky and showed some of these characteristics. The Metropolitan Museum owns a tea set of this type with gadrooned lobes and bands made by Boyce and Jones of New York (c. 1825). A tea set by John Ewan of Charleston, South Carolina (1823–1834), has a lobed body and heavy bands of grapes and grape leaves about the base, shoulders and covers, and the finial on each cover is a dolphin. Edward Lownes working in Philadelphia (1817–1833) also used heavy bands of gadrooning and leaves on his classic-shaped coffee pots. A coffee pot by Garret Eoff and John H. Connor of New York (c. 1833) is more delicate. Bulky tea sets covered with body gadrooning and bands of leaf scrolls and rosettes typical of the period were made by Frederick Marquand. A tea set by William Thompson (c. 1810) in the collection of Philip Hammerslough has a more refined boat-shaped body. The claw and ball feet, gadrooned bands, and cast lion finials show Empire influence.

In the Fletcher & Gardiner papers in the Pennsylvania Historical Society there are letters which give some information about the design of household silverware at this time. What is perhaps most interesting, however, are the comments which refer to the changes in the design of silverware. These were occasioned by the fact also revealed in other letters that Fletcher & Gardiner were usually slow in delivering orders. R. & A. Campbell, silversmiths of Baltimore, write to Fletcher & Gardiner: "We wish you to make us as fast as possible two sets of plate consisting of coffee, two tea, one Creampots, sugar dish, slop bowl to each set—Make them of the large size and newest pattern." (June 8, 1831) In another letter, May 28, 1831: "those in fashion here are low with heavy chased edges." A client from Boston writes: "let me have it before the very fashion of the article is gone by." (June 7, 1831)

Presentation and ceremonial pieces of the Empire period are more elaborate. They tend to follow classic forms such as that of the famous Warwick vase, cylix, and other Greek vase forms and are ornamented with borders of palmettes and cast or tooled bands of scenes from mythology. Symbolical figures of Greek gods and goddesses often form the handles and bases.

Although there were a great number of silversmiths working both in the cities and small towns in the Empire period in America there are certain well-known silversmiths who made the majority of the testimonials and other pieces for distinguished persons and important public places such as the White House. Samuel Kirk, the founder of the present-day firm of Samuel Kirk & Son, did much of this work. Although born in America, Kirk was descended from a line of English silversmiths and his designs were influenced by the work of London silversmiths. At first Kirk produced simple classic designs inspired by English Georgian silver. However, noting the changing tastes, Kirk was the first in America to use the technique of repoussé. In the years when the Empire style was popular Kirk produced massive shapes inspired by Greek and Roman urns and vases. Kirk not only made silver for influential Baltimore families but when Lafayette visited America in 1824, he commissioned Kirk to make a pair of goblets which he presented to David Williamson. The goblets are round with convex, partly fluted bodies. A narrow Greek key band decorates the rim and an anthemion border rings the base of the pedestals. About this date Kirk also made luncheon forks for Betsy Patterson Bonaparte, wife of Jerome, brother of the Emperor Napoleon. These were of oval-tipt shape and were engraved with the Bonaparte crest and shield.

LEFT. Silver fruit basket with leaf and grape rim. Inscribed "President's House." Robert Keyworth, Washington, D.C., c. 1830–1833. (*White House Collection*) RIGHT. Soup tureen with applied shell borders and cast reeded handles. C. Giffing, New York, 1815–1835. (*Gebelein Silversmiths*)

Kirk later made covered vegetable dishes for the Bonaparte family. These had classic leaf bands, the Bonaparte arms and a coronet finial. Through the years the firm of Samuel Kirk & Son continued to make silver for the Bonaparte family. Kirk also made a racing trophy with sculptured figures of horses in 1835. William Gale & Son, William Adams, Garret Eoff, Whartenby & Bumm, Shepherd & Boyd, Joel Sayre, Baldwin Gardiner, Andrew E. Warner, Edward Lownes and John W. Forbes were other important silversmiths working at this time. It was John W. Forbes (1808–1834) who made the three-section plateau for the State dining table of the White House in 1824. The railing of the plateau is engraved with a classic scene and the paw-footed pedestal shows a raised figure of Flora, goddess of flowers, produced by a re-usable die. John Targee used a design of Hercules battling the Nemean lion. This relief die pattern is seen on sword knuckle guards and on the cover of a snuff box in the Metropolitan Museum. However, the silversmiths who made the most ambitious pieces at this time were Thomas Fletcher and Sidney Gardiner who worked in Philadelphia from 1814 to 1838. They are known for the many important presentation pieces which are now in museums and other public institutions and important private collections. Because these pieces attracted public interest they played an influential part in the development of the Empire style in America. The pieces are formal interpretations of the Federal and Empire styles. The shapes are classic and the motifs of decoration are taken from Greek and Roman sources.

The final element of the Empire style is Egyptian. Because of Napoleon's campaign on the Nile and the publications on the archaeology of Egypt, motifs such as the sphinx and heavy animal legs were incorporated into silver design and shapes took on the heavy geometric volume of Egyptian architecture. An inkstand by Harvey Lewis of Philadelphia is supported by sphinxes with feathered American Indian headdresses. It was made in about 1815 and is now in the Yale University Art Gallery.

This last phase of classic which produced the Empire period in American silver is generally thought of as a decline in taste, but it must be judged in its own context as a counterpart of the architecture of the

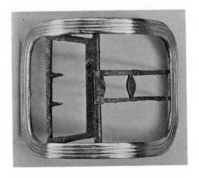

TOP. Shoe buckle, engraved decoration. Maker unknown, c. 1800. BOTTOM. Shoe buckle, moulded line decoration. Maker unknown, c. 1810. (*Metropolitan Museum of Art, bequest of A. T. Clearwater, 1933*)

Greek Revival. The classic influence lasted into the 1840's and overlaps the return of the romantic rococo of the Victorian era.

Although the elements of silver design of the 1820's continued to the 1840's, there was a gradual change in the shapes of hollow ware from round, bulbous vase and classical helmet shapes to pear shapes. Baroque and rococo elements gradually regained prominence and bands of egg and dart and foliate scroll borders and winged leaf borders mingle to create a romantic style.

Repoussé work was also popular in the 1840's. R. & W. Wilson made a pitcher with ovoid body covered with repoussé figures and landscape, and a scrolled handle draped with a United States flag on which an eagle is perched. Wood & Hughes of New York made tea and coffee services with repoussé grapes and garlands of oak and acorns and rustic twigs and pheasant finials. The tea and coffee pots made by Ball, Tompkins & Black had oval globular bodies covered with leaf patterns in repoussé and tulip finials. Bailey & Kitchen and William Gale & Son made similar pieces in the 1840's. There were also silversmiths in Boston and the Southern states making silver in characteristic rococo design.

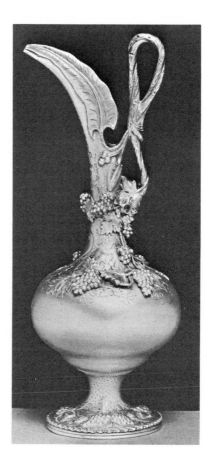

Wine ewer with pear-form body on moulded base, sculptured leaves and grapes. Samuel Kirk, 1828. (*Samuel Kirk & Son*)

III *American Victorian Silver · 1840–1900*

As the Victorian period opened two influences which had been in favor in the first quarter of the century—Greek Revival and repoussé decoration—were important factors in the design of silver. In classic forms the smooth surface of the silver was exploited while in the repoussé rococo ornamentation the malleability of the silver was used for a different decorative effect. In the 1860's Renaissance motifs of design came into vogue and the classical forms were decorated with cast bands of architectural ornament and sculptured figures. In the 1870's new techniques such as matted surfaces and Oriental, Assyrian and Indian styles were introduced. Finally, as a reaction to the complexities of the '70's and '80's, a revival of eighteenth century designs appeared in the 1890's and thus within sixty years the design pendulum had gone full swing. However, the rules and regulations of traditional ornamentation were completely rejected by the New Art enthusiasts with the introduction of Art Nouveau at the end of the century.

1. ROCOCO · 1840–1850

By 1830 the Victorian age was dawning. The day of the individual silversmith was ending and the style of American silver was changing. Although the Empire style persisted into the 1840's it was often used in combination with Romantic decoration which anticipated the Rococo revival. There were style influences from abroad but by 1840 silver began to be manufactured by machine and the coming of mass production brought about changes in design. Until now little mechanical progress had been made in sterling manufacturing. The application of machinery to the working of precious metal was only beginning. John Gorham was one of the pioneers in the use of machinery. In 1847 Gorham installed a steam engine in his plant at Providence, Rhode Island. He broadened the use of machinery in making flat silver and, later, silver hollow ware. Gorham's search for new and better ways to make sterling silverware was not confined to machines. He brought silversmiths from England who were skilled in the manufacture of hollow ware such as tea sets and pitchers with the aid of machine tools. The devising of mechanical methods such as spinning speeded up manufacture and produced cheaper goods and made silver available to an increasing number of people. Articles of gold and silver which had long been connected with the power and opulence of royalty were now available to persons of lesser wealth. Thus the machine, together with the discovery of new deposits of ore in various parts of the world, made silver so desirable that it became the chief status symbol of the Victorian Era.

The silver production of the Victorian Era was also influenced by both social and economic customs and events. First and foremost were the great international exhibitions. Beginning with the London Great Exhibition of the Works of Industry of all Nations at the Crystal Palace in 1851, there followed a series of international exhibitions. Among the ones which included the work of American silver companies were the exhibits in New York and Dublin, Ireland, in 1853, Paris in 1855, 1857, 1889 and 1900, Brussels in 1861, London in 1862, Vienna in 1873, the Philadelphia Centennial in 1876, the World's Columbian Exhibition at Chicago in 1893, and the St. Louis Exposition in 1904. However, the only American silver manufacturers who exhibited their products in most of these big exhibitions were Gorham and Tiffany. Tiffany had a Paris branch and was thus nearer the scene of the foreign exhibitions. Gorham, however, had a larger organization and their chief designer from about 1868 was Thomas Pairpoint who had worked his apprenticeship in Paris and later worked in London for the important firm of Lambert & Rawlings. These connections abroad brought the American firms in touch with the activities of English and continental silversmiths and were an important influence in American silver design of the last half of the nineteenth century.

The rococo style was well on its way in England and the Continent before it reached America. However, Samuel Kirk, who followed the English tradition, had initiated repoussé into his silver pieces early in the century, the first such piece having been made in 1824. Repoussé is a raised over-all naturalistic decorative pattern of rococo floral detail often combined with sentimental scenes. Repoussé was not generally popular in America until the 1840's when it became one of the most characteristic elements in rococo silverwork and one of the chief methods of decoration on Victorian silver.

The rococo was the first and also the most important style development in the decorative arts of the Victorian Era. It lasted for many years, flourishing side by side and intermingled with the other influences such as

ABOVE. Teapot and sugar bowl, gadrooned lobes continued into panels marked by engraving. Handles, flower finial and design on base are cast. R. & W. Wilson, Philadelphia, 1825–1846. (*Gebelein Silversmiths*) BELOW LEFT. Candlestick and matching trimmers. Classic design with rococo foliate borders. George Gelston, New York, c. 1837. Lent by Mr. and Mrs. Mark Bortman to the "Classical America" exhibition. (*Newark Museum*)

Gothic and Elizabethan strapwork. The revival of the exuberance of the curved line rococo in silverware was expressed in exaggerated shapes and florid ornamentation. Although many classical shapes were still used and motifs such as acanthus leaves and husks remained in style for a time, the curved forms were more popular and the handles, lids, and feet of articles tended to become engulfed with exaggerated curved leaf decoration. Tea and coffee pots and pitchers were of various shapes; high-shouldered, straight-sided with feet continuing the line of the body, pear-shaped forms with heavy rounded bases, fanciful curved forms with spherical bodies and lobed forms with wide, rounded shoulders. Ornament was now something added to the object, not an integral part of the form, and motifs of rococo or naturalistic decoration were applied indiscriminately to all forms. The

ABOVE. Tea set, Chased floral design. Marquand & Co. Waste bowl. Ball, Tompkins & Black, c. 1839. (*The New-York Historical Society*) BELOW AND LOWER RIGHT, PAGE 46. Tea set, all-over rococo design. R. & W. Wilson, c. 1825 (*Philadelphia Museum of Art*)

acanthus became of such luxurious growth that it often overpowered the form of the vase or other object that it decorated. The grapevine had twining branches with heavy bunches of grapes and gnarled oak branches were laden with acorns. Rococo motifs of design from the eighteenth century—waves, scrolls, and flowers—were again in vogue. Oriental influence is seen in chased floral repoussé designs and here there was a tendency to fill up every space with scrollwork, oval cartouches and flowers, or Orien-

ABOVE. Silver cake basket, oak leaf and acorn repoussé with rustic grip handles. Jones, Ball & Poor, Boston, 1840–1846. LOWER LEFT. Coffeepot Pear-form with floral chasing and gadroon bands. Lincoln & Foss, Boston, 1848–1858. (*Gebelein Silversmiths*) LOWER RIGHT. Teapot with oak leaf and acorn decoration. Jones, Ball & Co., Boston, 1850–1852. (*The Worcester Art Museum*)

tal landscapes, thus imitating the French silverwork of the earlier rococo period. Many ornate pitchers with floral patterns and landscaped scenes were made at this time. A pitcher with a scene of a Whig meeting was made by Osmon Reed of Philadelphia and presented by the Whigs of Philadelphia to the Governor of Tennessee in 1843. A pair of pitchers of ornate rococo design decorated with rural landscapes was made by Kirk for the president of Harvard College in 1860. This type of rococo work continued for many years, as is evidenced by the monteith bowl with similar repoussé background and a scene of General Israel Putnam leaving

Covered cream jug with engraved and chased decoration. Hayden & Whilden, Charleston, 1855–1863. Sketches of Laforme Brothers, Boston, 1850–55, show similiar design. (*Gebelein Silversmiths*)

ABOVE. Tea and coffee service. Bulbous pear shapes, chased vintage-leaf repoussé scrolls, vine-knotted handles and spout, grape finials. H.B. Stanwood & Co., Boston. Coin silver, c. 1855. (*Gebelein Silversmiths*) BELOW. Tea and coffee service, hand-chased rococo design. The foliated legs continue the body lines. William Gale & Son, New York, c. 1851. (*Gebelein Silversmiths*)

his farm to go to the Battle of Lexington. It was made by Andrew E. Warner of Baltimore (1786–1870). An article in Frank Leslie's Illustrated Newspaper, June 14, 1856, describes a presentation silver service of similar workmanship consisting of a salver, coffee urn, cream pitcher, sugar, and slop bowl. The service was made by W. T. and T. V. Gendar of New York. The description reads: "The different pieces were splendidly embossed and ornamented very appropriately with scenes from camp life. On the coffee urn was a representation of a sentry on duty before the guard tent, on the waste bowl appeared the whole regiment on parade, and on the sugar bowl an officer was represented giving the countersign to a sentinel. On the cream pitcher were several well-struck military figures. The lid-handle of each piece was the figure of a drummer sitting on his drum; the bodies of the different articles rest upon pedestals composed of eagles and live oak." The following inscription is engraved on each piece: "To Captain James Price from The Third Company National Guard, May 31, 1856." One of the important sets of American rococo silverware was the dinner service presented to Commodore Matthew Calbraith Perry by the Chamber of Commerce and Merchants of New York in 1855 which was made by William Gale & Son of New York and is described on page 133. This silver service is now in The New-York Historical Society.

The development of naturalism was an influential factor in the design of the rococo silver style of the mid-nineteenth century. The use of ornament based on natural forms was evident in English silver design as early as the 1830's and reached its height of popularity in the 1840's and undoubtedly had an influence on American silver design. Not only were design motifs naturalistic but objects themselves also took on the forms of flowers and leaves. There were shell and leaf dishes and vases in the form of convolvulus. Samuel Kirk made a pear-shaped pepper shaker set on a leaf. Naturalism at its height is most often seen in candelabra, dessert stands, and centerpieces. An oak tree with a pair of stags at its base rose from a rockwork ground and formed a pedestal which held glass dishes for fruit or bonbons. This was illustrated in an advertisement of Gorham Manufacturing Co. in 1853. Candlestick stems became twisted grapevines laden with bunches of grapes. A wine ewer made by Samuel Kirk as early as 1828 was decorated with a restrained design of grapes and leaves. At the end of the 1840's the grapevine designs became coarse and heavy and

ABOVE. Tea set with hot-water urn. Repoussé in Oriental style. Samuel Kirk & Son, 1846–1861. (*Nord Antiques, Inc.*) BELOW. Monteith bowl decorated with repoussé florals and scene of General Israel Putnam leaving his farm to go to the Battle of Lexington. Removable serrated rim and lion heads with ring handles. Andrew E. Warner, 1786–1870. (*Collection of Philip H. Hammerslough*)

naturalism also took on the forms of exotic tropical plants such as palm trees.

One of the most elaborate pieces of the period was a dessert service shown in an advertisement of Tiffany & Company, c. 1852. It consists of a tray with a tall branching column in rococo style ornamented with flowing acanthus foliage and "C" cartouches. At the top of the center column is a tall slender vase. Arms branching out about twelve inches below hold bowls for fruit and flowers. On a lower level shelves are grouped about the center column which hold a coffee pot, a sugar bowl and a cream pitcher. The lowest group of shelves holds teapots; and grouped around the tray at the base are twelve cups and saucers. This elaborate service was undoubtedly executed on special order, perhaps in Tiffany's Paris house.

The bodies of the tea sets of this period were ovoid with incurvate necks, and embossed decoration abounds in "C" and "S" scrolls, flowers, leaves, and grapes. The handles are often rustic twigs or grapes and leaves,

LEFT. Pitcher, repoussé floral decoration with medallions of landscape scenes, double "C" handle. Made for President Abbott Lawrence Lowell of Harvard, c. 1850. (*Samuel Kirk & Son*) RIGHT. Pitcher with scene of a Whig meeting. Presented to the Governor of Tennessee in 1843. Osmon Reed, Philadelphia. (*Philadelphia Museum of Art*)

while the finials are naturalistic roses or other blossoms. By mid-century Kirk's tea sets had elaborate naturalistic repoussé patterns made up of floral detail and sentimental scenes. The handles were tall and angular. Ball, Tompkins & Black also made tea sets in rococo style and Tiffany & Co. made tea sets covered with naturalistic grapes and leaves. One such set is now in the Museum of the City of New York. Similar tea sets were also made by Gorham Manufacturing Co. in Providence, Rhode Island, and by Bailey & Co., Krider & Biddle and J. E. Caldwell & Co., Philadelphia, as well as by silversmiths in Boston, Massachusetts; Charleston, South Carolina; and many smaller cities throughout the country.

A few years later designs appeared which were inspired by the Italian Renaissance which had now become popular in England and France. There were also forms and motifs from Greek and Etruscan art which influenced a return to the classical. These classic forms were exhibited at the London Crystal Palace in 1851. New shapes such as the elongated Greek oenochoë or wine pitcher with hoof feet were used for

BELOW. Covered vegetable dish, repoussé hand-chased. George Sharp for Bailey & Co., Philadelphia, c. 1850. (*Gebelein Silversmiths.*) RIGHT. Sugar bowl, rococo design. Part of set presented to Commodore Matthew Calbraith Perry. William Gale & Son, 1855. (*The New-York Historical Society*)

ABOVE. Tray with heavy bull's eye rim and engravings of early California life. Tiffany & Co., c. 1850–1855. (*James E. Birch Silver Collection, University of California*) (*Photo, East Bay Magazine*)
RIGHT. Coffee urn, repoussé leafage with scenes of California Gold Rush days. Finial figure of miner panning gold.

jugs and tea and coffee pots. The amphora, hydria, and cylix forms were also used. Other tea and coffee pots were low-slung, ovular or divided into angular panels. They were decorated with engraved acanthus, strapwork and other architectural details. Beading again became a favorite form of decoration and such motifs as the anthemion were used together with Grecian scenes of soldiers and horses. This classic style remained in popular use for several decades, but later the shapes became more exaggerated and design motifs were again more realistic and less formal.

The Great Exhibition of 1851 in London had brought forth elaborate hollow ware designs of the silversmiths of England and the Continent. There were massive ornate pieces which combined sculpture and ornament in symbolical groups of the Seasons, the Hours, and the Elements. Such fictional representations as the Story of Robert Bruce together with plants and people from exotic China and India also were used as subject matter for silver decoration. Rococo scrolls, flowers, and foliage were combined with enamels in the French and Elizabethan styles. The Renaissance style was especially favored in the French exhibits. The famous centerpiece designed by Prince Albert in 1842 which had naturalistic models of the Queen's dogs amid Renaissance ornament was also exhibited and this helped to bring about the demand for the Renaissance style in America which became the most popular design influence on the silver of the next few decades.

It was during this period that the silver industry was getting established in San Francisco, California. The discovery of the Comstock Lode near Virginia City in Nevada made a quantity of silver readily available. It also created millionaires with the desire for flashy living, and silver was one of the status symbols. During the Comstock era there were extravagant silver dining services made from Comstock Lode silver. There were also such items as silver place cards, menu cards, door knobs and hinges. Many of these larger articles were made by Gorham and Tiffany out of silver shipped direct to them from the mines. Although there were undoubtedly many silver services made, only two are definitely recorded. In Ellin Mackay Berlin's novel, *Silver Platter,* which is a fictional biography

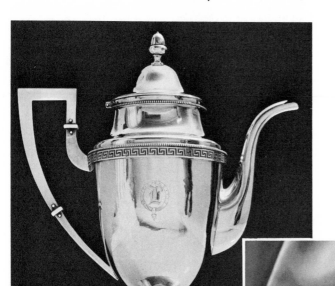

LEFT. Coffee pot, classic urn shape, beading and Greek Key borders, acorn finial. Stamped "V & Co. S.F. Cal. Pure Coin. Geo. C. Shreve" and Golden Bear hallmark of Vanderslice, c. 1863–1867. Made for Governor Low. (*California Historical Society*) BELOW. Covered vegetable dish, Empire style with Greek Key borders, cast ram's head handles and ox finial. Gorham Manufacturing Co., c. 1860. (*Blasdel Silver, Society of California Pioneers*) (*Photo, Western Collector Magazine*)

of John Mackay and the Comstock era, Mrs. Berlin records a conversation between John Mackay and his wife concerning the silver service made for them by Tiffany out of Comstock Lode silver, every piece made to their own design.

As fine as the Mackay silver service may have been, the most interesting service made of gold-rush silver is that which was made for James E. Birch who owned and operated a stagecoach line in the gold-rush days of the 1850's. This set was also designed and made by Tiffany and is now in the Hearst Memorial Mining Building at the University of California at Berkeley. There are twenty-eight pieces in all, including a tea and coffee service, fruit bowls, three trays, a soup tureen, pitchers, goblets and serving ladles and knives. The pieces are of characteristic rococo form and design. Flourishing rococo leaf motifs, etched and embossed, cover the pieces and in the cartouches are scenes of early California. Bears, miners' cabins and stagecoaches are repeated features. Mining scenes and stagecoaches are etched on the sides of the tea service. On the tops of the teapot, coffee urn and sugar bowl are figures of miners panning gold and the cover of a large tureen has an intricate model of an early stagecoach. California bears serve as handles and figures of bears decorate the covers of tureens. Bears also form the legs of trays. But the stagecoach was the most favored motif. A small unharnessed stagecoach rests on the top of a soup tureen and stagecoaches moving at full speed are found on the sides of several pieces. On a large tray which has a heavy bull's eye border there are views of Sutter's Mill, Sutter's Fort, an early California harbor, and a stagecoach drawn by four horses. Each scene is set within a rococo framework of leaves. The principal interest of this silver is derived from the scenes which picture history. The silver is also an excellent example of the fine workmanship and design of the era.

Although a great deal of Comstock Lode silver was sent to Eastern silversmiths there were also silversmiths working in San Francisco at this time and they too made silver for many important local people. The earliest and best known San Francisco silversmiths were George C. Shreve and W. K. Vanderslice. Shreve first manufactured and marked their silverware in 1852 when the two brothers, George C. and S. S. Shreve, opened a jewelry shop. The Bee was the oldest mark of George C. Shreve & Co. The Bell was used until 1920 when it was discontinued. Today "Shreve & Co." is stamped on articles made by Shreve. Although Shreve adver-

ABOVE. Coffeepot and teapot. Low upward-sloping bodies, angl[e]
handles. Renaissance lacework engraving, cupid finials. Made fro[m]
ore mined in Cerro Gordo Mine. Shreve & Co., 1875. (*Californ[ia]
Historical Society*) LEFT. Chocolate pot. Engine-turned, chased a[nd]
engraved. Beaded borders, cast dolphin spout and finial. W. Va[n-]
derslice, San Francisco, c. 1860. (*Blasdel Silver, Society of Ca[li-]
fornia Pioneers*) (PHOTO, *Western Collector Magazine*) BELOW. Silv[er]
tea service, floral and strapwork engraved decoration. Shreve & C[o.]
1873. Given to William Henry Smith, Superintendent of Belch[er]
& Crown Point Mine. Virginia City, Nevada, by miners at his ma[r-]
riage, January, 15, 1874. (*California Historical Society*)

tised in 1854 that he "manufactured to order" and again in 1859, in the *Daily Alta California,* the three silver services in the California Historical Society made by Shreve date from the 1860's and 70's. The set made for Governor F. F. Low who served as Governor of California from 1863 to 1867 is of classic design with borders of beading and Greek fret. The pieces are of urn shape with acorn finials. The pieces have the Vanderslice bear stamp in addition to "Geo. C. Shreve, Pure Coin, S. F. Cal." which suggests that Vanderslice may have done the actual work. The Society also owns two other services that were made by Shreve & Co. from Comstock Lode silver. Both date from the mid 1870's and their low-slung bodies which slope upward, angled handles and straight spouts are typical of the era, as is the etched design of lace work. Also in the California Historical Society there is a pair of 9-socket candelabra about four feet high which were made of Comstock Lode silver by Shreve in 1874 for William Chapman Ralston, the international banker and civic leader of San Francisco.

The other pioneer San Francisco silversmith was W. K. Vanderslice who opened a silver shop in San Francisco in 1858. Vanderslice learned silversmithing in Philadelphia and Maurice Brix lists him in *Philadelphia Silversmiths*—W. Vanderslice, Silverplate 1840. Vanderslice was in business in Philadelphia until 1857 before coming to San Francisco. In 1858 Vanderslice advertised "Better quality of silver and superior work from own natural silver. We are prepared to furnish all Premiums for State Fairs and County Fairs." In the 1860's, according to an article in the *San Francisco Business Director and Mercantile Guide 1864–65* (pp. 318–19), Vanderslice had a workshop that employed thirty artisans, while the large store on Montgomery Street had twelve workmen. It was at this time that Vanderslice made the silver service for the State of Nevada's first governor, Henry Goode Blasdel. This set is now owned by the Society of California Pioneers. It consists of five dozen pieces of hollow ware, including massive trays and tureens, coffee and chocolate pots, tiny nut dishes and napkin rings, and more than one hundred pieces of heavy flatware in Vanderslice's Medallion pattern. Gorham had patented the Medallion pattern in 1864 and Gorham pieces have been found with various retailers' marks in addition to the Gorham mark. Vanderslice merchandised Gorham wares and Shreve was their distributor or West Coast agent. There are also Medallion pieces marked J. W. Tucker & Co.

(San Francisco) and some marked Bailey & Co., both in addition to the Gorham mark. These marks are seen not only on flatware but on such pieces as salts and cups. However, the Medallion pattern of Blasdel flatware is a more refined pattern than the Gorham Medallion. Especially delicate is the banding on the stem and the scrolled leaves that connect the stem with the medallion circle. Smaller pieces of hollow ware such as the spoon holder also are of Medallion pattern. Classic borders including Greek fret decorate the pieces of hollow ware and handles are in the form of goats' heads, lions' heads and dolphins, while finials include lions' heads, a standing goat on the butter dish, and paired dolphins on the chocolate pot. Pieces are engine-turned, chased and engraved, and parts such as handles and finials are cast. Cast medallions are in the center of the compotes and on each handle. Most of the pieces have the Golden Bear hallmark of Vanderslice & Co. which was California's first registered trade-mark, although some pieces such as the vegetable dish bear the Gorham mark.

J. W. Tucker made a five-piece tea set from silver dollars minted from the first ore extracted from the Comstock Lode. It is in the style of the late 1860's with Greek honeysuckle decoration and classic borders and is marked "J. W. Tucker & Co. Coin silver." Similar sets of silver-

Spoons and forks, Medallion pattern. Gorham Manufacturing Co., 1864. (*California Historical Society*)

ware made from Comstock Lode ore are owned by many of the old families of the San Francisco Bay area. Among other silversmiths working in San Francisco in the 1860's were Schulz & Fisher (1868–1887). Their products included both flatware and hollow ware. In the 1890's Hammersmith & Field were important dealers and silversmiths in San Francisco.

An interesting silver trowel in the California Historical Society was made by Vanderslice & Co. and presented to Richard S. Floyd, president of the James Lick Trust, by William W. Story, sculptor, on the occasion of the laying of the cornerstone of the Francis Scott Key Monument, May 28, 1888. It has an ivory handle and an engraved replica of the monument and a pattern of Celtic scrolls surrounds the inscription. Several other pieces of presentation silver made by Vanderslice have recently come to light. A silver salver with beaded border and strapwork engraving surrounding four scenes of early San Francisco, including the Cliff House and Presidio, was presented to John S. Ellis in 1864, and is now in the collection of The New-York Historical Society. On October 4, 1876 a silver vase made by Vanderslice was presented to Edwin Booth, brother of John Wilkes Booth, by the Ladies of the Female Hospital. This piece was seen recently in a well-known New York shop that deals in secondhand

RIGHT. Dessert spoon, ice-cream server and berry spoon. Fiddle-handled, hand-engraved designs. Towle & Jones, 1860. (*Towle Silversmiths*) BELOW. Fruit knife and fork, acorn and oak-leaf pattern. c. 1860. Jones, Shreve, Brown & Co., Boston (*Worcester Art Museum*)

silver. A few years ago it would have been sold for junk silver; today the price almost equals that of some early silver. The inscription and the Vanderslice Golden Bear mark made it a collector's piece.

Old patterns of flatware continued to be popular in the 1850's. These included Plain, Tipt, French Thread, Plain Thread, Oval Thread, Mayflower, Shell, Grape, Kings and Queens. The Olive Leaf and Bead Leaf date from the 1850's. Ribbon was first made about this date by Theodore Evans & Co. and William Gale of New York. The Ribbon pattern, which consisted of bow-knots and borders of ribbons on a pointed tipt form, was designed by John Cook who worked for Marquand & Co. and also for Whiting Manufacturing Co. Ribbon pattern was especially popular in the Southern states before the Civil War. The Grape, Cox, and Le Cordon patterns were designed by Gibney for Whiting Manufacturing Co. They are knot patterns on oval thread forms. Gibney also made a pattern of oak leaves and acorns which was stamped "Gibney." Other patterns based on threaded forms included the Mayflower, an oval thread pattern with beaded design. It was first made in the 1840's but continued popular into the 1860's. The Olive was a leaf pattern combined with pointed thread and the Cottage was a simple variation of the oval thread form.

Spoon patterns. ABOVE. Oval Thread. BELOW, LEFT TO RIGHT. Fiddle; Tuscan, designed by Gibney for Marquand & Co., c. 1845; French Thread; Cox; Le Cordon.

2. THE RENAISSANCE REVIVAL · 1851–1870 (1900)

THE Renaissance Revival with its straight line architectural forms and classical ornament began to be felt in the 1840's. It had been introduced into the displays of silver in London in 1851, and at the Crystal Palace in New York in 1853 the silver exhibited by the English silversmiths was also classical in form and decoration. Although the naturalistic and exuberant rococo styles persisted there was an ever-increasing use of classical designs. Shapes and decoration were restrained and pieces were described as Greek, Etruscan, or Pompeiian. Numerous classical vase forms replaced the bulbous rococo shapes of teapots, coffee pots and jugs, which were now Renaissance versions of the high-handled Grecian vase with vase or helmet finial. While many different styles influenced display pieces and trophies or presentation pieces, the designs of domestic plate were simpler and the ornament more disciplined. There were also heavy round-shaped teapots with straight cylinder necks which combined both naturalism and more formal Renaissance details. Ornament was often reduced to surface engraving. Centerpieces and dessert stands resembled the tazza, or Pompeiian tripod with groups of draped female figures, swans or dolphins at their bases. Popular motifs of design included the anthemion or honeysuckle, stylized foliage and palmette. Borders were of beading, gadrooning, Greek key, waves, guilloche and heavy mouldings. Classical friezes ornamented the more elaborate pieces. Legs which supported the pieces were in the form of scrolled acanthus leaves, lions, rams, goats, griffins, sphinx, or even elephants' hoofs. Handles and finials as well as the body of pieces were ornamented with cast masks, putti, lion heads or swans. More elaborate pieces might be decorated with masks of Comedy and Tragedy or raised figures of Night and Morning, Apollo and Diana, or symbolic figures of Justice, Loyalty, Agriculture, Commerce or the Seasons. Designs combining the pictorial and the classical resulted in the literary, story-telling silver that depicted not only scenes with symbolical significance, but also illustrations of stories from contemporary literature and poetry. Charles Osborne designed a centerpiece illustrating Tennyson's poem "The Day-dream." The central motif of the Sleeping Beauty and the Prince were executed in satin finish ornamented with matting, chasing and parcel gilt. This piece was displayed in the windows of Whit-

Silver service presented to Mrs. Abraham Lincoln. Vase forms with repoussé florals, strapwork and vase finials. Gorham Manufacturing Co., 1860. (*The Smithsonian Institution*)

ing Manufacturing Co. in New York City in 1874. Thomas Pairpoint designed vases and tazzas for Gorham in the 1870's with representations of Thorwaldsen's Night and Morning and figures of Aurora and Venus. Pairpoint owed the literary character of his work to his association with Morel Ladeuil whose designs inspired by Renaissance examples also reflected the Victorian fascination for symbol and allusion.

Centerpieces for fruit and flowers allowed the designer to use his imagination and ingenuity both in the design and workmanship. Greek chariots drawn by cupids were ornamented with classic bas-reliefs whose edges were touched with gold. Centerpieces in Renaissance form were ornamented with chains. A silver fruit service made by Gorham consisted of a tall bowl set on a tripod of Egyptian design. Another centerpiece was composed of a large bowl and three small bowls upheld by a draped feminine figure set on a base with rams' heads and fastened to a burnished dome. A calla lily springs from the center of the large bowl. The finish is a rich combination of oxidation, gilding, and burnishing. An article entitled "The Silver Age" printed in *Scribner's Monthly Magazine,* December, 1873, and reprinted in *Jewelers' Circular,* May 15, 1874, describes the Gorham factory and many pieces of silver then in stock. The illustrations include a tankard decorated with a Grecian grapevine in gilt, a classic border of horses, and a figure of Bacchus astride a wine barrel atop the lid, in satin finish with burnished mouldings. A centerpiece for fruit and flowers reproduces a Grecian chariot drawn by cupids. The body of the chariot is engraved with a Renaissance leaf design and it is satin finished with gold edges and rims. Also illustrated is a silver tureen and stand with a bas-relief border and an engraved pattern of Renaissance lace-work. A silver tray with a wide relief border is "in the style of Benvenuto Cellini." The Raphael pattern of flatware was also in Renaissance style.

During the 1860's the vogue for Renaissance forms and motifs appeared in the silver made by Samuel Kirk. A water jug and tray has a handle ending in a dolphin's head. The body of the jug is covered with stylized Renaissance scroll and leaf designs and delicate engraved and chased ornament. Pompeiian designs with classical detail which were in-

LEFT. Water jug and tray, engraved and chased with Renaissance scroll and leaf designs. Dolphin handle and figure of a faun. 1879. (*Samuel Kirk & Son*) RIGHT. Renaissance vase design with classic figure. Designed by Thomas Pairpoint for Gorham and exhibited at Philadelphia Centennial. (*Art Journal,* 1876)

spired by the English display at the International Exhibition of 1862 decorated the dessert services. Some were in elegant urn shapes with the lower parts of the bodies fluted, with bands of palmette and key and wave ornament. The designs of less well-known manufacturers were often hackneyed expressions of the style. Tea sets of heavy awkward design sat on slender goats' legs and neo-Renaissance motifs were engraved on oval panels. Most of the decorative detail on the silver of this period was produced by engraving, flat chasing and casting. Some pieces were ornamented with pierced work and embossing or repoussé, which became one of the characteristic techniques of the period. Articles were spun on machines but finished by hand. The naturalism of the designs was increased by the use of gilding. Variety of surface textures such as a matte ground, which was a dull surface produced by light punch work or by oxidation, were contrasted with the burnished surface. Frosted or white surfaces were also used for contrast. Indented surfaces, too, produced a variety of highlights and shadows on plainer articles. Enameling in color was also developed at this time.

The 1860's saw the end of the individual silversmith and the beginning of wholesale production of silverware by the silver manufacturing companies. There were companies in Boston, New York and Philadelphia but there were also large centers of silver manufacture in North Attleboro,

LEFT. After-dinner coffee pot, repoussé Renaissance floral and leaf design with youths and maidens. Tiffany & Co. c. 1885. Lent by Mrs. Lawrence C. Ward to the exhibition, "Silver in Newark." (*Newark Museum*) BELOW. Centerpiece with engraved fret and grapevine borders and winged swan-head handles. Eoff & Shepherd, New York. (*Gebelein Silversmiths*)

Massachusetts; Providence, Rhode Island; Meriden and Hartford, Connecticut, and Newark, New Jersey. Other centers of nineteenth century silver manufacture were in Baltimore, Maryland; St. Louis, Missouri, and Cincinnati, Ohio.

Flatware patterns with Renaissance-inspired designs which were brought out in the 1860's and 1870's include Medallion which was first made by Gorham in about 1864. This pattern is often found with the marks of other silver companies alone or together with the Gorham mark. Medallion was also made by Vanderslice & Co. of San Francisco. The design consists of a circular medallion enclosing heads of Grecian warriors with helmets or of women with heads crowned with a diadem or wreath. Hollow ware pieces were also available. Gorham also made Renaissance-inspired patterns such as Grecian (1861), Ionic, Italian and Ivy (1865–1870). Other patterns made by Gorham at this time were: Bird's Nest, Byzantine, Olive, Pompeii, Princess, Rosette, and Fleur-de-Lis, all made between 1865 and 1870. Tiffany's flatware patterns during these years were Beekman (1869), King William and Saratoga (1870), Palm and Audubon (1871). The Beekman was Tiffany's first pattern. It has a shell at the tip of the handle which is supported by Grecian scrolls in the form of a modified antefix, an architectural ornament which was placed at the corner of the roof to hide the joints in the eaves. The Saratoga is also a combination of Grecian scrolls and honeysuckle while the Palm is a plain-tipt pattern with a conventional Grecian palm motif. The Angelo

Spoons. TOP. Chrysanthemum, 1880. BOTTOM, LEFT TO RIGHT. Saratoga, 1870; King William, 1870; Palm, Tiffany & Co., 1871; Fiddle, Towle & Jones, 1860. (*Towle Silversmiths*)

pattern of Wood & Hughes has an engraved design of a Renaissance vase and scrolls. It was brought out in the late '60's. They also made Cellini, Venetian and Murillo, which are ornamented with delicate tracery.

Joseph Seymour, Sons & Co., of Syracuse, New York (1850–1909), was also an extensive producer of sterling flatware. Seymour began as a silversmith in New York City in 1835 and worked in Utica during the 1840's before establishing in Syracuse. In common with other silversmiths he produced the old designs. In 1850 he introduced the Honeysuckle, an oval fiddle-shaped pattern tipped with a device representing the conventional honeysuckle. In 1852, he produced a plain fiddle-tipt, and in 1854 the Wreath, which was his first original pattern. It is a variation of the Oval Thread in outline ornamented with a wreath at the tip. The Twist Engraved, a spoon with a twisted stem, was brought out in 1860. It was one of the first engraved patterns made. In 1866 Seymour designed the Prairie Flower, a pattern with a head of an Indian girl in the tip. The Union was produced in 1867. The outline is squared and forecasts the more radical departures of the 1870's but its decoration consists of a thread with simple braided devices.

Paulding Farnham was the foremost exponent of Renaissance silver design in America in the nineteenth century. For that reason a discussion of his work is included here although the majority of his silver was made after 1880. As early as 1889 Paulding Farnham, like his uncle C. T. Cook, was a member of the firm and one of the chief designers at Tiffany & Company. His specialty was jewelry, but he also designed many pieces of silverware. Farnham was a classic designer. He had a thorough technical training in silversmithing and a knowledge of the detail of historic styles. But what is most important, he had a feeling for the nature of the material

Salver with Renaissance fruit and flower border. Paulding Farnham for Tiffany & Co.

TOP LEFT. Dessert plate, Renaissance fruit, flower and vase design, openwork border. Paulding Farnham for Tiffany & Co. (*International Studio*, vol. 29, 1906) TOP RIGHT. Mirror, Florentine style. BOTTOM LEFT. Cologne bottle, Florentine style. BOTTOM RIGHT. Silver teapot, Renaissance style, hammered and chased with vase and leaf designs and sculptured caryatid figures. All by Paulding Farnham for Tiffany & Co. (*Jewelers' Circular*, Nov. 2, 1904)

which may have been gained from his work as a sculptor. He also had a fine sense of color which he employed in the combination of different metals, gems and enamels. Farnham had been with Tiffany & Co. since youth and received his entire training in the factories and art departments of Tiffany & Co. under the guidance of Edward C. Moore and James H. Whitehouse. In 1892 Farnham was Secretary of Tiffany & Co., and a member of the Board of Trustees. Farnham was listed as an Applied Arts member of the Architectural League in 1892 and in 1895 he exhibited a sculpture figure, "Phoenicia and the Wind," at the National Sculpture Society exhibition although he was never recorded as a member. However, in the *New York City Directories* Farnham listed himself as a sculptor and he shared a studio with his sculptor wife, Sallie Farnham, in the old studio building at 57 West 57th Street, New York City. In the book *Charles L. Tiffany and the House of Tiffany,* a reprint from the article by George Frederic Heydt in *Godey's Magazine,* August 1893, Farnham is listed as the Secretary and as a Trustee of Tiffany & Co. At this time Paulding Farnham was the chief designer and director of the jewelry factory of Tiffany and all of the jewelry sent to the Chicago Fair in 1893 was designed and executed under his supervision. John T. Curran was the chief designer of the Tiffany silver works in Prince Street, New York City, and James H. Whitehouse was managing director of the engraving de-

Adams Gold Vase, Renaissance style with allegorical figures and design motifs of indigenous American flora and fauna. Paulding Farnham for Tiffany & Co., 1900.

partment. Tiffany also operated the Adams & Shaw plated ware factory at Forest Hill, Newark, New Jersey. According to a notice from *Jewelers' Circular Vol. VII* (August, 1876), reprinted in the catalogue (Fall-Summer 1966) of the Newark Museum exhibit of Newark silver, "Tiffany was interested in the manufacturing and wholesale business of the Adams & Shaw Company, Mr. C. L. Tiffany himself being its treasurer." As time went on and other designers, including James Whitehouse, who had been with Tiffany for forty years in 1898, became less active, Farnham assumed their responsibilities and also did more actual designing.

Many of the important pieces of Tiffany silver exhibited in Paris in 1900 and at the St. Louis Exposition in 1904 were designed and executed under the personal supervision of Paulding Farnham. The exhibits at Paris were notable in design, workmanship, and materials. Farnham also designed presentation swords, including the sword for Admiral Dewey which was made by Tiffany in 1899. In 1900 Tiffany was commissioned to design and make the Adams Gold Vase. This vase, which was 19¼ inches tall, symbolized the growth and development of cotton and the achievement in American finance and commerce. The vase is an example of the thoroughness of the research that characterized the work of Paulding Farnham who was responsible for its design. Every detail of the design, from the cotton blossom to the owl and falcons, was studied first hand from living plants and animals brought to the studio. The chief design motif was the cotton flower which also suggested the outline of the vase. Cotton leaves of delicate design and enamel make up the base of the vase while heavy purple cotton stems form the handles and contrast with the gold. On the sides the cotton flower is shown as it bursts into flower. The body of the vase is oval. The allegorical figures of Modesty and Genius are in chased repoussé and are worked in relief from the body of the metal. A lattice work covers the vase as a background and the roots at the base are studded with gems. All of the materials used in the vase are native American products. The gold was from the mines of Forrest City, California, and the rock crystal, spessartite garnets, tourmalines, amethysts, were all mined in America. The base of the vase was of agatized wood from Arizona. The combination of metal, gems, and colored enamels must have given a jewel-like richness. Tiffany put out a booklet with a description of the vase and a photograph, which is shown here only in photostat, however, the present whereabouts of this valuable vase being unknown.

The Tiffany exhibits at the St. Louis Exposition also recognized Paulding as the chief Tiffany designer. An article in the *Jewelers' Circular*, November 2, 1904, is headed "Tiffany & Co. Silver by Paulding Farnham" and begins thus: "In the Art Pavilion is a case, and on a card of information printed in gold on light lavender velvet is the following:

FAR LEFT. Goblets with Renaissance swags. Baldwin & Co., Newark, 1854–1869. (*Newark Museum*) CENTER LEFT. Water pitcher, Greek Revival. Chased band, ivy, grape and oak tendrils on matted background. Gorham, c. 1860. An entire tea and coffee service was available in this pattern. (*Gebelein Silversmiths*) RIGHT. Cream jug, gadroon borders, engraved shoulder ornament, gold lined. Characteristic Victorian knobs on handle. Crosby, Morse & Foss, Boston, c. 1870. (*Gebelein Silversmiths*) BOTTOM LEFT. Coin-silver pitcher, beaded rim, foliated handle. N. Harding & Co., Boston, c. 1850. CENTER. Syrup jug with fret and bead borders, twist rope handle. Shreve, Brown & Co., Boston, 1857. RIGHT. Covered jug, plain except for artichoke finial. Vincent Laforme, c. 1845. (*Gebelein Silversmiths*)

'These objects designed and executed under the personal supervision of Paulding Farnham. They are loaned by Tiffany & Co.' " The exhibits were in Renaissance and Florentine style, the revival of which had begun in the 1860's. Farnham, who was certainly the outstanding exponent of

TOP. Bud vases. CENTER PAIR, child with shovel. Gorham, c. 1860. LEFT. Greek Revival, 1869. RIGHT. Two-handled Greek vase form. William Gale & Son. (*Gebelein Silversmiths*) BOTTOM. Tea service, neo-classic style. Bowl-shaped bodies, fluted, engraved borders with fluted artichoke finials. Jones, Shreve, Brown, Boston, 1854. Sugar bowl, Bigelow, Kennard & Co., 1860. (*Gebelein Silversmiths*)

the Renaissance style in American silver, continued to favor this style and the majority of his important pieces reflect Renaissance influence. The pieces exhibited in St. Louis included a tea set in Renaissance style. The entire body of the pieces, which consisted of a teapot, sugar bowl and creamer, were hammered into form by hand, then chased as repoussé, hammering from the underside and chasing back again from the front to refine the ornament. The design consisted of delicate Renaissance formal scrolls and garlands of flowers. The bowls of the pieces were raised on caryatids, and the handles, the spouts, and the tops of the pieces have characteristic figures. The accompanying salver has a border of formal flower groups in repoussé and added bands of chasing. Also exhibited was a three-piece toilet set consisting of a mirror, powder box and cologne bottle in Florentine design, executed in gold repoussé and delicate chasing. The general decoration of the pieces shows caryatids, naiads and nymphs of the forest connected by garlands of flowers. On the cologne bottle caryatids are surmounted, one by Thalia, the other by Melpomene, muses of Comedy and Tragedy. Also shown was a tall, slender, gold-enameled vase, a silver gilt and enamel basket labeled Mandarin, which combined rock crystal with Chinese decoration in colored enamel. A repoussé gold and carved ivory inkwell was in East Indian design and another silver inkwell in Burmese style, with ivory top and ivory carved tusk. These pieces are all remarkable not only for their materials and exquisite workmanship but for the interesting content of their design which takes us back to the mythical figures of Renaissance ornament and the exotic details of Oriental design. They give us a picture of the ornate opulence of the silver made for the wealthy American in the late nineteenth century, and one regrets that they cannot be seen and studied today.

LEFT. Florentine black coffee pot and stand. Gorham, c. 1890. RIGHT. Silver salver in style of Benvenuto Cellini. The Gorham Co. (*Jewelers' Circular,* May 15, 1874)

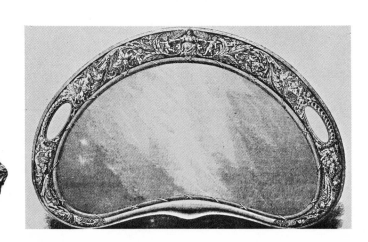

3. ECLECTICISM · 1870–1900

THE process of reviving the styles of the past which began in the first half of the nineteenth century reached its height in the decades 1870–1900, when the repertory of styles included every known decorative development. The styles were not only revived but were also combined and elements of two or more different styles were introduced on a single piece. Thus we find combinations of Renaissance and Elizabethan, Moorish and Persian, Japanese and Jacobean. These revivals—classical, medieval, Renaissance, baroque, rococo, and Oriental—continued to intermingle in the design of silverware as well as in the other decorative arts until the end of the century. There was an absence of a unifying style in much of the silver and in most instances the originality as well as the beauty and workmanship had disappeared. However, there were many large presentation and testimonial pieces made at this time that were not only extreme in style, but fine in workmanship. For these pieces the silver companies employed artistic designers and draftsmen, many of whom were trained in Europe. Although the majority of the designers at Gorham were Englishmen who had served their apprenticeship abroad, for the most part, those at Tiffany were American-trained in their own workshops. However, one of the foremost artists at Tiffany & Company was James Whitehouse who had his training under Morel Ladeuil in London. Ladeuil was of French origin and served his apprenticeship in France and his designs, which were shown in the various exhibitions, favored the Renaissance style. They were literary in character and he told a story with his hammer similar to that of the paintings of the era.

Although mythological figures and symbolism were characteristic of such large pieces as testimonials and trophies, the domestic plate of the 1870's tended to be more simple. A marked angularity was seen in the forms of jugs and tea and coffee pots with the main part of the body sloping toward the top and curving inward below to a flat base. These forms were sometimes ornamented with bands of moulding, and tall angular handles rose above the tops of vessels. Centerpieces and candelabra had a columnar stem with branches at right angles. A low wide dish combining

Bowl and spoon holder. Haddock, Lincoln & Foss, Boston, 1868. (*Gebelein Silversmiths*)

a glass container in a silver framework with cupids and draped classic figures became popular.

Flat patterns of engraved and chased historical ornament began to replace cast and relief decoration on domestic plate. The classical designs included scenes and motifs such as Greek frets and ovolos along with Persian, Indian, and Egyptian motifs and arabesques. By the 1870's flat surfaces with engraved Adam motifs were again popular and copies of Adam-style urn shapes decorated with engraved wreaths, swags and rams' heads characterized the tea sets of the period. The Japanese style, brought in by the ending of Japan's isolation, had been introduced at several exhibitions in the 1860's. It was also favored for domestic plate. Straight-sided shapes of Japanese derivation had handles of bamboo and dragon forms and engravings of exotic plants and birds.

By the 1880's mechanical copies of eighteenth century shapes and motifs called Queen Anne vied for popularity with other copies termed Louis Seize. Tea and coffee pots were straight sided, handles were scrolled with acanthus leaf decoration or fluted, and spouts were slightly curved or fluted. Engraved patterns of leaves, wreaths, swags, and formal borders had center medallions. A debased rococo decoration was also typical of the 1880's and 1890's.

Elaborate epergnes and candelabra were out of style. A large silver or cut glass lamp and small shaded candlesticks with pierced silver shades at each place and baskets or bowls for flowers was the usual dining table decoration of the 1890's. In 1895 there was a revival of Colonial and Old English styles in both hollow ware and flatware. The designs were a combination of garlands of leaves and beading and the forms were modifications of the classic Adam vase. Teapots and coffee pots were octagon in shape with beaded borders and simple leaf ornament. The finials repeated the form of the vessel. These sets were made in an entire line comprising silver tea sets, tête-à-tête sets, black coffee sets, cup and condiment sets, ice cream dishes and plates.

After-dinner coffee pots were made in long-necked exotic shapes taken from Persian and Turkish models. A Gorham advertisement of

After-dinner coffees showing classic, Persian and other influences. Gorham Plate, 1888. Similiar shapes also made in sterling silver. LOWER RIGHT, PAGE 77. Adam-style coffee. (*Jewelers' Circular*, March 25, 1891)

the 1890's reads: "After Dinner Coffees. In odd and unique designs, Turkish, Moorish and Old English decoration, in combination with Sugar Dish, Tongs and tray to match. The assortment comprises both plain and elaborate decoration." Their decoration, however, was often naturalistic and original, such as the coffee pots, one of which is ornamented with oak leaves and acorns in relief, and the other with a design of thistle leaves and blossoms.

Jewelers' Weekly reports the exhibits of Tiffany and Gorham at the Paris Exposition Universelle in 1889. The Tiffany exhibit included pieces in Saracenic and native American themes. The American pieces employed native materials and the designs incorporated American flowers and foliage, American animals, and American sports and Indian scenes. The display included household articles such as tea sets and dinner sets as well as more elaborate costly "made to order" vases and loving cups. The articles, many of them in repoussé, were decorated with a combination of enameling, niello, etching, inlaying and gilding. Coffee pots and teapots were decorated with a combination of repoussé and enameled lines with a groundwork of etching. Open-mouthed pieces such as sugar bowls were decorated on their inner surfaces. Chief among the pieces with American decoration was the tea and coffee service in a design of American flowers and ferns in repoussé. The service consisted of a salver, teapot, coffee pot, sugar bowl, cream ewer, waste bowl, kettle and stand. A small tête-à-tête tea set was ornamented with mountings and repoussé bosses set with baroque pearls. The price was $1,200. A coffee pot of butterfly design was ornamented with parcel gilt, inlay of pearl shell and opals. There were also cases of spoons, knives and forks, bonbon dishes, compotes, an enameled tea caddy, a water pitcher and a tankard, both decorated with chased and etched foliage or flowers.

The designs of silver in the Gorham Manufacturing Company's exhibit were predominantly East Indian. There was a massive tea service, chased and engraved in East Indian design and a pair of candelabra ornamented with silver and gold oxidized on the chasing. The base was casket shaped and the pedestal which held the candelabra rested on a representation of a sacred elephant. There were also dinner and tea sets chased and engraved in Greek designs and a group of silverware of Louis XVI style decorated in rococo with figures of cupids. Other pieces include water pitchers, jardinières, punch bowls, a group of tankards, prize and loving

cups in combinations of silver and bronze. The loving cup of the Massachusetts Humane Society was inlaid with gold, silver, and bronze medals. The prize cup of the yacht *Sachem* was also in the exhibit as was the American Shield, a patriotic plaque designed and modeled by F. A. Heller for the Centennial Exposition in 1876. The exhibit also included scent bottles, puff boxes, manicure sets, inkstands of silver and cut glass, and many other small useful articles.

ABOVE. Tea set, late English revival. Fluted, half gadroon-chased, bead rim and vase finials. Goodnow & Jenks, 1893–1900. BELOW. Tea set, matted and chased with tendrils. The Gorham Co., 1872. (*Gebelein Silversmiths*)

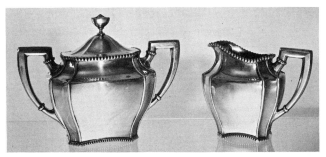

UPPER RIGHT. Small after-dinner coffeepot, classic vase form, applied festoons. Ferdinand Fuchs & Son, New York, 1898. UPPER LEFT. Creamer and sugar bowl, 18th century revival. Crosby & Foss, 1868. (*Gebelein Silversmiths*) LOWER. Sugar and creamer, classic revival with vase finial and heavy gadrooned borders. Towle Manufacturing Co., c. 1900. (*Towle Silversmiths*)

Gorham's exhibit at the Chicago Fair was much more impressive than their Paris exhibit a few years earlier. Many special exhibition pieces were made, including the silver statue of Columbus which was a reproduction of the statue by the sculptor Bartholdi. Silver sculpture had enjoyed great popularity in England from the middle to the end of the century. English scenes with horses and figures of riders were put at the bases of hunt cups and on centerpieces for the table. Pieces were also made with scenes from English history and symbolical scenes from Greek mythology. It was the influence of the latter which was seen in the Gorham exhibits at Chicago and many of the vases and bowls had sculptural scenes from mythology.

H. J. Barrett, who had long experience in England where he was connected with Hunt & Roskell of London, was now at Gorham. His vase on the theme of "Ulysses defying Polyphemus" from the *Odyssey* represents the story in high relief showing figures of Ulysses, Boreas the wind and the blind giant Polyphemus about to hurl a boulder. At the base are figures of water nymphs and on the handle a full relief figure of a mermaid. The remainder of the vase is covered with elaborate scrollwork in high relief. Another artistic production was the "Jaeger Bowl" which reproduced a scene with the god Neptune and figures of dolphins and sea nymphs in bold relief. Another elaborate punch bowl was designed by Granville Hastings, and one of the most striking pieces in the show was the cup representing Andromeda and Perseus. The figure of Andromeda is in full relief chained to the cup in the form of a nautilus shell and at the base is Perseus mounted on the winged horse Pegasus. A repoussé tea set in Renaissance design by George Wilkinson was also exhibited. Gorham's ecclesiastical exhibit at Chicago was also of special note. Although Gorham had maintained an ecclesiastical department for many years it had developed recently under the direction of the Superintendent, William

Centerpiece. Plateau, bowls and flower vase. Gorham Manufacturing Co., c. 1890. Catalogue.

ABOVE. Oriental East Indian tea service exhibited at Paris Exposition in 1889. BELOW.
Tea service with fluting and floral chasing. Special catalogue in French and English,
Paris, The Gorham Co., 1889.

ABOVE LEFT. After-dinner coffee pot and tray. Gorham Manufacturing Co. (*Jewelers' Circular*, 1890) RIGHT. Silver tea kettle and stand, repoussé chased in elaborate rococo style. Gorham Exhibit, Columbian Exposition, Chicago, 1893. BELOW. Tea service. Repoussé with American flowers and ferns exhibited by Tiffany & Co. at Paris Exposition, 1889. (*Jewelers' Weekly,* vol. 8.)

SUGAR BOWL.

CREAM EWER.

J. Codman. The masterpiece of the exhibit was an altar cross 42 inches high which was designed by Codman. The body of the cross was bronze plated with gold and set with crystal, amethyst, topaz, garnet and other stones and enamel work. The cross was set on a base of hemidecagonal form and at the foot of the cross on branches are the figures of the Virgin and St. John. The figure of Christ on the cross is in oxidized silver and the flowered extremities of the cross have the symbols of the Evangelists. A communion set, alms basins, a sanctuary lamp and a paschal candlestick made for St. Patrick's Cathedral, New York, were also in the exhibit.

This silver exhibited by Gorham and Tiffany at the World Columbian Exposition at Chicago in 1893 gives a picture of the elaborately decorated silver show pieces made by American manufacturers in the 1890's. Tiffany exhibited many and varied designs with distinctive American characteristics including the Magnolia Vase of Pueblo Indian design. This was covered with decoration of native American blossoms and buds. The design, which was chased with relief enameling, had a lattice work of cactus leaves in high relief and a border of goldenrod executed in gold. The base was studded with opals. The heavy frieze of magnolias was richly enameled in natural colors. John T. Curran, the chief designer in the Tiffany works in Prince Street, New York, was the designer of the vase.

Tiffany had been interested in the possibilities of American Indian design motifs for some years. In 1885 Charles T. Grosjean of New York City, who was a Tiffany designer, filed application for a patent on twenty-four designs for spoon handles. These were designs of American Indians performing the various war dances. The patents were assigned to Tiffany

BELOW. Salted-almond dish in shape of an almond. RIGHT. Olive dish in form of an olive. Gorham Manufacturing Co., Catalogue, 1888.

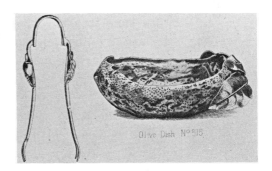

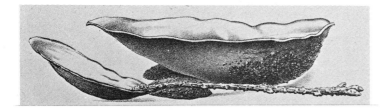

Jaeger Bowl. Gorham Manufacturing Co., World Columbian Exhibition, Chicago, 1893.

& Co., and these spoons were made by Tiffany between this date and 1891 when Charles Moore was still at the company. Sets of Indian War Dance spoons were exhibited at the World's Columbian Exposition at Chicago in 1893. The spoons and other Indian-inspired articles were exhibited and sold in cases, the forms of which suggested Indian flint arrows, knife sheaths, etc. The coverings used were buckskin and soft ooze-finished leathers, decorated with fringes and imprints of Indian signs and hieroglyphics. A unique feature was the applied work decorations of wampum, cut beads, American turquoise and tassels of native Indian workmanship. The other exhibits of Tiffany were also characteristic of American and native materials.

The gold used in the Tiffany exhibit was from California, Alaska and the Klondike; the silver from Colorado, Nevada and New Mexico, and the semiprecious stones and crystals were from American mines. The design influences ranged from Byzantine and Burmese to Viking, and the pieces included wine coolers, vases, candlesticks, presentation pieces and dinner and dessert services. A tea set described as chased "sou-chow" was ornamented with a design of various native American flowers including dogwood, azaleas, clover, buttercups, poppies, apple blossoms, ragged sailor roses, eglantine, marguerites, carnations, heliotrope, chrysanthemum, marigold, pansies, sweet peas, nasturtium, lily-of-the-valley and anemone. The influence of the Southwest American Indian is seen in many designs. An Indian-shape loving cup had a design of an Indian war dance and the handles were buffalo horns. Other vases had goat-foot handles or elephant tusks. A silver vase in Aztec style had a design motif of ears of corn; a bowl in the form of a Zuñi Indian basket was hand hammered and inlaid with niello and turquoise. Another bowl in the form of a Hupa Indian basket had rattlesnake handles. An entirely new and dainty creation was a bouquet basket for brides to carry. The baskets were made of silver and silver gilt in rich openwork designs of flowers suggesting appropriate ideas, such as violets for constancy, pansies for thoughts, daisies for innocence, etc., and the handle was in the form of a silver ribbon bowknot.

Magnolia vase, John T. Curran for Tiffany. (*A Glimpse of the Tiffany Exhibit, Chicago,* by George Frederic Heydt)

Space was left to insert fresh flowers. There is no information as to price but if one of these baskets were located today the price would certainly run into three figures.

Tiffany exhibited many of these same pieces in the Paris Exposition in 1900. There were also coffee pots etched and enameled in Byzantine and Egyptian style and a Greek tête-à-tête tea set with ornament of laurel. A gold-plated silver service of two hundred pieces was Italian XVth century design richly pierced and chased. Another dinner service was pierced and chased in George III style. There were 110 pieces in this set with no two pieces alike. A large oval centerpiece had carefully modelled figures. There were also such sporting articles as silver-mounted rifles, cowboy whips, coaching horns, silver-mounted hunting belts, gun cases of grizzly bear leather and buffalo skin mounted in silver, and an elephant skin and moose-hide bags with a set of hunting knives with buck-horn handles mounted in silver.

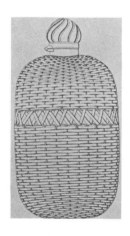

Silver vases were enameled in Celtic, Viking, and Pompeiian style. In 1900 there was a new design influence called Cymric based on Celtic design and characterized by low relief hand-hammering. A chased and pierced vase was in New Zealand style as was a smoker's set which had sharkskin and ivory inlays. A toilet set and a pair of wine coolers were in Burmese style with green enamel disks and silver candlesticks with carved jade sections in the shaft were labeled Byzantine. The extent and variety in the design of these objects is characteristic of the eclecticism of the period.

Eclecticism also is seen in the flatware of the era. The Renaissance style influence in the flatware of the 1860's remained popular through the 1870's. Naturalism and Renaissance details were often combined. The popular old patterns such as Cottage, Rosette, Antique, Palm, Threaded, Plain Tipt, Kings, Queens and Grecian continued to be made. But there were also new influences in silverware design in the 1870's and 1880's. These included the revival of old French designs and the interest in the decoration of the Orient and the Near East as seen in such patterns as Celestial and Japanese by Wood & Hughes; Japanese (Bamboo) and Honeysuckle by Whiting Manufacturing Co.; and Audubon by Tiffany & Co. There were elaborately engraved handles with arabesque designs and ornament such as the Cashmere pattern taken from a Cashmere shawl. Similarly engraved patterns with arabesque work were made by Joseph

Sterling-silver flasks. Gorham Catalogue, 1888.

Seymour Sons & Co. These included Windsor, 1870; Duchess, 1876, and Patrician, 1880. Heavier die-cast designs in related styles included Gorham's Raphael, Lady Washington, and Hindostanee. The chrysanthemum was a favorite motif and a Chrysanthemum pattern was brought out by Tiffany in the 1870's which continues popular today. The well-known Chrysanthemum by Wm. B. Durgin & Co. was not made until 1893.

The forms of the majority of the handles of these spoons were variations on the old traditional oval and pointed Tipt, Threaded, and Kings patterns but there were several patterns made by Wood & Hughes in the 1870's, including Zephyr,

RIGHT. Bride's bouquet-basket, openwork, chased and pierced flowers. BELOW. Pieces of dinner service, Chrysanthemum pattern. Tiffany & Co., first made in 1880. (*Nord Antiques, Inc.*)

Humbolt and Viola which had angular handles and were radical departures from the traditional flatware forms. There were many more of these forms, typical of the 1870's, with panels that resembled the walnut paneled furniture of the era. Some had Egyptian motifs, others had masks, while others had acorns and oak leaves. All were considered outdated in a few years. John Cook had brought out the Centennial pattern in 1876 to commemorate the Centennial Exposition at Philadelphia. It had a simple classical design on a modified angular handle.

The names of flatware patterns in the 1880's reveal eclectic taste and the continued interest in the many styles of the past. There were patterns such as Cellini, Venetian, Murillo, Byzantine, Medici and Fontainebleau. Engraved floral patterns such as Woodbine, Rose, Wheat, and Lily were also popular. Floral, leaves, and shell rococo designs such as Undine, Luxembourg, Louvre and Louis XV were made by Wood & Hughes and others. These had outlines based on Oval Thread and old Kings patterns, but other designs had squared handles and did not follow any well-known standard. The oblong, square-handled, engraved patterns continued into the 1890's. Some of these handles were decorated with engraved flower and leaf designs such as the Gem Leaf made by Whiting Manufacturing Co. This company also made several berry and leaf patterns with designs in relief on the square handles. Pomona was a similar pattern made by Towle Manufacturing Co. The design consisted of various kinds of fruits

TOP TO BOTTOM, IN ORDER. Raphael, Hindostanee, Kings, Cottage, Swiss, New Tipt. Patterns of Gorham flatware in advertisement. (*Jewelers' Circular*, 1881)

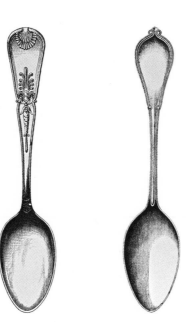

and leaves with the design different on each handle. In 1886 the Meriden Britannia Co. was offering nine patterns in sterling silver—and of these, six were patterns also made in 1847 Rogers Bros. Silverplate. These were Tipped, Embossed, Arcadian, Newport, Lorne and Armenian.

Pierced designs were also popular in the late '80's and '90's. One of the loveliest and most delicate pierced patterns was the Trianon Pierced, first made by Reed & Barton in 1885. A few years later Reed & Barton offered the unique and fascinating pattern called Labors of Cupid. This pattern had first been made by Dominick & Haff, but when Reed & Barton purchased the company in 1928 they took over the moulds and dies and thus the pattern is available by special order today. The handles have a pierced design of rococo scrolls which surround a figure of Cupid working at a different task on each handle. Appropriately the fish forks and knives and the small sardine fork show Cupid fishing and the decoration includes shells and fish. Other handles picture Cupid on a ladder gathering fruit or picking grapes, while the dinner fork has a design of vegetables and two cupids carrying a platter with a roast chicken or other fowl. A set of this silver would certainly be a conversation piece. A design of repoussé

RIGHT MARGIN. Teaspoons. Pomona and Orchids patterns. Towle Manufacturing Co., 1888. BELOW, LEFT TO RIGHT. 1847 Rogers Bros. Lorne-pattern salad fork, hand-engraved sterling silver. Cheese scoops, silver plate. Arcadian-pattern sliver pie-knife with flower and fruit decorated blade. The International Silver Co., Catalogue, c. 1886.

flowers called Number 10 was made by Dominick & Haff in 1896 and this is also now available not only in antique shops but on order at Reed & Barton. Other patterns of the 1890's era include Louis XIV, Trajan, Mazarin, and L'Elegant, La Touraine, La Marquise, and La Rocaille, which give evidence of the elaborate French influence. Whiting Manufacturing Co. brought out Louis XV and Pompadour, and Durgin's Empress Josephine, Pompadour, and Watteau also met the demand for French design. St. Cloud, Cluny, Marie Antoinette, Luxembourg, Louis XVI and Versailles were the Gorham patterns of the 1890's that show French influence. In 1900 Gorham made the Paris pattern which was designed by F. A. Heller. The Versailles was considered the most elaborate design produced at this time. Other Gorham patterns of the 1890's that reflect the eclectic character of the silver design included Acanthus (1885–90), Acorn (1894); Baronial, Bristol, Cambridge, Chippendale, Kensington, Lenox, King George and Lancaster showing English influence; Chrysanthemum, Carnation, Clematis, Buttercup, Daisy and Hawthorn reveal the interest in nature derived from Japanese design. To meet the demand for a plainer pattern the Colonial was made. Such simple designs as Old Basket-of-Flowers, Pointed Antique, and a new version of Kings was also made and many patterns still followed the oval thread and Kings pattern outlines to which were added bold rococo details or heavy gadroon borders, flutes

UPPER LEFT. Number ten. Reed & Barton, 1896. LOWER LEFT. Revere, International Silver Co., 1897. BOTTOM LEFT. Hand-engraved dessert spoon, A. F. Towle & Son, 1873. BOTTOM CENTER. Old Basket-of-Flowers, Reed & Barton, 1895. LOWER RIGHT. Indian War Dance, Tiffany & Co., c. 1893. (*Collection of Helen R. Hoegsberg*)

or curling leaves. There were also beaded patterns such as the Colonial, Bedford, and New Castle which reflected the fashion for Colonial and Old English. These were new patterns in the fall of 1895. The New Castle was a Gorham pattern. According to an article in *Jewelers' Circular,* September 18, 1895, "no originality in design for this pattern [New Castle] is claimed, as the dies were purchased by the company in England. These dies were the property of the celebrated Soho Works, having been designed and cut by them about the year 1830." However, Gorham recut the designs and modified the pattern. Sappho by R. Wallace & Sons Mfg. Co., and Colonial and Canterbury (Towle Manufacturing Co.), Florentine (Alvin Manufacturing Co.), Hope (Howard Sterling Co.), Lexington (J. B. & S. M. Knowles Co.) were also beaded patterns of 1895. The Colonial pattern is an excellent design which follows the old Kings pattern in outline. It has beaded borders and a pierced head which encloses a classic vase. Gorham's Chippendale was also a beaded design. The Medici showed the continued interest in Italian design. The International Silver Company, the largest silver manufacturer in existence today, was made up of a number of independent New England silversmiths including Ashbil Griswold, Rogers Brothers, H. C. Wilcox & Co., Meriden Britannia Co., and a dozen or so other companies. At first their products were pewter, Britannia and coin silver, later they specialized in silver-plated ware. International Silver Company did not get into sterling silver in an important way until about 1897. Their first pattern, Revere, was a conservative design.

BELOW LEFT. Labors of Cupid, Reed & Barton. Paris pattern. Gorham Manufacturing Co., 1900. LOWER RIGHT. Bread knife and fork. Gorham Catalogue, 1894. UPPER RIGHT. Fork, Mazarin pattern, Reed & Barton, 1892. LOWER RIGHT. Spoon. Trianon Pierced, Reed & Barton, 1885.

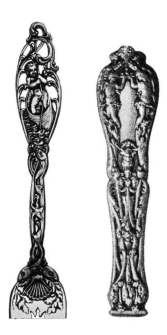

ABOVE. Sterling-silver coffee service, hand-chased. A. G. Schultz & Co., Baltimore, c. 1899. BELOW. Coffeepot, creamer and sugar bowl, floral repoussé. Samuel Kirk & Son, 1890–1896. (*Gebelein Silversmiths*)

ABOVE. Helmet-shaped creamer and boat-shaped sugar bowl, Classic Revival. Crosby & Foss, Boston, 1870. (*Gebelein Silversmiths*) RIGHT. Silver sugar sifters. Whiting Manufacturing Co. Catalogue, 1895.

When buying spoons or other flat silver, it is not only important to get the desired design, but the workmanship and weight of the silver should be considered. Some patterns of flat silver such as Gorham's Raphael and Tiffany's Olympian patterns were made in extra heavy weight, other patterns including the Swiss and the Cottage were of lighter weight. The various threaded, tipt, and Kings patterns were made in several different weights.

Dining in the great mansions of this era was a ceremonious affair with many servants in attendance. The table was long and narrow and covered with a linen damask cloth. In the center of the table was a plateau which held a large epergne or centerpiece of silver and cut glass bowls whose stems were classic female figures. On either side of the centerpiece were seven-branch candelabra with shades of pierced silver. The complete service was of silver including plates, goblets, and serving dishes, and by this date the flatware included an individual knife and fork for each course and serving knives, forks, and spoons for each kind of food. There were meat dishes, cutlet dishes, vegetable dishes, salad dishes, fried oyster dishes, tureens, sauce tureens, gravy boats, bread trays, mustards, salts and

93

peppers (table and individual), butter dishes, casters, and olive and pickle dishes. Dessert ware included: "Dessert Services consisting of Center and Side Fruit or Flower Pieces; Bon-bons; Coffee Sets, Coffee Cups and Saucers, Black Coffee Pots and Trays, Berry Sets, Berry Bowls, Punch Bowls, Jelly Dishes, Cheese Dishes, Cake Stands, Fruit Plates, Stands for Ices, etc., Fruit or Flower Pieces, Ice Cream Plates, Cutlery, Grape Scissors, Bottle Stands, Wine Coolers, Claret Jugs."

Centerpieces and large casters were in Egyptian style upheld by sphinx figures or in Renaissance style with draped classic female figures as stems. Symbolism was evident in the design and decoration of each article and related to the special purpose of each vessel and utensil. On the bread plate was a bas-relief of Ceres. The meat platter was engraved with stag or boar, the fish platter with a huge salmon with mermaids for handles, while the fish knives had decorations of fish, seaweed, and even fishing rods and tackle, and the sauce was served in a boat. Wine coolers were ornamented with a Bacchanalian scene. The water pitchers were engraved with fountains, lakes, and oases of palms, and ice bowls had pendent icicles and Arctic scenes of icebergs and polar bears, and even the ice spoon was perforated with an appropriate design. Arctic scenery also decorated the ice cream service and the saucers were frost-finished. Fruit bowls were ornamented with garlands of fruit, and berry bowls and spoons

LEFT. Silver flagon. Fanciful mixture of classic and Egyptian motifs. Designed by James Whitehouse for Tiffany & Co. (*Art Journal*, 1876) RIGHT. East Indian-design candelabrum exhibited in Paris in 1889 by The Gorham Co. (*Jewelers' Weekly*, 1889)

had embossed designs of berries. The patterns of flatware were also impressive and elegant and ornamented with engravings of Renaissance tracery.

A note from the San Francisco silver firm of Hammersmith & Field published in *The Argonaut,* May 26, 1890, gives another picture of the dining table of the era:

"The dining-tables of today are ablaze with the brilliancy of silver and cut-glass. It is marvelous to what dazzling perfection silversmiths have brought their art. By reverting to the old styles for shape, and working in *repoussé* design, some exquisite pieces of table-ware are produced.

"Nothing could be more artistic than a silver punch-bowl, gold lined, and belted by an antique Greek frieze, or chorus, of cupids. It presents the effect of a double ornamentation, for on the outside of the bowl the silver figures appear in bas-relief, and in the inside of the hemisphere, they sink into the golden depths in alto-relief. The handles of the punch-bowl are the hoary head of old Silenus on either side, and the ladle is a deep cup with a grape-grown handle weighted at the upper end by a vine-crowned Bacchus.

"A silver dinner-set, consisting of an elegant soup-tureen, small vegetable dishes, a swinging hot-water kettle, a tea and a coffee-pot, a milk-pitcher, and a sugar-bowl, are extremely chaste and elegant, noble specimens of the silversmith's art.

"Nor is the precious metal kept by itself. Silver table-knives are mounted with handles of *fleurs d'argent,* with silver tracery entwining heavily carved ivory."

"Ice Berg" ice bowl decorated with polar bears and icicles. Gorham, c. 1875. Property of Class of 1912, Bowdoin College, Brunswick, Maine. (*Gebelein Silversmiths*)

IV *Art Nouveau·*
1895–1910

THE Art Nouveau style which had been bred by the British idealists William Morris and John Ruskin was based on originality and the personal expression of the artist. Charles Rennie Mackintosh of Glasgow started the movement in design in the 1880's. It was taken up by the Belgian artist Henri van de Velde. The British Arts & Crafts Movement also became an important inspiration in Scandinavia and at the turn of the century Danish Art Nouveau silver was developed.

Louis Comfort Tiffany had contact with the Art Nouveau influence in England and France but his interest centered in the decorative arts, jewelry and glass. Tiffany has been given the credit of introducing Art Nouveau to America. His wealth and personal connections gave Tiffany standing in social circles. He formed the Louis C. Tiffany Company in 1878. In 1892 the firm became the Tiffany Glass and Decorating Company, and Tiffany Studios from 1900 to 1936. This firm executed many important commissions such as churches and the redecoration of the White House. However, the Louis C. Tiffany Company made no silver, and Tiffany & Co., Jewelers and Silversmiths, made only a small amount of Art Nouveau silver. It was left to the Gorham Manufacturing Co. to produce the finest expression of Art Nouveau in America in their line of

TOP. Hand mirror, peacock motif; silver, enamel and sapphires. Louis Comfort Tiffany, c. 1900. (*The Museum of Modern Art, New York, Joseph H. Heil Collection*) CENTER. Silver mirror; Paul and Virginia pattern. Theodore W. Foster & Bro. Co. (*Jewelers' Circular*, Aug. 27, 1902) BOTTOM. Mirror, Art Nouveau style, Oriental influence. The Sterling Co. (*The Jewelers' Weekly*, vol. 8)

96

Martelé silver. Because of the size and impersonal set-up of the company and the fact that Gorham was a wholesaler and made silverware which was distributed and sold by jewelers and small silver companies throughout America such as Spaulding & Co. of Chicago, Black, Starr & Frost of New York and Shreve & Co. of San Francisco, Gorham never attained the prestige of Tiffany and it is only recently with the revived interest in Art Nouveau that the true worth of Martelé as an art expression is being realized.

Silversmithing reached its lowest ebb in America in the 1890's. Design had become simple copying of past styles with little originality or imagination and the future of good design in silver seemed dim. However, a new force with fresh ideas had developed in the decorative arts in England under the inspiration of William Morris, Arthur Mackmurdo, Walter Crane, Lewis Day, and others in the 1880's. In about 1890 these influences began to penetrate silversmithing. The New Art, or Art Nouveau as it was called, started with a genuine search for the new. It stood out as something original and recognizable among the enormous quantity of eclectic factory production of traditional silver designs. Although Art Nouveau borrowed from the past it never copied. Instead, the curvilinear organic movement of fantastic lines signaled the end of the romantic past. It was also the beginning of applied art designed to accept machine processes, and it became an international style that was popularly accepted.

Art Nouveau is easily recognizable. Its free-flowing organic line is characterized by an elegant interplay of undulating curves. Imaginative and fanciful as the designs are they are based on nature, but flames of fire, wreaths of smoke and waves of water take one to the world of the mystical. There are curvilinear motifs of abnormal flowers, leaves, twisted and undulating plant forms and tangled seaweed. Serpents, octopi and other writhing and ''amorphous'' oozing forms had a fascination for the artists.

TOP. Hair brush, "Butterfly Girl." Woodside Sterling. (*Jewelers' Circular*, Oct. 15, 1902) CENTER, Mirror, The Mauser Manufacturing Co. (*Jewelers' Circular*, Sept. 10, 1902) BOTTOM. Mirror; "La Paris" design, scrolls and flowers. William B. Kerr & Co. (*Jewelers' Circular*, Sept. 23, 1903)

Roots of trees, treetops and stems of flowers and plants are swayed by the wind. One of the most recognizable motifs of Art Nouveau silver is the willowy woman's head with flowing tresses and eyes suggestive of the pre-Raphaelite women of Burne-Jones and Rossetti. Forms of nude veiled women with mermaid curves were also characteristic of the style. The

LEFT. Designs for silver hairpins; Art Nouveau style. The Sterling Co. (*The Jewelers' Weekly,* vol. 8) LOWER LEFT. Hat brush, Martelé. (*The Gorham Manufacturing Co.*) UPPER RIGHT. Brush, brooch and tray, Unger Brothers, c. 1903. (*Collection of Dr. and Mrs. Robert Koch*) CENTER. Hat brush, Martelé. LOWER. Clothes brush, Martelé (*The Gorham Manufacturing Co.*)

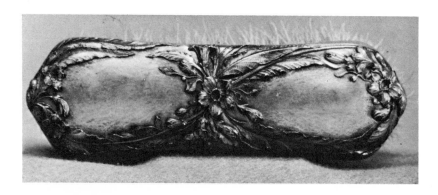

peacock with its spread-out fan feathers which fascinated Whistler became a favorite motif as did the butterfly wing.

Although much of the inspiration for Art Nouveau design came from the Orient, the style was also influenced by Byzantine arabesques and especially by the tortuous animal forms that decorate the borders of the *Book of Kells* and other Celtic manuscripts. Louis Comfort Tiffany, who had studied in Europe, was an early exponent of Art Nouveau as were Adolph Mucha, Emile Gallé and René Lalique in France, Victor Horta

LEFT. Symbolical silver figure, "The Awakening of Columbia." Geo. W. Shiebler Co. (*Jewelers' Circular*, 1893) UPPER RIGHT. Bud vase, Woodside Sterling Co. (*Jewelers' Circular*, Mar. 25, 1903) CENTER. Candlestick, Dominick & Haff. (*Jewelers' Circular*, Jan. 14, 1903) BOTTOM. Silver tray, Oriental influence. The Sterling Co. (*The Jewelers' Weekly*, vol. 8)

and Henri van de Velde in Belgium, and Jan Toorop in Holland. However, although some of these designers were producing silver, Tiffany's interest remained in glass and pottery. Except for the work of Louis Comfort Tiffany, Art Nouveau was late in getting to America and the most of American Art Nouveau silver dates from 1900 and later. The influence of William Morris was manifested in the craft of silversmithing in England at this time and in 1887 C. R. Ashbee had founded the School and Guild of Handicraft in London. This is described in Ashbee's book *Modern English Silverwork* published in 1908. The Guild of Handicraft

RIGHT. Silver pitcher, chased design based on nature. N. Heitzelman for Gorham. (*Jewelers' Circular*)

TOP LEFT TO BOTTOM RIGHT. Spoons, Art Nouveau patterns. Majestic, Fleur-de-Lis and Raphael, Alvin Manufacturing Co. (*Jewelers' Circular*, Mar. 2, 1904) Violet designs, R. Wallace and Whiting Manufacturing Co.

TOP. Three-handled bowl, "Society of Arts and Crafts" influence. CENTER. Teapot; silver and enamel, Art Nouveau influence. Tiffany & Co., 1900. (*The Metropolitan Museum of Art, gift of a friend, 1897*) BOTTOM. Pair of candlesticks and pitcher. Goodnow & Jenks, Boston, c. 1897. (*Gebelein Silversmiths*)

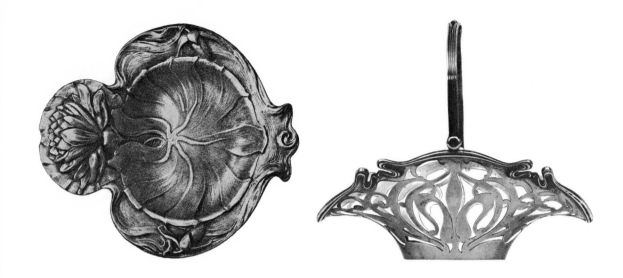

ABOVE LEFT. Bonbon dish, water lily design. Alvin Manufacturing Co. (*Jewelers' Circular*, 1903) RIGHT. Bonbon basket; open work, Art Nouveau. J. E. Caldwell & Co., c. 1900. (*Chrysler Museum of Provincetown*) BELOW LEFT. Martelé tankards. (*The Gorham Manufacturing Co., c. 1900*)

first exhibited in 1889 at the Arts and Crafts Society. The Guild idea was adopted in several other places in England and in Boston, Massachusetts. The foreman of Goodnow & Jenks, the foremost silversmiths in Boston at this time, was James T. Wooley. Wooley and Barton P. Jenks embraced the Guild idea and when the Arts and Crafts Movement held an exhibition in Boston in 1897, the silver displayed was entered under the name of Barton P. Jenks. George C. Gebelein was apprenticed to Goodnow & Jenks at this time and worked in the Handicraft Shop of Boston until he started his own business.

1. MARTELÉ

IN 1891 Gorham had brought over from England the talented artist William J. Codman to direct their design department. Codman had been trained in the traditional manner and his specialty was ecclesiastical design; however, he was acquainted with the new art movement in Europe. In 1895 Gorham decided to produce a new line of silverware that would be essentially an art production. It was felt that the limit of mechanical perfection had almost been reached and that art was being sacrificed to

102

mechanics. The problem was to develop a line of silverware which should be essentially an art production. With this idea in mind, the creation of an entirely new set of designs was started, and these designs were unfettered by the conventions of historic styles, but at the same time they were not as extreme as some of the examples of Art Nouveau. It was an extremely difficult and expensive task to train the workmen to the point where they were able to turn out satisfactory pieces. The artisan was given a design and a flat sheet of metal and told to work it out by hand with a hammer and such tools as were necessary for the design he saw before him. Gorham's wares had the new art credo and under the direction of Codman the best craftsmen in the Gorham workshop were educated in the new design. These wares were marketed under the names Martelé and Athenic. The Athenic, although Art Nouveau in feeling, was Grecian in inspiration. The Athenic combined metals other than silver and was never as popular as Martelé. John S. Holbrook in his book *Silver for the Dining Room,* includes a chapter on Martelé in which he describes it thus: "Forms variable, frequently classic, often fantastic. Decoration subservient to form largely natural, not conventional. Ornaments raised but melting into the background, nonsymmetrical, no mouldings, plain surfaces always hammered."

RIGHT TOP. Martelé tankard, capacity 5 pints. CENTER. Martelé tankard, capacity 1 pint. BOTTOM. Original drawing for Martelé rose water ewer and tray, c. 1900.

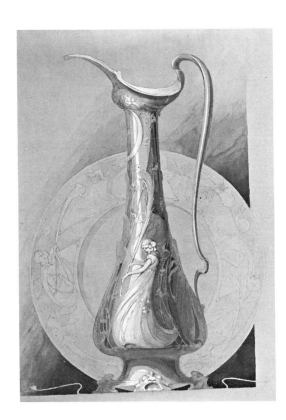

The hammer marks gave the undecorated surfaces a misty texture. Each piece was worked by hand and since no mechanical aids were used no two pieces were exactly alike. The quality of the silver used was finer than sterling and each design is unique. Martelé is expensive. Every piece is marked with the Martelé stamp. Martelé was not put on the market until 1901 but it became the finest expression of Art Nouveau silver in America. Vases, bowls and tankards were the first articles made. Later the line was increased and even dinner services were made. Martelé was exhibited at the Exposition in Turin, Italy, in 1902. The pieces shown included a tall vase in naturalistic floral design; candlesticks in the form of flowers and animals and decorated in unique ribbon chasings; a loving cup with wheat and hop vine chasing; an inkstand with matching cigar holder, ash trays, and match boxes. A tea set with panels and floral decoration and an after-dinner coffee set with a tall slender-necked coffee pot were also exhibited.

LEFT. Martelé vases with shaped lips and floral designs. BELOW. Martelé vases. LEFT TO RIGHT. Peacock design; waves and figures; Athenic vase, silver with copper appliqués of peacock feather decoration, enamelled peacock eyes. (*Chrysler Museum of Provincetown*)

The Gorham Company's exhibit for the St. Louis Exposition in 1904 was directed by Codman and it also featured many pieces of Martelé including a centerpiece with a large center bowl and four small bowls. The centerpiece was 35 inches long and 22½ inches in height. The flowing-shaped bowls were ornamented with figures, heads, and detailed scroll-work. A Martelé punch bowl entitled "Toilers of the Sea" was one of the finest pieces in the collection. The figures in the water, the sunburst and the conquering human figures, a female on the obverse and a male on the reverse, skillfully portrayed a mythological scene told in the relief work. There were also vases and loving cups of various sizes; one, a tall form with mermaid handles and topped with a sailing ship, was graceful in form and suggestive of the sea. The exhibit also included tea, coffee, and

RIGHT TOP AND BOTTOM. Martelé vases with floral designs and flowing floral rims. BOTTOM LEFT. Rose water ewer and plateau. Martelé design of waves and nudes with nude figure handle. BOTTOM RIGHT. Martelé vase. Design of waves and figures of maidens, with sea urchin handle. (*The Gorham Company*)

LEFT. Ewer and plateau elaborately ornamented with waves, seaweed, dolphins and figures of nude women with flowing tresses. Handle, figure of man grasping a fisherman's net. BOTTOM. Martelé punch bowl; grape design. (*The Gorham Company*)

chocolate services, waiters and candelabra in Martelé. Some of the tea services were in plain bright finish and some sets were finished in dull gray and various other finishes.

Although Martelé was an expensive ware made of 950/1000 fine silver with no two pieces alike there was a large group of workmen trained to make this ware and hundreds of exclusive pieces were made, ranging from ink sets and desk sets, including paper knives and cigar lighters, to important punch bowls with a capacity from 8 to 16 pints. The designs

RIGHT. Martelé punch bowl; design of lilies and nudes, capacity 30 pints. BOTTOM LEFT. Martelé hot water kettle; flower and scroll design. RIGHT. Martelé punch bowl; design of draped figures of women, morning glories and butterflies. (*The Gorham Company*)

ABOVE. Martelé punch bowl and ladle; design of grapes and foliage encircling scene of satyr and nymphs; satyr figure handles. BELOW. Martelé punch bowl, twelve cups and two ladles; design of seaweed and nude figures with sculptured heads of women on base of plateau. (*The Gorham Company*)

on these outstanding pieces included nude female figures playing in the waves, sea serpents and floral and leaf decorations. Claret sets also gave the designer an opportunity for elaborate design as did coffee, tea, and chocolate sets. There were also trays and waiters in various sizes and shapes—oval, square, and oblong. The many floral designs included iris, daisy, water lily, fuchsia and leaf motifs.

Hollow ware pieces also included bonbon dishes, covered serving dishes, bread trays, dessert plates and other plates and goblets. Fish platters had elaborate fish and seaweed patterns and meat platters were ornamented with deer and boars' heads. There were many children's sets which consisted of plates, cups, porringers, knives, forks, and spoons. No complete sets of flatware were made in Martelé but serving forks, spoons and fish knives and a set of coffee spoons in Orchid pattern were made. Dresserware was also an important item which included every toilet article and also large dressing table mirrors.

Although Martelé was made in the hundreds as against the thousands of other silver products by Gorham there were many pieces made over a period of a dozen years. However, few large important pieces have come on the market. Martelé because of its artistic value as well as its intrinsic silver value is in the realm of the collector with a good-sized pocketbook.

Martelé punch bowl and ladle; design with head of Neptune, figures of maidens on handles and ladle, dolphins on base. (*The Gorham Company*)

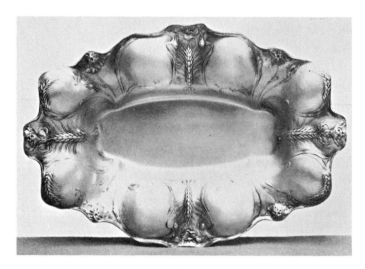

TOP. Martelé fish set including platter, sauce boat, knife, fork and ladle; fish and shell design. LEFT AND BOTTOM. Martelé bread trays with chased designs of wheat. (*The Gorham Company*)

Even the small pieces are rare and expensive. The beauty of the designs and the hand-wrought form make each piece a unique work of art. The beautiful texture made by the hammer also gives an aesthetic value to even the undecorated surfaces.

Tiffany & Co. made little Art Nouveau silver although Louis Comfort Tiffany designed silver frames and supports for his Favrile glass vases. A small oval tray in Art Nouveau style made by Tiffany & Co. has an Oriental design. It is a combination of silver, brass and copper. A tea set deco-

RIGHT. Martelé tray with floral rim. Made for Theodore B. Starr, New York. BELOW LEFT. Martelé tray; grape design. RIGHT. Flower and foliage design. (*The Gorham Company*)

rated with colorful enamels also made by Tiffany & Co. shows Far Eastern influence and a modified Art Nouveau influence. Tiffany & Co. also made several trophies in Art Nouveau style. The loving cup presented to Kingsley Post No. 113, Massachusetts Grand Army of the Republic, Comrades

TOP. Martelé pitchers. LEFT. Conventional swirl design. RIGHT. Water lilies, cattails and fish. BOTTOM. Martelé pitcher and matching tray; design of waves, fish and nudes. (*The Gorham Company*)

of the Mess, August 15, 1904, has a design of iris, a flower which grows in a natural Art Nouveau design.

J. E. Caldwell & Co. of Philadelphia made some pieces of Art Nouveau silver with simple cut-out line designs. However, the silver of

TOP. Martelé tea set and kettle; design of iris with flower finials on covered pieces. BOTTOM. Martelé tea set; conventional foliage design with flower finials. (*The Gorham Company*)

the firm of Samuel Kirk & Son shows little Art Nouveau influence. Indeed comparatively few hollow ware Art Nouveau pieces for domestic use were made in America. Although there were few tea services there was a quantity of small trays, bonbon dishes, cake dishes, berry bowls, bread trays, vases, and candlesticks. There was considerable output of Art Nouveau pieces by such large companies as Reed & Barton and R. Wallace & Sons but the large majority of Art Nouveau pieces were made by the smaller companies who seem to have capitalized on the popularity of Art Nouveau style with the person of average means. At the turn of the century the big output of such companies as William B. Kerr & Co. and Unger Brothers of Newark, New Jersey; Alvin Manufacturing Co. and the Sterling Company of Providence, Rhode Island; the Mauser Manufacturing Co., Dominick & Haff and Woodside Sterling Co., of New York, was Art Nouveau design. Small trays made at the Sterling Company showed Japanese influence and one tray had a group of growing iris at one end balanced by a large winged bee. A small tray made by the Mauser Manu-

Martelé black coffee sets. LEFT. Iris pattern. RIGHT. Daisy. (*The Gorham Company*)

Martelé claret set. Glass specially designed to harmonize with the design of the silver tray and the heavy silver mounting on the claret jug. (*The Gorham Company*)

facturing Co. has a swirling line pattern with a flower and a woman's head with flowing tresses. This company made many small bowls such as bonbons, berry dishes and bread trays in Art Nouveau flower designs. They also made dresserware sets, including patterns such as L'Art Nouveau and Du Barry, the latter a design of a dreamy girl with flowing hair. Another set had the artist Bouguereau's Satyr and Nymphs embossed and set within a framework of Art Nouveau lines. A similar framework enclosed a reproduction of a Watteau painting and another pattern was called La Vision. There were dresserware sets decorated with Netherlands scenes and a gentleman's toilet set called Meadowbrook which was ornamented with hunting scenes, including a coach and a man on horseback. In 1893 William B. Kerr & Co. advertised Bouguereau's Great Masterpieces, Satyr and Nymphs and Psyche and Love. These and other related designs were also put on match box covers.

Dresserware in Art Nouveau patterns was very popular and there

Martelé lavatory set; iris, water lilies, insects and amphibious animals. (*The Gorham Company*)

were many companies making these sets at the turn of the century. One center for such pieces as well as other small articles of silverware was North Attleboro, Massachusetts, where F. M. Whiting & Co., R. Blackinton & Co., and Webster Co. were located. In Providence, Rhode Island, there were companies such as W. J. Braitsch & Co., and Theodore W. Foster & Bro., in addition to many smaller firms and the large Gorham Manufacturing Company. In the 1901 *Jewelers' Circular*, Theodore W. Foster & Bro. advertised a new pattern in toilet and manicure sets called Paul and Virginia which had a vignette of a boy and girl clothed in drapery sitting in a swing. The border was of iris and wavy lines in Art Nouveau style. One of the companies specializing in toilet and desk sets was Woodside Sterling. They made patterns called Iris and The Butterfly Girl, and silver bowls in designs of realistic oak leaves and acorns, strawberries, grapes and poppies, as well as a long list of small articles including table bells, ash trays, book marks, inkstands, pencils, pen wipers, muff clips, sewing emeries, tape measures, table covers, garters, glove hooks, hatpins, pin boxes, soap boxes, liquor flasks, and champagne corks. One liquor flask, although not Art Nouveau, would intrigue the present-day collector. It has a design of a dog in a blanket watching over kittens eating out of a bowl, and an inscription "Welcome." R. Wallace &

116

Sons Mfg. Co. also made many small articles and dresser sets including one pattern in Art Nouveau with poppies. Such small novelties as hairpins, hatpins, belt buckles and girdles, and chatelaine bags were also designed in Art Nouveau style and many are in excellent design as well as the highest grade of workmanship.

The history of the firm of Unger Brothers of Newark, New Jersey, gives an excellent picture of the various types of silver articles as well as the style and design of the output of the average small silver firm of the late nineteenth century in America. The company was established in 1870; however, the two brothers are listed separately as engravers in the *Newark Directory* of that year. From 1871 to 1874 the firm is listed as Unger & Keen, Jewelers. H. Unger & Co., gold jewelry, is the listing in 1878–80, and the firm of Unger Brothers (Eugene and Herman) is not listed until 1881 when the title reads, "Manufacturing Jewelers." However, a few years later, the sign on a cut illustrating their factory reads, "Unger Brothers, Jewelers, Manufacturing Silversmiths and Glass Cutters." For some years Unger Brothers also had a showroom in New York. This was closed in 1897. Unger Brothers employed three artists: Philemon O. Dickenson, a painter of watch dials and engraver, Otto Leigh, and Edward P. Beach, a painter. Dickenson and Beach were members of the firm. These men made the designs for the patents taken out for Unger Brothers silver patterns. At the beginning the designs of Unger Brothers silverware were in rococo style. Spoon handles, mirrors, brushes, belt buckles, and garter buckles were made in designs of elaborate rococo leaf scrolls. A

RIGHT. Cigar lighter with moulded free-form naturalistic floral decoration. BELOW. Martelé wine cooler and punch ladle; water lily design. (*Chrysler Museum of Provincetown*)

garter buckle had a scene of a sleeping cupid enclosed in flower and leaf scrolls, a folding buttonhook design was called Cupid and Venus, and in 1895 a violet holder had a border design of simple rococo scrolls. However, in the catalogue of the company which was circulated in about 1900 the majority of the designs are Art Nouveau although the Cupid and Venus theme persisted, and contemporary designs of popular motifs such as the man and woman smoker and the golfer were included. Tea sets and other hollow ware were now made by the firm and there were also exclusive designs of flatware. There were tea sets in designs labeled Rose, Iris, Colonial and Rococo. Sets in which both flatware and hollow ware were made were Narcissus, an Art Nouveau pattern; Passaic, rococo style; and Fontenoy, a design of simple rococo curves. Spoon sets were made in patterns called Cupid's Nosegay, Evangeline, The Wave, La Fantaisie, Love's Dream, He Loves Me, Cupid, Sunbeam, Dawn, and La Fleurette. Fork sets included Secret des Fleurs, The Wave, Les Circes, and Reine des Fleurs, all Art Nouveau patterns. A set called Douvaine which was Art Nouveau with a satyr figure, was made in knives, forks and carving pieces. There was also a line of berry bowls in flower patterns including wild rose, poppy, daffodil, hibiscus, daisies, water lilies, and sweet peas. Other pieces made were serving trays, bread trays, compotes on stands, butter dishes, gravy boats, bonbon dishes, wine coasters, and tall and chamber candlesticks. A large output of Unger Brothers was toilet or dresserware sets. These were made in Art Nouveau patterns incorporating flowers and heads of women with flowing tresses. The patterns included Le Secret des Fleurs, a design of a woman's head with swirls and iris. The Queen of Flowers or Reine des Fleurs pattern included a nude woman and roses. Love's Dream was a pattern of cupids and dolphins with a Medusa head in the handles. Peep O'Day was a woman's head with poppies while Evangeline set the same dreamy head among wild roses. Other patterns were called Dawn, Love's Voyage, and Bride of the Wave. The Jersey wild Day Lily was used on still another set. He Loves Me was a favorite pattern. The design consisted of a girl with a crown of daisies as a center motif and this was surrounded by flowing lines and groups of larger daisies. According to their advertisement in *Jewelers' Circular*, October 1, 1902, this was "One of 5 new patterns produced this year, making twenty-one sets in all. The strongest line of Toilet Goods on the market." The advertisement also states: "We make everything in Sterling Silver from a

TOP TO BOTTOM. Martelé salad spoon, salad fork, Martelé paper knife. (*The Gorham Company*)

Tie Clasp to a Tea Set." The listing and illustrations of the small items in the catalogue reveal the truth of this statement and the numerous articles shown give a picture of the many small articles of late nineteenth century silver, especially Art Nouveau items, available to collectors. Every imaginable article of dresserware or toilet articles for both men and women was made with a silver handle or cover. These included mirrors, hairbrushes, jewel cases, pincushions in round, slipper and fan shapes with silver rims; combs, files, buttonhooks, shoehorns, toothbrushes, cuticle and corn knives, curling irons, powder boxes, and covers for tooth powder and toilet water bottles and Listerine. There were folding combs for gents' pockets and folding cigar cutters, shaving brushes, razor strops, garters, suspenders and shaving mugs. Desk sets include calendars, pen wipers, inkwells, blotters, paper cutters, erasers, seals and corners for large blotters. A group of designs made to interest the sportsman included the Golfer, a boy carrying caddy clubs and a woman golfer. Other designs included a man smoking and a woman smoking, a woman on horseback taking a hurdle, and a man in the moon. These designs were put on shaving mugs, smoking accessories, match and cigarette cases, corks, corkscrews, cuff links, key tags, key rings, bag tags and watch fobs. Liquor flasks were made in three sizes: ½ pint, ¾ pint, and 2½ ounces. Flask designs included The Golfer, a man smoker, a woman smoker, Indian, a nude with harp, a woman on horseback taking a hurdle. There were also cut glass flasks with silver bottoms. Items especially for women included lorgnettes, hatpins and hatpin holders, violet holders, belt buckles, and girdles with chains and links of Art Nouveau heads, chatelaine bags and mesh purses. For the needlewoman there were tape measures, needle cases, strawberry emeries, scissors, thimbles, and thimble cases. For children there were spoons, knives and forks, mugs, and rattles. Rattles with mother-of-pearl handles were mounted with silver in designs including cupids, jesters, figures of children in nineteenth century dress and the Billikin. All had small silver bells attached.

Unger Brothers also made a line of cut glass articles with silver tops. These included bowls, pitchers, perfume bottles, jewel, glove and powder boxes, and vases. The company did their own glass cutting, and some of the patterns were original with the company.

Small pieces of Unger Brothers silver are seen in many shops. These include match safes with golfer and smoker designs, nail files, buttonhooks

TOP TO BOTTOM. Martelé salad spoon, salad fork, paper knife. (*The Gorham Company*)

and brooches in rococo and Art Nouveau designs. Mirrors, flatware, tea sets and other hollow ware are more difficult to locate but there should be many pieces of Unger Brothers silver in Newark and nearby New Jersey towns and in New York City. Unger Brothers silver is usually marked with their trade mark.

There were many other Art Nouveau patterns of flatware besides those made by Unger Brothers. Tiffany and Gorham did not take up the fad but continued making more conventional patterns. However, a few patterns such as Tiffany's Chrysanthemum variations and Gorham's Orchid, Poppy, Tulip, Violet and Virginia, the latter dating from 1905, do show Art Nouveau influence. The first group of Art Nouveau flatware patterns were made by William B. Durgin Co. between 1898 and 1900. These were Iris, Jonquil, Tulip, Magnolia, Orange Blossom and New Art. In 1902 Charles Osborne patented the Lily design for Whiting Manufacturing Co. Also in 1902 William J. Codman designed Patrician for Gorham; R. Wallace & Sons brought out Apple Blossom and Irian. La Viola and #80 were also Art Nouveau patterns by R. Wallace & Sons. Reed & Barton's La Parisienne, 1902, was followed by Intaglio, Love Disarmed, Les Six Fleurs and Les Cinq Fleurs. International Silver brought out Les Saisons, a cupid pattern in 1903, and in 1905 Cleota. The Alvin

Martelé candlesticks and candelabra. (*The Gorham Company*)

Manufacturing Company's Art Nouveau patterns were Bridal Rose, Raphael, Fleur de Lis, and Majestic, a poppy design. The Wave and Fiorito by George W. Shiebler & Co. were made in dresserware as well as flatware as were many of the other Art Nouveau patterns. Frank M. Whiting Co.'s pattern was Helena; Simpson, Hall, Miller & Co. brought out Berwick, a plated floral pattern resembling a nasturtium, in 1904; and Fessenden & Co. made McKinley, Tulip, Daisy, and Narcissus, all showing Art Nouveau influence.

These patterns scorned for many years are available in secondhand silver shops today. Many of the patterns were made in heavy weight sterling silver. They are usually marked with the manufacturer's name or trademark.

2. SILVER DEPOSIT WARE AND SILVER-MOUNTED CUT GLASS

SILVER Deposit Ware was a combination of crystal and silver. The effect was produced by depositing a coating of precipitate of silver on crystal glass. This silvering by chemical reduction was done by three different processes, all using chemicals as the reducing agent. The Brasher Process

BELOW LEFT. Decorated glass and silver-mounted toilet bottle and silver repoussé tray. (*The Gorham Company*) RIGHT TOP TO BOTTOM. Silver deposit decanter, whiskey jugs and perfume bottle. Meriden Britannia Co. and Alvin Manufacturing Co. (*The International Silver Company*)

which uses a combination of potassium hydroxide and ammonium hydroxide as the reducing agent is the process most favored today. The delicate fruit, flowers and conventional abstract designs of the silver patterns were also enhanced with engraving, etching or oxidation and some were executed in relief, such as the grape design on wine bottles and decanters. At first the process left the inner surfaces of the silver pattern black, but later a new process was developed which made the inner surfaces white. Although Silver Deposit Ware was first made in the 1880's it was most popular in the 1890's and in the first decade of the twentieth century and it is still being made today. Electro-deposit work was not only attractive but it also utilized electricity in a new channel.

The popular articles made in silver deposit included decanters, wine and whiskey bottles, claret sets, flasks, perfume bottles and atomizers, vases, pitchers, loving cups, bonbon dishes, cigarette boxes, picture frames, tiles, candlesticks, plates, finger bowls, cane heads, buttons, and hatpins. The designs include conventional scrolls and foliage, grapes and leaves, and such flowers as iris, tulips, carnations, wild roses and chrysanthemums. A cartouche of plain silver was usually left for an initial, monogram or crest. The Alvin Manufacturing Co., which was founded in 1886, specialized in Silver Deposit Ware and they ran many advertisements in the *Jewelers' Circular* advertising their various pieces. Other makers of Silver Deposit Ware were Scharling & Co., Inc.; Whiting Manufacturing Co.; E. & J. Bass; the Mauser Manufacturing Company; Fishel, Nesser & Company; New York Silver Deposit Co., and National Silver Deposit Ware Co., Inc. As late as 1913 Reed & Barton formed the Hopewell Silver Company which among other high quality items put out a line of Lenox China tea and coffee sets with gold and silver deposit. They also made pierced silver stands for Lenox after-dinner coffee cups, tea and chocolate cups, bouillon cups and ramekins. The Lenox China backgrounds were usually cream, dark blue, or a rich orange brown. Silver deposit patterns were also put on metal and wood. In 1893 Alvin Manufacturing Co. made a bowling trophy of ebony and silver deposit and in 1905 they made an ebony and silver deposit trophy for the Northwestern Curling Association.

Alvin Deposit Ware. (*Jewelers' Circular,*1903)

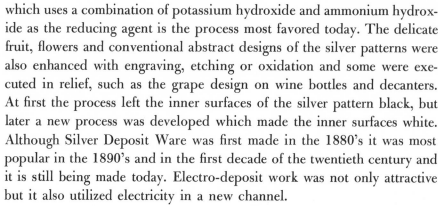

They also made cane and umbrella heads and hatpins with silver deposit, and silver deposit patterns with angels blowing trumpets enriched with blue enamel were put on bibles and prayer books. Silver deposit on purses and card cases also became the style and Deitsch Brothers of New York specialized in these.

Indeed non-metallic objects decorated with gold and silver had become a feature of the silverwork of the 1890's. Elaborate pieces were manufactured by such important firms as Tiffany & Co. and the Gorham Manufacturing Co. Tiffany added silver mountings not only to crystal and cut glass, but also to Tiffany Favrile Glass articles which were mounted in gold-plated silver designs of mermaids and sea horses and studded with aquamarines and pearls.

Gorham's output of silver-decorated objects can be divided into two general classes: first, pieces made by the generally used electro-deposit process called silver deposit, and second, the simple mounting of a piece of glass or pottery or metal other than silver by the silver ornament, thus forming a clasping framework. At the exhibit of the Gorham Manufacturing Co. at the Chicago Exhibition in 1893 pieces of Rookwood Pottery decorated with designs of silver deposit were exhibited. The beautiful colors varying from light yellow to almost black-brown were delicately entwined by a design adapted to the vase which was heightened by the silver ornament. This method of decorating Rookwood Pottery was introduced by Gorham. A third class of objects with combinations of silver and glass included those with a metal framework into which the glass was blown. The effect produced by the bulging glass forms is similar to jewels, especially where the color of the glass is varied. This process was invented by the Gorham Manufacturing Co.

Another innovation of the silver industry of the late nineteenth century was silver-mounted cut glass. Pieces of cut and engraved glass were mounted with borders of ornamental engraved or repoussé silver. The pieces included vases, fruit bowls, claret and champagne pitchers, punch bowls, ice bowls, centerpieces, plates, and loving cups. One set was composed of a champagne pitcher, with ladle and twelve glasses with silver

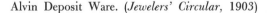

Alvin Deposit Ware. (*Jewelers' Circular*, 1903)

deposit enriched with gilt and enamel. Cut glass for mounting was made especially for Gorham and cut to the patterns of their designers. Later, they added a department to do their own cutting. The glass used was not only crystal but also came in delicate shades of ruby, sapphire, and rich ambers. Some of the mountings were richly chased and some were repoussé. Such pieces as wine flagons, pitchers for champagne and three-handled loving cups had silver mountings with elaborate designs, sometimes including figures in full relief.

Silver-mounted cut glass was made by the majority of the silver companies during the years of its popularity and the large scale production of cut glass (1890–1915). The glass for mounting was also made by many companies. In the *Jeweler's Circular*, 1898, Fostoria advertised glass for mounting. "Cut and pressed in various patterns and shapes. Powder puff, Pungents, Cigar jars, Pomades. Cut pungents a Specialty." Cut glass for mounting was also made by L. Straus & Sons, Hawkes, and the majority of the larger companies. Unger Brothers of Newark, New Jersey, had a glass cutting department and cut their own glass.

According to E. P. Hogan, Historical Research Librarian of the International Silver Company, the records of the purchasing department of the company for the last fifty years show purchases of glass blanks from

TOP. Whiskey jug and glasses; silver deposit. Reed & Barton. BOTTOM LEFT. Claret jug; Alvin Deposit Ware. RIGHT. Ale Set; silver deposit on crystal. Meriden Britannia Co., c. 1910. (*The International Silver Co.*)

ABOVE LEFT. Silver-mounted cut glass vase and bowl. RIGHT. Silver-mounted cut glass ewer. (*The Gorham Manufacturing Co.,* c. 1889) CENTER RIGHT AND BOTTOM. Silver-mounted cut glass claret jugs. Rogers Smith & Co., 1896. (*Catalogue*) (*The International Silver Company*)

the following companies: Cambridge Glass Works; Heisey; Duncan & Miller; Macbeth-Evans Glass Company; Corning Glass Company and Pairpoint Corporation. In the 1902 *Jewelers' Circular,* International Silver Co. advertised that they cut their own glass for mounting. A. Christian Revi, in his book *American Cut & Engraved Glass,* says: "Mrs. Nolan recalled that the Wilcox works were supplied with cut glass for their silver-plated fittings by the Meriden Flint Glass Company and later by Bergin & Niland." In the book, *American Cut Glass for the Discriminating Collector,* by J. Michael and Dorothy T. Pearson, the silver-mounted cut glass articles illustrated include a vase with sterling top and a box with silver knob and inlay (Hawkes, Millicent pattern); a perfume bottle with sterling top (Tuthill, Wild Rose); a fern pattern pitcher with an ornate hinged sterling top; a cheese plate with an openwork rim of sterling silver; a basket with sterling rim (Hawkes); an L. Straus & Sons silver-mounted bowl and a perfume bottle of Russian pattern with sterling top. In the *Jewelers' Circular,* January 19, 1898, L. Straus & Sons of New York advertised "a new line of Glassware, etc., for mounting purposes." Reed & Barton, Meriden Britannia, and many smaller companies made silver mountings for glassware.

Besides the larger articles for dining table use, there were many small articles made of silver-mounted cut glass such as napkin rings, cruets, sugar sifters, knife rests and syrup jugs. There were also articles of dresser-

125

ware including powder boxes, sachet jars, toothbrush bottles, glove boxes and jewel boxes. For the desk there were inkwells with silver tops, paste boxes and stamp boxes. In 1897 W. K. Vanderslice of San Francisco made a unique cut glass bowl mounted with gold nuggets from the Klondike which was presented to Captain Constantine of the Canadian Police by the miners of the Northwest Territory.

Silver-mounted cut glass was never cheap. Decanters with silver stoppers sold for $100 a pair; a Milieu de Table or centerpiece mounted with sterling silver was priced $80 in the catalogue of the Wilcox Silver Plate Co. in 1896. In the same catalogue a cheese plate seven inches in diameter was priced at $12.50 and a ten inch sandwich plate was $24, while an eleven-inch plate of the same design was $27. Claret jugs with silver-plated mounts were cheaper—priced at $6.75 and $12.50. These were made in 1896 by Rogers Smith & Co., which was at that time owned by Meriden Britannia Co.

LEFT. Silver-mounted cut glass plate. BELOW RIGHT. Silver-mounted Milieu de Table. Wilcox Silver Plate Co., 1896. (*Catalogue*) (*The International Silver Company*) CENTER. Lenox china cups with hand-pierced and engraved silver stands and saucers. (*Reed & Barton*)

V *American Presentation Pieces and Trophies*

THE presentation pieces of the first third of the nineteenth century are examples of the late classic style in American silver. This late classic style was influenced by the grandiose designs in books of drawings from the antique and many pieces were exact copies of the urns and vases of Roman emperors which were displayed in these engravings. The work of the French silversmiths which celebrated the victories of Napoleon also served as pompous models to honor the heroes of American nationalism. The tea service made for Napoleon in 1810 which was elaborately decorated with emblems of the Emperor provided the motifs found on many American pieces of this late classic period: the eagle, the winged-claw foot, winged Victory, the dolphin, the serpent-head spout, the bulbous Renaissance swags of leaves and flowers, the anthemion and borders of classic figures in relief are all motifs used by the American silversmith of this period.

One of the earliest pieces of presentation silver which displays these characteristics is the pitcher presented by the 2nd Regiment N.Y.S.A. to Colonel James A. Moore. The seal of the State of New York is on one side and the inscription on the reverse. This was made by John W. Forbes c. 1808. Forbes also made the classic plateau which is in the White House. However, Thomas Fletcher and Sidney Gardiner who worked in Philadelphia (1813–1825) were the most prolific makers of large-scale presentation pieces in this period. At the close of the War of 1812 the nation was paying homage to its heroes in silver which was often pompous and declamatory and a large proportion of these pieces was made by Fletcher and Gardiner. Fletcher and Gardiner made the massive silver urn which the citizens of Philadelphia presented to Captain Isaac Hull, the famous naval hero, on September 5, 1812. A document in the Pennsylvania Historical Society which lists the names of contributors includes those of

ABOVE LEFT. Silver ewer with New York Coat of Arms. John W. Forbes, c. 1808. Inscribed: "Presented by 2nd Regiment/N.Y.S.A. to Col. James A. Moore, as a token of Respect/Geo. W. Heelas, Major/Augts. Cleveland, Captn. Committee/Enoch Armitage, Adjut." Collection Stuart P. Feld, (*James Graham & Sons, Inc.*) RIGHT. Ewer. Shepherd and Boyd, c. 1810–1830. Presented to Captain Isaac Hull after the capture of the *Guerrière* and engraved with a picture of the battle. (*Courtesy Wadsworth Atheneum, Hartford*) BELOW. Soup tureen and pitcher presented to Captain James Lawrence by the citizens of Philadelphia; classic Empire style; beaded and acanthus leaf ornament and cast heads of Grecian gods; topped with figure of Athena. Simon Chaudron, 1813. (*Courtesy of The New-York Historical Society, New York City*)

well-known Philadelphians of the time and also many lesser known people, some giving only five or ten dollars. The urn is classic in form and decoration and stands on a base supported by four claw feet. The handles are rams' heads and a panel contains a representation of the frigate *Constitution* in full sail. The panel on the reverse contains the presentation inscription and the top of the vase is crowned by an eagle with outspread wings. Classic leaf borders fill in the spaces between and the dull hammered background contrasts with the polished silver of the panels. The urn is now in the custody of the Naval Historical Foundation. A collection of Fletcher's silver drawings in the Metropolitan Museum of Art includes a large urn with serpent handles, an eagle finial and a scene of the Battle of New Orleans (1814) which was designed for presentation to Andrew Jackson. The firm also designed the important punch set which was presented to Colonel George Armistead by the citizens of Baltimore in recognition of his services in the defense of Fort McHenry against the British attack in 1814. The service includes an oval tray supported by six winged-claw feet. The ball-shaped punch bowl is held by four eagles mounted on a round base. The round bowl duplicates in size and design the mortar bombs used by the British. On one side of the bowl is an engraved view of Fort McHenry and Baltimore harbor and on the other is the following inscription: "Presented by a number of the citizens of Baltimore to Lieutenant Colonel George Armistead for his gallant and successful defense of Fort McHenry during the bombardment of a large British force, on the 12th and 13th September 1814 when upwards of 1500 shells were thrown;

Silver urn presented by citizens of Philadelphia to Captain Isaac Hull in appreciation of the victory of *U.S.S. Constitution* over the British frigate *Guerrière*. Fletcher & Gardiner, 1812. (*Courtesy U.S. Navy*)

RIGHT. Sporting challenge bowl, Thomas Fletcher, 1828. The round medals bear the names of the champion archers. (*Lent by the Historical Society of Pennsylvania to the Newark Museum exhibition "Classical America." Photograph courtesy of the Newark Museum, Newark, N. J.*)

LEFT. Tureen presented to Com. John Rogers by the citizens of Baltimore for his part in the defense of the city against the British in 1814. Fletcher & Gardiner, 1814 (*The Smithsonian Institution*)

RIGHT. Punch set presented to Colonel George Armistead by the citizens of Baltimore in recognition of his services in the defense of Fort McHenry and Baltimore harbor. Fletcher & Gardiner, 1814. Ten matching cups. Andrew E. Warner. (*The Smithsonian Institution*)

400 of which fell within the area of the Fort and some of them of the diameter of this vase." The ten silver cups and ladle which match the design of the bowl were made by Andrew E. Warner, a Baltimore silversmith of the same era. Fletcher and Gardiner also designed the dinner service which was presented to Com. John Rogers for his part as a naval officer in the defense of Fort McHenry and the silver set presented to Nicholas Biddle by the Directors of the Bank of United States. Philip Hone comments on this set in his *Diary* (Wed. Feb. 14th, 1838): "The Biddle Plate. I was shown this afternoon at the shop of Messers Fletcher & Co. in Chestnut Street the most superb service of plate I ever saw to be presented by the directors of the old Bank of The U. S. to Mr. Nicholas Biddle. It is to cost $15,000. The inscription recites all his valuable services to the institution and to the country at large and among other things his having 'created the best currency in the world' . . . Fletcher & Co. are the artists who made the Clinton vases. Nobody in this 'world' of ours can compete with them in their kind of work."

The most important and most beautiful of all the presentation pieces made by Fletcher and Gardiner were the two urns presented to Governor DeWitt Clinton. In 1825 the merchants of Pearl Street, New York, presented these vases to Governor Clinton in testimony of their gratitude due for the work he accomplished in constructing the "Northern and Western Canals." The engraved panel on one vase shows Little Falls on the Mohawk, a view of the aqueduct at Rochester, and the Falls of Genesee. The corresponding panel on the other vase depicts the falls at Cohoes and the grand lock and basin at Albany where the canal connects with the Hudson River. The Van Rensselaer Mansion is also shown. The form and many of the motifs of decoration were taken from the famous Warwick Vase. The silversmiths have added animal claw feet, a cover topped with an eagle finial, and panels with classic figures. The original sketch of the design, which is in the Metropolitan Museum of Art, included a base panel with a scene of classic figures but this has been left off the vases and the presentation inscription is put in its place. These vases are owned by the Chamber of Commerce of the State of New York and are on view on the rostrum of the Great Hall.

There were numerous presentations honoring heroes of the War of 1812. Captain James Lawrence was presented with posthumous awards from both New York and Philadelphia. The City of New York gave a pitcher and two fruit dishes made by John Targee of New York and the City of Philadelphia gave a soup tureen and pitcher made by Simon Chaudron. In Albany, New York, Commodore Isaac Hull was honored by the presentation of a pitcher after the capture of the *Guerrière,* and Commander Stephen Decatur, another Navy officer of the War of 1812, was honored by several cities. A wine cooler made by Whartenby & Bumm of Philadelphia is in the Historical Society of Pennsylvania. In the letter book of Samuel Hildeburn and Hildeburn & Woolworth, Philadelphia Jewelers, in the Historical Society of Pennsylvania, a letter to Charles W. Scott, March 16, 1817, states: "I can safely say they (Whartenby & Bumm) are the best house in the city and most to be relied on both for the quality of the silver and workmanship." The Decatur salver made by Andrew E. Warner is in the Metropolitan Museum of Art. There were also presentation pieces given in recognition of services in the Mexican War and several of these are in the Smithsonian Institution in Washington, D.C.

A set of silver consisting of 381 pieces, including soup tureens, gravy

Cooler presented to Commodore Decatur by the citizens of Philadelphia; Federal style with acanthus chasing, winged-paw feet, surmounted by an American Eagle. Whartenby & Bumm, 1816. (*Lent by the Historical Society of Pennsylvania to the exhibition "Classical America," The Newark Museum*)

boats, tea and coffee pots on trays was made by William Gale and Son of New York and presented to Commodore Matthew Calbraith Perry by the Chamber of Commerce and Merchants of New York City in 1855 in acknowledgment of his success in the negotiation of a treaty with Japan in 1854. Although the pieces have no engraved scenes they have embossed floral sprays and rustic handles with pendent bunches of grapes which are representative of Victorian rococo silver. Their forms are graceful and the workmanship excellent.

A sugar bowl made by Tiffany & Company in 1862 was presented to Alban C. Stimers of the *Monitor*. The motifs of design are unique and suitably related to the occasion. Around the center of the bowl is a band of anchors and chains and the inscription is enclosed within an oval of rope crested with an eagle and dolphins. The finial incorporates cannon and cannon balls and on the handles are heads of Neptune.

There were other pieces given to Civil War heroes; however, the most popular item of the Civil War period was the presentation sword.

Punch bowl given by the Merchants of New York to District Attorney Hugh Maxwell; Empire style; classic vase with heavy base, sphinx figures and massive claw feet. Baldwin Gardiner, 1829. (*Courtesy of The New-York Historical Society, New York City*)

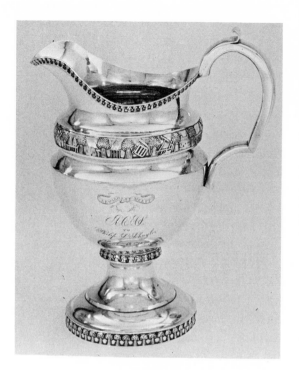 

LEFT. Pitcher decorated with borders of agrarian motifs. Joseph T. Rice, Albany, 1819. Given by the Academy County Agriculture Society to Philip S. Schuyler. (*Albany Institute of History and Art*) RIGHT. Pitcher decorated with grape and leaf meander in high relief and cast relief classic figure groups. Presented to Col. John Hare Powel by the Pennsylvania Agricultural Society. Edward Lownes, 1817. (*The Historical Society of Pennsylvania, lent to the exhibition "Classical America," The Newark Museum*)

The sword had been a presentation favorite for military men of all the wars beginning with the Revolution, and there was a great deluge of presentation swords at the time of the Civil War. These swords were massive with gaudy sculptured symbols and precious metals which reflect the opulence and ostentation of the Victorian Era. Presentation swords are discussed in Chapter VI.

Another category of American presentation silver includes the pieces with engravings of military conflicts, historical buildings, and monuments. These also include such scenes as rescues from fires and rescues at sea. One of the most interesting and earliest pieces of this type is the pitcher made by Ebenezer Moulton of Boston which depicts the Old South Church fire. The so-called "Manumission Society Pitchers" made by Joel Sayre, New York (1778–1818), have a connotation with the present-day racial problem. They were presented to Joseph Curtis for his efforts in obtaining the passage of the Manumission Act of 1817 which freed the slaves in New York State. Each pitcher bears a vignette representing Curtis as the slave's champion, holding a mirror in one hand which reflects the light upon two slaves whose manacles the Goddess of Liberty is loosing, while his other hand points to a black child holding a book.

Early industry was recognized in the presentation of several pieces of silver including the teapot to Philip Ten Eyck and the bowl given to Frederic Uhl in 1811 which were made by Isaac Hutton of Albany and

LEFT. Presentation salver; floral border, applied cast feet. Hayden Bros. & Co., 1853-55. (*Gebelein Silversmiths*) BELOW. Presentation salver; classic laurel border and scrolls, inscription and army insignia. William G. Forbes, 1856. (*Courtesy of The New-York Historical Society, New York City*)

presented for the best specimens of woolen cloth. A covered ewer made by William Gale of New York in 1823 is particularly interesting not only because of the bands of wheat sheaves and agrarian motifs but because of the engraving which shows a mill, a dam, and the ship *Mary & Hannah* on the river. A pitcher made by Joseph T. Rice of Albany has similar bands and borders of agrarian motifs. A pitcher made by William Adams of New York in 1852 is engraved with a scene of the Croton Aqueduct and Highbridge.

Loving cups, trays and bowls were also given in token of respect and admiration to heads of companies, professors and clergymen. Silver with engravings of buildings is especially interesting because of the historical significance and several pieces of gift silver given to the clergy have engravings of their churches. A tray in The New-York Historical Society has an engraving of the old Brick Church, New York, in 1860, and the loving cup given to the Rev. M. Morgan Dix has an engraving of St. Paul's Chapel, New York.

Awards to encourage agriculture had been made by the Farmers of New York in the eighteenth century and by the Connecticut, Pennsylvania and other agricultural societies in the early nineteenth century. The cup made by H. A. Goodwin for the Hartford County Agricultural Society which was awarded to Frederick Oakes in 1823 for the best cultivated farm is now in the collection of Philip Hammerslough. It has an engraved wreath of oak leaves with agricultural implements and an inner wreath of wheat which encircles an engraving of a plow. A jug-shaped pitcher with applied grape and leaf border and Bacchanalian group of infants is inscribed: "Presented to/Col. John Hare Powel/ by the Pennsylvania Agricultural Society not only in the testimony of their personal/ regard, but of their high respect for his/talents, zeal and liberality in promoting/the agricultural interests of this country." Such early pieces are examples of fine silversmithing, but the late nineteenth century pieces,

Bowl with inscription: "Given to Frederick Uhl by the Society for the Promotion of Useful Arts for the Best specimens of Woolen Cloth." Isaac Hutton, 1811. (*The Metropolitan Museum of Art, gift of Earl D. Pabst, 1953, in memory of Alice Edwina Uhl Pabst*)

although not as good design or workmanship, seem to express the plenty and abundance of the American harvest.

There is a group of these late nineteenth century American trophies whose unique design motifs relate closely to the products of American

RIGHT. Pitcher presented to Isaac Harris for his efforts in fighting the Old South Church fire, Boston, January 29, 1811; barrel-shaped with hoops, engraved scene of fire, acorn finial. Ebenezer Moulton. (*Courtesy, Museum of Fine Arts, Boston*) BELOW. Pair of silver pitchers. Joel Sayre, 1817. Presented to Joseph Curtis by the Manumission Society of New York. (*Courtesy of The New-York Historical Society, New York City*)

agriculture. The first of these cups was the Keystone Cup made by Tiffany & Company for H. J. Heinz & Company. It was exhibited at the United States Food Exposition in Madison Square Garden, New York, in October, 1892. The piece, which is in the form of a loving cup, is ornamented with fruit and vegetables used in the pickling and preserving business. Encircling the rim of the cup is a vine of cucumbers, each cucumber bearing the name of a city where Heinz had a branch. Below the neck of the vase are tomato vines with tomatoes, gherkins, horse-radish, onions, apples, pears, grapes, peaches and currants strewn on the body background of cabbage leaves. The handles are stalks of celery. In 1904 four silver cups were awarded at the 11th National Irrigation Congress held at Ogden, Utah. The cups, which were designed and made by the Mauser Manufacturing Company of New York City, were examples of American silversmithing at that time. The four prizes were for the best exhibits of fruit, hops, barley, and sugar beets grown under cultivation and the design of each cup was appropriate for its purpose. The award for the best fruit was known as the Pomona Cup. In the center of the cup is a graceful figure of the goddess Pomona pictured distributing the products of the soil. The handles are elm trees entwined with grapevines whose branches

LEFT. The Hops Cup presented for the best exhibit of hops. RIGHT. The Pomona Cup for the best exhibit of fruit. Mauser Manufacturing Co. (*Jewelers' Circular*, 1904)

encircle the rim of the vase. The base of the vase consists of four cornucopias resting upon waves of water. The Hops Cup has a wavy Art Nouveau outline suggesting water movement, while the ornamentation from
the bottom of the bowl upward is a growing hop vine which extends along
the bowl and twines about the rim of the vase. On the body of the bowl
is a relief figure of a nude woman. The base of the cup shows water falling
over rocks. The Sugar Beet Cup was a massive vase which embodied a
unique design significant of the purpose for which it was intended. The
decoration included a combination of beets and beet leaves and stalks in
relief. The Barley Cup while not so unique is decorated with borders of
growing barley. All of those designs show Art Nouveau influence.

Perhaps the most important presentation piece of the American Victorian Era was the Bryant testimonial vase. It is representative of the best
work of the American silversmith of the late nineteenth century. The idea
of presenting a testimonial to the poet William Cullen Bryant originated
with the members of the Century Association in New York. The committee appointed consisted of the Rev. Drs. Samuel Osgood, Henry S.
Bellows, and Henry Codman Potter; and Messrs. Asher S. Durand, William H. Appleton, Frederick de Peyster, Franklin H. Delano, Benjamin H.
Field, Theodore Roosevelt, Joseph H. Choate, and others. The committee decided that the testimonial should be in the form of a vase to be
executed as a work of art and ornamented in an appropriate manner with
designs illustrating the most important events in the life of the poet. On
the invitation of the committee, the leading silver workers of New York—
Tiffany & Co.; Starr & Marcus; Black, Starr & Frost; the Whiting Manufacturing Co. and Gorham Manufacturing Co. of Providence, Rhode
Island, submitted designs. The design accepted was by Tiffany & Co. and
was the work of their head designer, James H. Whitehouse. The vase is
thirty inches in height and was executed in oxidized silver. It is of classic
Greek form but the outside ornamentation is original and related to the
occasion. The words of the artist explain his motif: "When the Bryant
testimonial was first mentioned to me, my thoughts at once flew to the
country—to the crossing of the boughs of trees, to the plants and flowers
and to a general contemplation of nature, and these, together with a certain Homeric influence, produced in my mind the germ of the design—
the form of a Greek vase, with the most beautiful of American flowers and
plants growing around and entwining themselves gracefully about it, each

LEFT. William Cullen Bryant Vase. J. H. Whitehouse for Tiffany & Co., 1875. (*The Metropolitan Museum of Art, gift of William Cullen Bryant, 1877*) RIGHT. Design of Starr & Marcus for Bryant Vase.

breathing its own particular story as it grew." Thus the vase as we see it is entirely covered with a fretwork of apple branches and blossoms which not only were a favorite of Bryant, but, after the fashion of the Victorian era, bear a fruitful moral as the apple tree blossoms in the Spring, and in Autumn produces fruit. Continuing the allegory under the fretwork are the eglantine and amaranth suggesting the spirit of poetry and immortality. Medallions contain the portrait bust of the poet and low relief scenes of his life and works. On the neck of the vase the "Water-fowl" and the "Fringed Gentian" are illustrated. A lower portion of the vase is ornamented with a design of American cotton blossom and Indian corn. The ornament at the foot of the vase is the water lily, a symbol of eloquence, while the handles are decorated with Indian corn and cotton and a perched bobolink, relating to the poem, "Robert of Lincoln." The finished vase, which cost $5,000, was exhibited at the Centennial. Facsimiles were sold

140

for $500, but how many were sold is not known and so far none have come to light. The Bryant vase, which was presented June 20, 1876, received considerable attention at the time. The poet gave the vase to the Metropolitan Museum of Art where it now is and from time to time it is put on exhibit.

The propositions for vases which were submitted by the other silver companies received little notice from the public and, the original sketches being lost, nothing remains but the descriptions and illustrations in the magazines and newspapers of the times. Today, with the revived interest in American Victorian art and silversmithing, these vase designs seem worth our attention. First of all, their form and motifs of design are characteristic of the era, and secondly, they represent the best craftsmanship

LEFT. Design by Whiting Manufacturing Co. for Bryant Vase. CENTER. Design by Gorham Manufacturing Co. for Bryant Vase. RIGHT. Design by Black, Starr & Frost for Bryant Vase. (*The Art Journal,* 1876)

of the period and give us a record of the work of the leading American silver companies of this period and the names of their designers. The vases illustrate the historic, story-telling characteristics of late nineteenth century art and important silver pieces of the period. Classic form and detail was combined with naturalistic floral motifs which included indigenous flowers and plants. Motifs of design were executed in repoussé and high relief and sculptural subjects were often conceived in the round and attached to the form of the piece. Emblematic figures and symbolic design are combined to produce pieces of monumental significance.

The Bryant vase design by Thomas J. Pairpoint of Gorham & Co. of Providence, Rhode Island, stressed the poetical and was conceived as a monument to the poet's genius rather than to his person and fame. The central figure of the vase was a medallion bust of the poet and this was surrounded by a richly ornamented background with a variety of emblematic borders and designs. Around the pedestal base were six groups in bold relief each composed of figures representing one of Bryant's poems including "Thanatopsis," "The Death of Slavery," "Waiting at the Gate," "The Conqueror's Grave," "A Day Dream," and "Odyssey of Homer." The lower part of the vase is covered with Greek ornament introducing wheat and violets which relate to the poems, "Song of the Sower," and "The Yellow Violet." The handles contain birds illustrating the poems on birds.

The vase design by C. Witteck submitted by Starr & Marcus was also classical in form, being a variation of the famed Warwick Vase used earlier in the century by English silversmiths and by the American Thomas Fletcher in the vases presented to De Witt Clinton in 1825. The graceful urn has a rim of rich arabesques representing fruits, flowers, and grains such as the azalea, fringed gentian and maize, and the handles are supported by heads of fauns festooned with garlands of American pine and hemlock. Around the neck are graceful amorini and on the top of the vase is the symbolical figure of the poet in Grecian costume and crowned with a wreath of leaves wrought from gold and enameled. About the body of the vase are four classical panels in relief with scenes representing four of Bryant's poems. The octagonal base is flanked at each corner by a pedestal supporting emblematic figures of Truth, Meditation, Inspiration, and America, seated in niches.

The vase design submitted by Whiting Manufacturing Co. was the work of their head designer, Charles Osborne. The outline of the vase was classical. In the center of the vase is a relief medallion of Bryant which is flanked by relief illustrations of "The Song of the Sower" and "Sella," and illustrations of other poems surround the base of the neck. The graceful handles decorated with sugar cane, corn, and cotton spring from the body of the vase. The figure of Truth surmounts the vase. The marble base was designed to have four panels in silver repoussé illustrating scenes from Bryant's poems. The height of the vase was to be thirty-eight inches and it was to be wrought of oxidized silver relieved at points by gilding.

The design of the vase presented by Black, Starr & Frost is also Grecian in form and is a combination of classic motif and emblematic figures such as Apollo seated in the center of the vase and the figure of Pegasus that surmounts the top. The vase rests upon a square base with statuette figures of History and Mercury which stand on either side of the medallion portrait of the poet. The base is further enriched with mouldings and circular panels which were to include poems. The vase was to be executed in oxidized silver accented with gold. It was designed by C. Witteck.

When all of the vase designs are carefully considered, one cannot help but commend the committee for selecting the most dignified and simple design. As seen today, the vase is not only an example of American Victorian silver, but it is evidence of the excellent work done by Tiffany and a credit to the good taste and restraint of their designer.

The earliest existing American racing trophy was made by Jesse Kip in 1699 and presented to Jacob and Maria von Dorn whose colt won the one mile race on King's Highway, Middletown, New Jersey. It is now in the Henry Ford Museum. *The New York Gazette*, May 31, 1762, ran the following announcement: "Horse Race to be run for on Tuesday the first of June next at the Beaver Pond in Jamaica, a Silver bowl, Value Twenty Pounds, free for any Horse, Mare or Gelding, the best of three two mile Heats, Paying Two Dollars Entrance, or double at the Post. . . ." It is not known what silversmith made the bowl. A silver tankard of Twenty Pounds value was to be run for at Morris Town in 1771 (*The New York Gazette* and the *Weekly Mercury*, October 7, 1771). A racing trophy was also given to "Kitty Fisher," the winner of the Maryland Jockey Club sweepstakes in 1773, and silver trophies continued to be the popular awards in racing and other sports down through the years.

However, it was in the late nineteenth century before horse-racing and yachting trophies were regarded as major products of the silversmith. As was typical of the decorative art of the era, they were characterized by extreme style and decorative abandon. Every type of silversmithing technique including frosting, matting, burnishing, oxidation and parcel gilt added to the exuberance of their ornamentation. They were not only chased and engraved, but also covered with cast reliefs, sculptured figures and repoussé decoration. At first the shapes were based on Grecian forms and classic decoration was combined with naturalistic designs and motifs with local color. Although few pieces of American Victorian silver reached

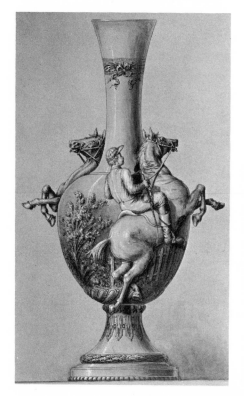

LEFT Original sketch for Jockey, 1889. BELOW. Original sketches for Hunt trophies, 1900. (*The Gorham Company*)

the decorative exaggeration of similar pieces of English Victorian silver, the chief characteristics of Victorian design are seen especially in American yachting and racing trophies. By the mid-nineteenth century classic forms had been discarded in favor of the rococo by most companies. Rococo curved forms were covered with exuberant "C" and "S" scrolls, naturalistic grapevines, and other floral and leaf motifs such as rustic oak branches. One of the most important trophies of the mid-nineteenth century was the Belmont Cup which was first awarded in 1869 to August Belmont for his winning horse, Fenian. It is a solid silver punch bowl with sculptured figures of horses at its base and on the cover. The technique is a combination of shiny silver and repoussé and is typical of the rococo silverwork done at the time. Other trophies have story-telling scenes, and sculptural figures of deer, Indians, and patriotic figures also cling to the sides of vases and urns, sometimes completely obliterating the form of the object. Symbolic figures from classical mythology were used as finials and in sculptural groups about the bases of urns, and Grecian-gowned figures told the story of the event commemorated. By the 1890's the forms of American silver were eclectic. In some pieces we see the influence of the Orient, in others Egyptian and Etruscan motifs are

Belmont Cup; Rococo border of oak leaves and acorns, sculptured figures of horses. Tiffany & Co., 1869. (*New York Racing Association*)

TOP LEFT. Original sketch for Yachting Trophy, 1884. RIGHT. Astor cup for Sloops, c. 1895. LEFT. Original sketch for Yachting Trophy, 1893. (*The Gorham Company*)

LEFT AND CENTER. Martelé Prize vases, 1900–1904. (*The Gorham Company*) RIGHT. The Goelet Cup won by *Volunteer* in 1891; classic vase design of sea horses. Whiting Manufacturing Co. (*Jewelers Circular*, 1891)

used and on still others there are Renaissance details such as dolphins, amorini, shells, acanthus leaves and classic figures. Later trophies reflect the influence of Art Nouveau.

The popular shapes for trophies were vases, urns, and centerpieces of bowl form. Elaborate decorative effects of contrasting surfaces which were popular earlier were seldom seen and the techniques most commonly used were engraving, chasing, and repoussé decoration. The companies who made the majority of these silver pieces were Gorham Manufacturing Co. of Providence, Rhode Island; Tiffany & Co., Black, Starr & Frost, and Whiting Manufacturing Co. of New York; J. E. Caldwell & Co., of Philadelphia, and Samuel Kirk & Son of Baltimore, Maryland. These firms employed excellent designers, many of them with European training, but the names of the designers seldom received mention.

147

ABOVE LEFT. Ewer ornamented with agrarian motifs and engraved scenes of the Erie Canal, presented to the owners of the boat *Mary & Hannah* that took the first load of wheat through the Erie Canal. William Gale, New York, 1823. (*Lent by the Albany Institute of History and Art to the exhibition "Classical America", The Newark Museum*) RIGHT. Teakettle and stand given to Gen. Montgomery C. Meigs by the citizens of Washington for his work on the Washington Aqueduct. M. W. Galt & Bro., c. 1853. (*The Smithsonian Institution*) BELOW. Pitcher and goblets, Rococo style, with engraved scenes of Croton Aqueduct. William Adams, 1831–1850. Presented to Nicholas Dean, President of the Croton Aqueduct Department. (*The Museum of the City of New York*)

Although the general characteristics and motifs of decoration followed Victorian influence there was considerable individuality and indigenous symbols appropriate to the occasion were used on many pieces. Hunt cups not only show scenes of horse racing, but incorporate such motifs as jockey caps, saddles, stirrups and horseshoes. Yachting trophies are covered with waves, shells, dolphins, sea horses and figures of Neptune and other mythological figures. Many of the more elaborate trophies kept to the classic theme of decoration but there are cups with handles composed of sailors in American Navy uniform of the era.

One of the most important cups made by Tiffany & Co. at this time was the Commodore's Ocean Challenge Cup of the New York Yacht Club, made in 1876. The design of the vase is of classical origin, but its ornamentation is emblematic of nautical sports. The standard of the vase is a miniature capstan supported by dolphins' heads. On top of the capstan is a fluted cup and from this springs the body of the vase. Its front is ornamented by a panel with an illustration of an incident from Longfellow's "The Wreck of the Hesperus." From either side of this medallion spring handles which represent the prows of Egyptian barges. They are ornamented with cables and anchors. Spread eagles fill the space between the handles and the pennant-hung neck, and the top is surmounted by the figure of Columbus. The figures and designs in relief are all hand

LEFT. Larchmont cup. (*Whiting Manufacturing Co., 1892*) RIGHT. Original sketch for shipping trophy. (*The Gorham Manufacturing Co., 1889*)

wrought and a combination of rich oxidization and gilding adds to the beauty and the imposing appearance. The mixture of Grecian and Egyptian influence and the grandiose concept of the vase is typical of the ostentatious Victorian taste, but the medallion of Longfellow's poem makes the vase unique and distinctly American.

In 1893 Tiffany made a silver punch bowl for the Society of Colonial Wars. The story of the colonial wars and the scenes of the period are pictured on the bowl in bas-relief, repoussé and etching. At the base of the bowl is a figure of an American Indian and an old colonial soldier. Around the body of the bowl are the arms of nine of the original colonies. There are also two scenes etched on the bowl. One pictures a three-masted boat

LEFT. Commodore Bennett's Ocean Challenge Cup. Tiffany & Co., 1876. BELOW. Cape May Challenge Cup. Tiffany & Co. (*The New York Yacht Club*)

LEFT. Cup presented to Dr. Morgan Dix, Rector of St. Paul's Chapel. Tiffany & Co.

sailing into a harbor along the Massachusetts coast. The other is a battle scene between the Puritans and Indians. On the front of the bowl is the inscription "Society of Colonial Wars in the State of New York, 1607–1775." A rare collection of old colonial silver coins decorates the side of the bowl and a gold coin is in the bowl of the ladle. Probably no piece of silverware produced in the nineteenth century has told the story of an epoch more interestingly.

In the 1890's trophies and prize cups were made for almost every event from horse racing and yachting to bowling, lawn tennis, football and dog shows. Among the late prize cups made by Tiffany were the Goelet and Astor cups of the New York Yacht Club made in 1893; the Harvard-Yale University Track Cup, 1891; the "Football 1891" cup and the silver match boxes made for the players; the Morris County Golf cups; and the Charles J. Glidden Auto Trophy. The Salmon Cup presented to Henry de Forest by the Restigouche Salmon Club is ornamented with a design of salmon, pine cones and ferns seen on the banks of streams where salmon are found. The Pigeon Shooting Trophy made by Tiffany in 1891 has a flock of flying pigeons about its rim. In 1899 Tiffany made a cup which President McKinley presented to Ambassador Cambon of France. The series of cups which President Cleveland presented to sea captains who rescued American sailors from shipwrecks in 1895 were made by the Mauser Manufacturing Co. Gorham also made many trophies in the 1890's including the Oarsman's Trophy, the Astor Cup for Sloops in 1898 and New York Yacht Club Trophies in 1892. The silver bowl for the Tammany Society which has a reproduction engraved in silver of the photos of well-known Tammany leaders was made by Simpson, Hall, Miller & Co.

The workmanship of many of these trophies is excellent but the design is often poor and in bad taste and the pieces generally have more pictorial value than artistic worth in that they illustrate the subject but do not relate to the form of the piece. However, the pieces are representative of a certain category of silverware made in America in the late nineteenth century.

Especially interesting because of their indigenous and appropriate motifs are the many yachting trophies designed and made by the New York silversmiths, Whiting Manufacturing Co., in the 1890's. These include the cup won by the *Priscilla,* which was a covered flagon with a figure of the Puritan maid Priscilla Alden and the inscription, "Why don't you speak for yourself, John" from Longfellow's poem, "The Courtship of Miles Standish." The vase given to the *Vigilant* to commemorate her victory over the *Valkyrie* in defense of the *America's* Cup in 1893 has a standing figure of an Indian with bow and arrow and a figure of symbolical victory. A cup won by the *Mayflower* in 1886 is decorated with figures in Puritan dress. The Seawanhaka Corinthian Yacht Club cup won by *Cinderella* has a slipper-shaped neck and the bowl of the vase is covered with shell forms. Other vases show sea shells of various kinds. The New York Yacht Club Schooner prize won by *Fortuna* is a tall tankard with an ear-of-corn handle and a nude maiden standing amid a design of waves. The Lawn Tennis trophy made by Gorham for the High Rock Club in 1891 illustrated Cooper's *The Last of the Mohicans.* Indian war plumes form a bold decoration about the rim of the cup. Other designs showed Art Nouveau influence both in their form and design motifs.

RIGHT. Goelet Prize for Schooners. Tiffany & Co. (*The New York Yacht Club*) CENTER. Larchmont Yacht Club Commodore's Cup, 1894. Whiting Manufacturing Co. (*Harper's Monthly Advertizer*, May, 1894) (*Courtesy of The New-York Historical Society, New York City*)

LEFT. The *Genesta* Cup; sea urchins on body, handles of sculptured nude figures. Whiting Manufacturing Co. (*Century Magazine*, February, 1892)

The Martelé department at Gorham Manufacturing Co. also made prize vases and loving cups, and these were the finest trophies made in this era in design, materials and workmanship.

Another piece of presentation silver available to the collector today is the silver trumpet. The brass speaking-trumpet was used by the foreman of the volunteer fire department to shout directions and to encourage the men fighting the fire. Similar trumpets of silver were presented for heroism at fires or for work in volunteer fire companies.

Still another presentation piece was the silver trowel. The use of a silver trowel to lay the cornerstone of a public building was a late nineteenth century custom. These trowels were inscribed with the occasion, date, and names of the person who laid the stone, the building committee and the architect. A collection of these presentation trowels would be interesting from the historical viewpoint and also would not be too expensive to assemble. Trowels can be used as serving pieces for meat and other foods.

TOP. Souvenir spoon with facsimile of the *America's* Cup. Howard Sterling Co. (*Jewelers' Circular*, September 20, 1899) BELOW LEFT TO RIGHT. Silver trumpet presented to the Philadelphia Hose Company, July 1843. Maker unknown. (*Philadelphia Museum of Art, photograph by A. J. Wyatt, Staff Photographer*) Presentation trumpet, c. 1850. (*The H. V. Smith Museum of the Home Insurance Company*) Sketch of silver trumpet presented by the officers and members of Sacramento Engine Co. No. 3, April 21, 1853. (*Index of American Design*)

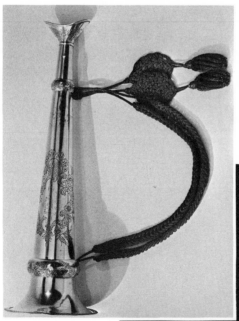

ABOVE LEFT. Silver trowel used in laying of the corner stone of the Francis Scott Key Monument, San Francisco. (*The California Historical Society*)

VI American Presentation Swords

THERE are many facets of interest for the collector of swords. The serious collector is concerned with the terminology and the understanding of the sword as a weapon. He is usually also interested in the historical significance—who owned the sword, and the events connected with the owner's career. The sword is also collected as a work of art and this phase of sword collecting which relates to the design of the sword hilt with its decorative pommel and guard is now a popular field for many collectors. The appreciation of the sword as a work of art has turned the attention not only to the design and workmanship but to the silversmith who made the hilt.

According to Harold Peterson, the authority on American swords, the great period for collectors of American swords is from 1700 to 1815. There were no swords hilted by American silversmiths before 1700 and after the first decade of the nineteenth century the silversmiths began making ponderous hilts of decadent design with rococo pommels and large counter-guards. During the colonial period many civilians wore swords and there were various types of swords, including the cutlass, the saber, the hunting sword and the small sword. There was also a variety of pommel designs such as sculptured lions, dogs' and birds' heads, cones, mushrooms and spheres. There are many fine collections of these early swords with hilts made by well-known early American silversmiths and these swords which date from the seventeenth and eighteenth centuries have become an important and advanced field of antique collecting.

Another category of sword collecting is that of the presentation sword. The history of American presentation swords begins with the Revolution. Presentation swords were given by the Continental Congress. States, cities and organizations also followed the practice. Such swords were presented as a mark of esteem or in recognition of some heroic act.

155

Presentation swords more than any other type of sword are usually connected with important personages or events in American history. With the exception of the diplomatic swords, swords were no longer used by civilians in the nineteenth century. Thus the collector of nineteenth century presentation swords must concentrate on those belonging to army or navy personnel. Nineteenth century presentation swords include those given to heroes of the American wars of the century: the Tripolitan War, the War of 1812, the Mexican War (1842–1848), the Civil War in the 1860's and the Spanish-American War at the end of the nineteenth cen-

TOP. Sword of Lt. O'Bannon. Johnson & Reat, Baltimore, 1810. BOTTOM. Detail of oval medallion depicting raising of U.S. flag over Derna. (*Marine Corps Museum, Quantico, Virginia*)

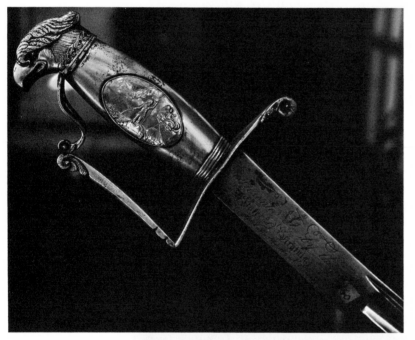

tury. The enlisted man's sword was a fighting weapon, but the officer's sword was a decoration, thus it offers more variety of design and fine workmanship. Especially is this true of the presentation sword since it was made to personal specifications and to indicate rank, and was used as an ornament of dress. Elaborate presentation swords often cost as much as $1,500. Others given by a company to their commander might be simpler in design and less expensive.

The design of presentation swords relates to the decorative arts of the period in which the sword was made. Those of the early nineteenth century reflect the influence of the Federal period and show motifs of classical inspiration and also such patriotic motifs as heads of Washington and the American eagle. Later, as the rococo style dominated the decorative arts, elaborate rococo motifs are seen on sword hilts. Not only was the hilt topped with an ornamental pommel but the blades were usually blued and gilt or bright-etched and ornamented with foliage sprays, patriotic symbols, stars, military trophies, mottoes, and scenes of battle. Presentation swords were often not made until many years after the event or happening commemorated so that there were swords given for heroism in the Revolution which were not made or presented until early in the nineteenth century and which thus relate to the designs of the later period rather than those of the eighteenth century.

In the Federal period the eagle head pommel was the most popular because of its patriotic significance but classical heads with helmets and Indian head pommels were also made. The motifs of design on these swords include classical figures and borders of beading and laurel.

One of the earliest nineteenth century American presentation swords was the Marine Corps presentation sword given to Presly O'Bannon for his service in the Tripolitan Wars. O'Bannon led the charge against the fortress at Derna and is credited with raising the American flag over the city. The sword, which has a silver hilt with an eagle-head pommel, was presented by the State of Virginia. The inscription, which is surrounded with decorative scrolls and a fouled anchor, reads: "Presented by the State of Virginia to her Gallant Son Priestly [sic] N. O'Bannon." The following is inscribed on the reverse: "Assault & Conquest / of the / City of Derna in Africa / April 27th, 1805." The oval medallion of gold depicts the raising of the U.S. flag over Derna. The sword was made by Johnson & Reat of Baltimore in 1810 and the makers' touch (partly worn) is in a rectangular cartouche. Thus the sword is not only valuable from the historic angle but also as a record of the work of an American nineteenth century silversmith.

During the War of 1812 many fine eagle-pommeled swords with classical motifs were made for presentation. The flat curved guards sometimes had a large decorated counter-guard. The Congressional Naval presentation sword of the War of 1812, which was issued at the conclusion of the war, had blades made by William Rose of Philadelphia. These swords were decorated with bright-etched designs of floral sprays, a military trophy or picture of the engagement, and a presentation inscription. The classical helmet pommel is cast. The large counter-guard is ornamented with an eagle, anchors, flags, a cannon, and floral sprays. The underside bears the letters "U.S."

The State of New York also presented swords to prominent officers of the Army and Navy. All of these were similar in design. The blade is blued and etched in gilt with bright panels. The designs include an American eagle with a ribbon inscribed with the motto "E Pluribus Unum" and on the reverse, Liberty wearing an Indian headdress. The hilt is gold and the pommel is an eagle's head while the large counter-guard is embossed with classical figures such as Hercules and the Nemean lion. Although the sword has a silversmith's mark it has never been identified. There were many silversmiths working at this time who are known to have made silver sword hilts. Among those working in Philadelphia who made hilts with eagle-head pommels were Emmor Weaver (1808–1820); Philip Hartman c. 1813; Jacob Kucher (1806–11); William Ball Jr. (1784–1815) and Robert Swan (1795–1831). Baltimore makers included John Lynch (1761–1848); Johnson & Reat (c. 1810); and Christian Wiltberger (1766–1819). In New York, Hugh Wishart (1784–1816); Elias Pelletreau (1736–1810); and Christopher Giffing (1815–1835). Ball, Black & Co., c. 1851, were among nineteenth century makers. There were also silversmiths in such cities as Albany, New York; Hartford, Connecticut; and even smaller cities, who are known to have made decorative sword hilts at this time.

The most important firm of silversmiths who made presentation swords in the first quarter of the nineteenth century was Fletcher & Gardiner of Philadelphia. Several of these swords made by Fletcher & Gardiner exist today, two in the collection of Jay P. Altmayer and several in the Maryland Historical Society. In beauty of design, workmanship and richness of materials these swords surpass all other American presentation swords of the nineteenth century and are also worthy to be placed beside those of well-known American silversmiths of the eighteenth century. When the project was undertaken of a sword to be presented by the Commonwealth of Virginia to Major General Winfield Scott, Scott himself suggested Fletcher & Gardiner, as shown in his letter to Governor Randolph dated Philadelphia, July 9, 1821. The part referring to the design of the sword is as follows: "Messrs. Fletcher & Gardiner, Manufacturers in Chestnut Street, Philadelphia, are the workmen whom I beg leave to recommend for all the parts of the sword. I have seen several of their make, ordered by public bodies, executed with superior taste and workmanship. They make the best steel blades, and have a great variety of antique models, from which to compose the ornaments of their work." Although Scott wanted the sword made by Fletcher, the Virginia Assembly selected Harvey Lewis instead, according to information in letters in the Virginia Historical Society.

"Scott's sword, along with those voted for General Gaines and Captain Lewis Warrington, was made under the direction of General Thomas Cadwalader at Philadelphia by Harvey Lewis. We have a letter from General Cadwalader dated April 5, 1825, announcing that the swords were ready for shipment. I have no information yet on the presentation date. According to the executive letter book for March 30, 1824, the sword cost Virginia $500. General Cadwalader informed the governor in a letter of 20 April 1825 that the swords had been shipped, and described them in detail."

The Scott sword as seen today has a gold hilt with helmet pommel. The grips are ornamented with diagonal ropes of laurel and oak with a mask in the center of each side and a band of beading at the top and bottom. The knuckle-bow and quillons are ornamented with acanthus leaf decoration. The large counter-guard is ornamented with helmets, a laurel wreath and borders of acanthus. Three wide bands of silver acanthus leaf decoration centered with an oval containing an antique scene decorate the scabbard. The sword presented by the State of Maryland to Lt. Henry C. Ballard, gunnery officer on the *Constitution* in the War of 1812, was designed by Thomas Fletcher. This is probably the finest and earliest American gold presentation sword in existence. The pommel is an eagle head with elongated neck. The other parts of the sword including the scabbard are ornamented with classic motifs and medallions of antique scenes. The blade engraving includes a scene of the battle between the *Constitution*

and the *H.M.S. Cayenne* and *H.M.S. Levant* together with an inscription of presentation.

In the Thomas Fletcher collection of manuscripts in the Pennsylvania Historical Society there are several letters which refer to swords. One letter relates to a sword to be made for the Governor of Matanzas,

LEFT. Gold-hilted sword given to Major General Winfield Scott by the State of Virginia for service in the War of 1812; helmet head, classic masks, acanthus and laurel decoration. Harvey Lewis, Philadelphia, c. 1825. CENTER. Gold-hilted sword presented to Lt. H. C. Ballard by the State of Maryland for his services in the War of 1812. Thomas Fletcher. (*Both, collection of Jay P. Altmayer*) RIGHT. Sword and scabbard presented by the State of New York to General Jacob Brown for his services in the War of 1812. (*The Smithsonian Institution*)

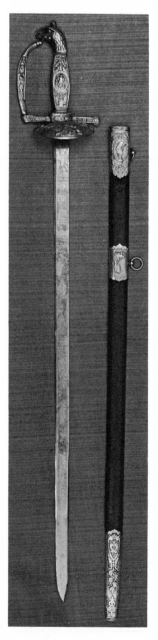

Cuba. "1200 (Twelve hundred Dollars) is the amount to be employed in a Sword & belt to correspond. The ornaments must be Spanish & no Republican emblems of any kind can be admitted, the sword being presented to a distinguished Spanish Off. lately Governor of Matanzas. I have the Escutcheon of the City which with the initials, C.A. will be a

LEFT. Sword awarded Sailing Master John Percival by Congress in 1811. (*U.S. Naval Academy Museum*) CENTER. Sword presented to Alfred Davis by the State of New York in 1817. (*The Metropolitan Museum of Art, gift of Francis P. Garvan, 1922*) RIGHT. Sword presented to Lt. General Ulysses S. Grant by his Friends in Kentucky. Canfield Bros. & Co., Baltimore, 1864. (*Collection of Jay P. Altmayer*)

part of the ornaments—Two mottos must be worked into the material of the blade, one in Spanish, the other in Latin or English—I have not yet determined which. I presume the clasp of the belt shud be a golden Lions head; & the belt itself, red & blue morroco?" (Newport R. I. 23 July 1832. E. A. Grace.) The letter was addressed to Mr. Thomas Fletcher (late Fletcher & Gardiner) Goldsmith & Sword Cutter, Philadelphia. It is not known if this sword was ever made.

A sketch for a typical presentation sword of the period 1830–1840 is in the collection of the Maryland Historical Society, as is a sword of similar design. The sword commemorates an engagement of the Tripolitan War although its presentation was not authorized until 1834. The blade marked "Rose" is engraved with floral sprays and a representation of an engagement with a Tripolitan gunboat. One side bears the inscription "Presented to Edmund P. Kennedy of the United States Navy By His Native State of Maryland For His Gallant Services Off Tripoli in 1804." The grips have oval medallions with eagles surrounded by laurel wreaths. The quillons which resemble the arms of a Maltese cross are a typical form of the period. At the crossing is an oval medallion with an eagle

Sword presented to Major General John C. Robinson by his friends and the City of New York for his gallantry at Gettysburg. Tiffany & Co., 1865. (*Collection of Jay P. Altmayer*)

clutching burning brands. The pommel is in the form of a stylized helmet. Other cross-hilted swords in the Smithsonian Institution have vase-shaped and sculptured eagle pommels. These were made as presentation swords for heroes of the War of 1812. The decorative details of these swords are larger and include a variety of materials and completely cover the surfaces. The grips are of mother-of-pearl and are decorated with strips of silver gilt and set with diamonds, garnets, topaz and other precious stones. The engravings, in addition to floral sprays, eagles and military trophies, often bear more complicated military groupings including cannon.

The majority of the swords made for presentation to Mexican War heroes have hilts with elaborate rococo designs but a few were of simpler design. Regulation army presentation swords were made in two designs. One has an eagle-head pommel holding a wreath of oak leaves and acorns which is attached to a knuckle-bow of rococo leaf and rosette ornament. Another army presentation sword of this period is cross hilted with a vase-shaped pommel. The rococo counter-guard has an engraving of a fortified city and a military trophy marked "Mexico," "Vera Cruz," and "Cerro Gordo," together with the presentation inscription, connects the sword

Silver-hilted sword and scabbard presented to Captain R. Suydam Grant for Civil War Service. Schuyler, Hartley & Graham. Tiffany & Co. (*Collection of Jay P. Altmayer*)

with the Mexican War. A variation of this sword has a panel on the grips with a cast relief scene of Hercules strangling the Nemean Lion. The inscription reads "Presented by the citizens of Mobile as a testimonial of their admiration of the gallant conduct of Major Braxton Bragg in the defense of Ft. Brown, the attack on Monterey, and more particularly in contributing greatly as he did to the glorious victory at Buena Vista." An interesting feature of the sword is the 1849 version of the map of the State of Alabama. One of the finest presentation swords of the Mexican War was that presented to Colonel A. H. Gladden by the City of Charleston, South Carolina. The design of the hilt and pommel are adapted from the palmetto palm, the symbol of South Carolina and the Palmetto Regiment. The hilt is cast in the shape of a palm trunk and the pommel is silver gilt depicting the crown of the palmetto palm. A rattlesnake in high

Silver-hilted sword presented to Major General Andrew Jackson Smith for gallantry at Vicksburg, Pleasant Hill, Yellow Bayou and Tupelo by the Commissioned Officers of the 16th Army Corps, Sept. 19, 1864. Tiffany & Co. (*Collection of Jay P. Altmayer*)

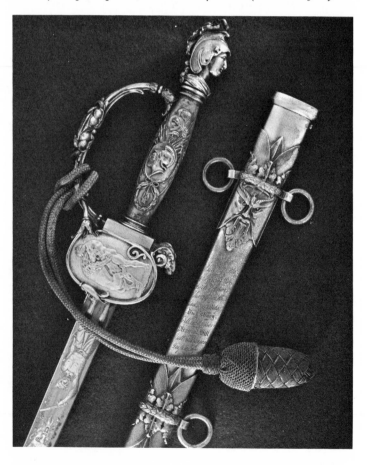

relief is entwined about the trunk. Although there is no mark, the design and the workmanship point to a silversmith of outstanding ability and the sword certainly ranks with those made by Fletcher & Gardiner some twenty years earlier. The sword has remained in the family and is now owned by Mr. Marion E. Wynne, Jr.

In 1851 Ball, Black & Co. made nineteen gold-sheathed swords for presentation by the State of Illinois to officers of the Mexican War. This firm was founded by Isaac Marquand in 1810 and after several different partnerships and changes in name became the present firm of Black, Starr & Frost.

Sword hilts became more elaborate in the mid-nineteenth century and reflected the gaudy taste of the period. The cross-hilted sword continued to be made. Straight swords with cross quillons in the form of eagles

Silver-hilted sword presented to Brigadier General John C. Pile. Marked "M" (Old English) Tiffany & Co. (*Collection of Jay P. Altmayer*)

with pommels of helmet shape were made for generals in the Civil War by Tiffany & Co. Other Tiffany designs at this time had pommels with sculptured eagles, classic heads and heads of Washington. The straight

LEFT. Sword and scabbard presented by the State of South Carolina to General James Shields for his services in the Mexican War. Gregg Hayden & Co., by Ames Manufacturing Co. CENTER. Staff officer sword and scabbard, 1860, owned by General George B. McClellan during the Civil War. Ames Manufacturing Co. RIGHT. Sword and scabbard presented to General Nelson Miles in 1887 by the People of Arizona for services in capturing Geronimo. Tiffany & Co. (*All three, The Smithsonian Institution*)

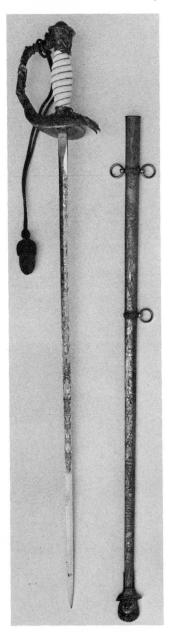

quillons had acorns, flower buds, ram's head, or scrolled leaf finials. This post Civil War era was the heyday of the American presentation sword. Massive swords with heavy rococo ornamentation and mountings of gold and silver set with precious stones reflected the gaudy taste of Victorian America. Grips were ornamented with massive sculptured forms of classical figures, the Goddess of Liberty or figures of soldiers or sailors.

Navy presentation swords were decorated with motifs such as sea

Swords presented to Rear Admiral John W. Philip including Tiffany sword (right) designed by Paulding Farnham. (*U.S. Naval Academy Museum*)

LEFT. Sword presented to Major General Frémont, by "The Men of The West". CENTER. Sword presented to Major General Burnside by the State of Rhode Island. RIGHT. Sword presented to Major General Halleck by the Union Ladies of St. Louis, Missouri. Tiffany & Co., c. 1862. (*Catalogue*) (*The Metropolitan Museum of Art*)

monsters, waves and anchors. Scenes of naval encounters were embossed on panels and figures of Neptune, dolphins and naval trophies were also included in the elaborate etched and gilt decorations.

Between 1860 and 1870 there were over twenty-five sword manufacturers and distributors in the United States including Ames Manufacturing Company, Nathan Starr, W. H. Horstmann & Son, and Schuyler, Hartley and Graham, but Tiffany & Company was pre-eminent from the standpoint of design. Although Tiffany carried stock presentation swords for both officers and generals they also produced original designs for special presentations. According to Jay Altmayer, the owner of the largest collection of American presentation swords and the author of a monograph on the subject, the designs of Tiffany swords were influenced, through the French firm of Tiffany, by Nicholas Noel Boutet, the famous gunsmith of Versailles. Tiffany swords are usually marked Tiffany & Company together with the letter "M" in old English or block type in a circle. In an elaborate catalogue circulated from 1854 to 1868 the swords made for Major General Halleck, Major General Burnside and Major General

168

Frémont are illustrated. Swords of similar design are also shown in the 1864 catalogue of Schuyler, Hartley and Graham. The grips are composed of classic figures from mythology, the Goddess of Liberty or figures of army officers in Civil War uniform. A cavalry sword in the Schuyler, Hartley and Graham catalogue has a figure of a cavalry officer on horseback. Ornamental motifs of design are also taken from classic sources or have patriotic significance. These include medallions with classic heads or scenes such as Hercules and the Nemean Lion or a head of the hero for whom the sword was designed. Decorative motifs include swags of twined laurel or oak and acorns, ribbons and tassels, stars, acanthus, and patriotic insignia such as flags, crossed swords, cannon and anchors. The blades are also engraved with appropriate patriotic designs. At the exhibit of the Metropolitan Fair in New York City in April, 1864, presentation swords were displayed by the following companies: Tiffany & Company; William Deitrick; Schuyler, Hartley & Graham; Bailey & Company; Staderman &

Silver-hilted sword and scabbard presented to Bv't Major Daniel H. McPhail, 5th Infantry, U.S. Army by the citizens of Baltimore for his services in the Mexican War. Detail shows crossguard in shape of two dolphins back to back and pommel in high relief with full modeled head of George Washington. Samuel Jackson, Baltimore, c. 1849. (*Collection of Norm Flayderman*)

Shapter; Emerson & Silver; Ball, Black & Company; Ames Manufacturing Company; Horstman Brother & Company, A. W. Spies; Shreve, Stanwood & Company; and William Rose & Sons. An Army sword and a Navy sword of silver, sculptured and engraved and set with precious stones, were donated by Tiffany. These were to be given by popular vote to the favorite general and admiral. The whereabouts of these swords today is not known but existing descriptions show them to be typical of the elaborate over-decorated swords of the post Civil War era.

At the time of the Spanish-American War presentation swords attempted to conform to United States military regulations for service swords. Enamel work supplanted the fine castings and engraving on the hilt of the presentation swords and thus color took the place of rich castings and carvings and cheap paste stones were set in red, white, and blue enamel. There was also often a deterioration in workmanship as well as materials. In 1899 Tiffany executed a presentation sword for Admiral Dewey as a gift from the nation in memory of his victory at Manila Bay. The sword combines fine craftsmanship together with enamel, precious stones and gold. The designer of this sword was Paulding Farnham, one of Tiffany's chief designers. A sword made for Captain John W. Philip, U.S.N., is of similar design and is now in the United States Naval Academy Museum at Annapolis, as is another Tiffany sword designed by Paulding Farnham.

Collecting swords is an expensive hobby but rewarding if you can afford it, since there are many swords on the market. Certain dealers specialize in swords and data is readily available. There are historical swords that belonged to well-known persons, but any sword that is connected with a battle of any American war has value even though it may not have belonged to an historic figure.

Contour cased silver-hilted presentation sword presented to Colonel A. H. Gladden by the City of Charleston for Mexican War service. (*Collection of Mr. and Mrs. Price Russ*)

VII *American Navy Presentation Silver*

ONE of the most interesting and little known fields of American silver-smiths' work was the production of presentation silver for battleships and cruisers of the United States Navy. A considerable amount of presentation silver had been made for officers of the ships of the War of 1812 in appreciation of their services for the defense of the country and there were also presentation pieces given to officers of the Army and Navy who fought in the Civil War, as already mentioned in chapter V. However, it was not until the United States began building its modern navy in the 1880's and 1890's, prior to the Spanish-American War, that the silver service as a presentation to the ship became the custom. It was amid the opulence and ostentation of this late Victorian Era that these ornate pieces were made. Battleship and cruiser services became one of the major products of the late nineteenth century American silver companies, including Gorham, Tiffany, Reed & Barton, J. E. Caldwell & Co., Shreve & Co. of San Francisco, and Samuel Kirk & Son. Today the battleship has vanished from the seven seas, made obsolescent by the airplane, the airplane carrier and other inventions of modern war. The great battle wagons of the United States Navy have gone into "mothballs" and nothing remains except the memories and the silver—the magnificent silver services that rode the oceans in their wardrooms.

These pieces were characterized by extreme style and decorative abandon. Every type of silversmithing technique added to the exuberance of their ornamentation. They were not only chased and engraved, but also embellished with cast reliefs and enriched with repoussé decoration. Classic ornament was combined with naturalistic motifs. Rococo curved forms were covered with exuberant "C" and "S" scrolls and motifs symbolic of patriotism and the sea. These elaborate silver sets which were given by the city to a cruiser, or by a state to its namesake battleship, were

171

Punch bowl and other plate from the service made for the battleship *Maryland* by Samuel Kirk & Son, 1906.

designed to promote the feeling of state and local pride. They were laden with motifs of sentimental import which related to the history, tradition, and achievements of the state. State seals, and scenery including the flora and fauna, together with the engraved picture of the ship, make them records of state and national history.

The punch bowl was the favorite navy presentation piece and these ornate and ostentatious bowls exuberant with eagles and dolphins; state, national, and navy seals; anchors, flags, and cannon, became the rallying point for the social life of the ship. When the ship was in foreign ports, the silver service was often put to use in entertaining visitors of state and

172

royalty and enhancing the prestige of our nation by adding to the dignity of official functions. It did not matter that the elaborate design of many of the pieces was in poor taste and the workmanship stereotyped. Nor is that of consequence to us today, for the pieces are notable for their historic value in preserving pictures of ships, places, and a way of life which is no longer in existence. The services are also records of nineteenth century silver design and of the important silver companies working at that time.

One of the earliest and most historic of these services was that made by Gorham Manufacturing Co. for the *U.S.S. Maine* in 1891. The *U.S.S. Maine* was built at the Brooklyn Navy Yard, now itself a casualty of pro-

Tureen and vegetable dishes from the battleship *Maine.* Gorham Manufacturing Co., 1891. (*Courtesy, the State of Maine*)

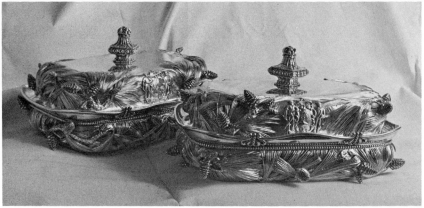

gress. She was launched November, 1890, commissioned nearly five years later, September 17, 1895. With less than three years' service, she was sunk in Havana Harbor at 9:45 p.m. on February 15, 1898. Her silver consisting of a centerpiece and two covered bowls was recovered and presented to the State of Maine, where it is now on public view in the

Tray and punch bowl, *U.S. Cruiser Detroit*. Gorham Manufacturing Co., 1893.

Governor's Mansion in Augusta, Maine. The pieces are massive and are decorated with repoussé pine cones and pine needles. Each piece has a central panel of the pine tree seal of the State of Maine. The borders are a design of shells and waves, and the handles are decorative capstans.

A punch bowl, cups, and tray which were made by Gorham Manu-

Tray, punch bowl, ladle and cup. *U.S. Cruiser New Orleans.* Gorham Manufacturing Co., 1899.

Punch bowl and ladle, *U.S. Gunboat Helena*. Gorham Manufacturing Co., 1896.

facturing Co. were presented to the cruiser *Detroit* by the city of Detroit in 1892. The bowl is covered with a bacchanalian scene in relief and the borders are of grapes and leaves. A similar design of grapes and bacchanal figures decorates the border of the tray, but in the center of the tray are engraved scenes of the Detroit City Hall, the skyline of the city, Belle Isle, and ferries on the river. Another interesting punch service was the one given to the cruiser *U.S.S. New Orleans* by the city of New Orleans in 1899. The punch bowl has a center engraving of the ship enclosed with rococo scrolls and cotton foliage and blossoms. The handles of the bowl are eagles' heads holding laurel wreaths and the base is a design of shells and seaweed with a rope border. The tray has engraved scenes of the New Orleans waterfront, showing ships loading bales of cotton and a grove of trees with ribbons of hanging Spanish moss. The border of the tray is of sugar cane stalks. Four medallions of seals, those of the State of Louisiana, the City of New Orleans, the Navy, and the United States Seal embellished with wheat or cotton blossoms, are set in the center of each side. The set also includes a ladle, twenty-four punch cups and two compotes. The punch bowl given to the U. S. gunboat *Helena,* a ship which was with Dewey at Manila, was made by Gorham in 1896. The bowl has a center medallion of the seal of the State of Montana with sprays of native plants. The handles are dolphins.

The elaborate service presented to the *U.S.S. Minneapolis,* by the city of that name in 1895, was also made by Gorham. The pieces have bas-relief panels which include sailors standing at attention and such local scenery as Minnehaha Falls. These panels are framed by a border of draped flags and sprays of wheat. The feet of the standing dishes are dolphins; the handles, eagles' heads, and the finials on the lids of bowls are dolphins and shells. The seals of the City of Minneapolis and of the Navy are also incorporated in the designs. Gorham made punch bowls and cups for the cruiser *Montgomery* in 1893, and for the *U.S.S. Nashville* in 1896. Later services made by Gorham for the Navy include those made for the *U.S.S. Rhode Island,* the *U.S.S. Providence,* the *U.S.S. Delaware* and the *U.S.S. Florida.* In addition to a punch bowl and plateau, a centerpiece and a seven-light candelabrum, the set for the *U.S.S. Delaware* included many hollow ware serving pieces. The set was Colonial style and was designed by William J. Codman. It was made in 1910. Also in 1910 Gorham made the service for the *U.S.S. South Carolina.* This was in the Louis XVI style but the flowers, fruit and agricultural products of the

Punch bowl, battleship *Florida* silver service. Gorham Manufacturing Co., 1911. (*Courtesy Governor & Mrs. Claude Kirk*)

state were illustrated as well as epochs of history and portraits of illustrious men. There were medallions with portraits of Governor Rutledge and John C. Calhoun. The Battle of King's Mountain, and Marion's sweet potato dinner to the British was illustrated. The techniques used were repoussé and flat chasing. In 1911 Gorham made a silver service for the *U.S.S. Florida* which was then flagship of the North Atlantic Fleet. The service consisted of twenty-five pieces including a punch bowl and candelabra. In addition to seals it was ornamented with scenes of Seminole life and the landing of Ponce de Leon, and native flora and fauna. The handles of the cups were alligators. The main shafts of the candelabra were palm trees, and alligators formed the bases with egrets on the arms; surface ornamentation included orange blossoms, jasmine and palmetto. The service is now in the Governor's Mansion at Tallahassee and is used on State occasions. In 1912 Gorham made silver services for the *U.S.S. Idaho* and the *U.S.S. Wyoming* and in 1914 for the *U.S.S. Oklahoma* and the *U.S.S. Texas.*

Punch bowl, ladle and twelve cups. *U.S. Cruiser Montgomery.* Gorham Manufacturing Co., 1893.

Pieces from service of *U.S. Cruiser Minneapolis;* scene of Minnehaha Falls on tureen. Gorham Manufacturing Co., 1895.

The *U.S.S. Minnesota* was launched April 8, 1905, and commissioned March 9, 1907. In 1909 the State of Minnesota presented the ship with a silver service consisting of forty-one pieces. It was made by Reed & Barton and over a year was spent in preparation. "The general style is of the later Louis XV period and many of the pieces are rich in symbolic and emblematic ornamentation. The ornamentation throughout the whole service consists of stars and star points, representing the title of the state, The Star of the North, the state seal, the state flower (the moccasin), the eagle, and all the emblems of the sea, such as flags, prows of vessels, cables, mythological characters, tritons, dolphins, sea horses, shells, seaweed, etc. In the centerpiece for the Admiral, the decorations are hulls of

179

modern war vessels alternating with cannons belching forth their fire in the form of electric lights. To be used in connection with this centerpiece are vases for flowers and a system of lighting by tiny electric lamps, the wiring to be run from the ship's regular current. Other pieces include two branching candelabra, centerpiece for captain, coffee urn, sugar bowl and cream pitcher, making a total of forty-one pieces. In order that this stately gift might have the proper setting, an elaborate bronze table was made. Upon this stands the "plateau" from which rises the circular platform to support the punch bowl and its twenty-four cups. At each end of the plateau are handles supported by figures of mermen, and just within the handles, on the floor of the plateau, are etched pictures of the state capitol. The punch bowl is the most ornate of all the pieces and bears on its front panel the inscription, 'Presented to the Battleship Minnesota by the State of Minnesota, 1909.' The silver made by Reed & Barton in 1916 for the *U.S.S. Arizona* has an appropriate design of cactus. The *Arizona* was sunk at Pearl Harbor in 1941, but the silver service is now in the State of Arizona.

Many ships were built at the Union Iron Works in San Francisco. Of these Shreve & Co. made sterling services for the *U.S.S. Oregon* (1897), the *U.S.S. Nevada,* the *U.S.S. Ohio* (1905), and the *U.S.S. California* (1908).

The silver service presented to the cruiser *U.S.S. Charleston* by the City of Charleston in 1905 was designed by Carrington, Thomas & Com-

Punch bowl, ladle and tray, *U.S. Cruiser Charleston;* engraved scene of Ft. Sumter and Charleston, cast eagle handles. Made by Gorham Manufacturing Co., 1905 for Carrington, Thomas & Co.

Punch bowl, ladle, tray and cup, service *U.S. Cruiser Nashville*. Gorham Manufacturing Co., 1896.

Punch bowl, ladle and cups. *U.S. Cruiser Chattanooga;* cast figures of Indians, American Eagle and engraved scenes of Lookout Mountain and other historical data. Gorham Manufacturing Co., 1907.

LEFT. Water pitcher from *U.S.S. Maryland* service. Historical ornament includes the Great Seal of Maryland; first telegraph set; St. George slaying the dragon, symbol of religious tolerance in Maryland; scene of St. Mary's; and the Ark and the Dove. Samuel Kirk & Son, 1905–1906. BELOW. Punch bowl and cups from service of *U.S.S. Pennsylvania*, J. E. Caldwell & Co., 1903. (*Jewelers' Circular*, June 24, 1903)

pany, Charleston silversmiths. Each piece carries the seal of the City of Charleston with engraved scenes of Fort Sumter, Fort Moultrie, St. Michael's Church, City Hall and the Battery. The service is now in view in the Charleston City Hall. J. E. Caldwell & Co. of Philadelphia made five silver services for U. S. battleships. They were for the *U.S.S. Iowa* (1896); the *U.S.S. Kentucky* (1899); the *U.S.S. Pennsylvania* (1904); the *U.S.S. Nebraska* (1909); and the *U.S.S. Mississippi* (1909). The most notable service was that made for the *U.S.S. Pennsylvania*. The large elaborate punch bowl has American eagles on either side of the rim and figures of tritons on sea horses at the ends. Etched scenes of groves of trees and state industries including a view of an oil field are set in oval rococo panels on the body of the bowl. The base is ornamented with dolphins and is set on a standard in the center of a tray which also holds several dozen punch cups. This silver service has been used and displayed in the *U.S.S. Valley Forge* since retirement of the battleship *Pennsylvania* in 1946. But perhaps the finest and most interesting set of silver ever made for a United States battleship was that made by Samuel Kirk & Son for the *U.S.S. Maryland*. The silver was first made for the armored cruiser *Maryland* in 1906 but in 1921 when the battleship *Maryland* was commissioned the silver service was transferred to her. Although it was made in 1906, it follows the tradition of the sets made in the nineteenth century, in that the forms are classical in inspiration, but the decoration is for the most part original, and motifs are indigenous. The design of the service developed the following themes:

NATIONAL—symbolized by the eagle.
STATE—symbolized by the Great Seal of Maryland.
COUNTY—symbolized by local scenes, flowers, fruits and vegetables.
HOSPITALITY—symbolized by overflowing horns of plenty.
NAVAL—symbolized by a view of the *U.S.S. Maryland*.
NAUTICAL—symbolized by rope borders.

Every piece of the service was different and there was practically no duplication of detail. The service consists of forty-eight pieces including a complete dinner service with platters, compotes, entrée dishes, covered vegetable dishes, trays, gravy boats, tea and coffee pots, sugar bowl, cream pitcher, water pitcher, centerpiece for flowers and six candlesticks. In addition there is a large punch bowl, ladle and punch cups set upon a plateau. The set is decorated with two hundred local and historical scenes

Silver punch bowl presented to the battleship *New Jersey* by the State of New Jersey; decorated with seals and figures of Justice and Plenty on plateau. Tiffany & Co., 1906. (*Courtesy of Governor and Mrs. Richard J. Hughes*)

in relief, including battle monuments, historical houses and the story of the birth of the "Star-Spangled Banner." There is also a view of the ship itself and the punch cups are inscribed with the the names of naval heroes. The seal of the United States is also incorporated into the design. The handles of the punch bowl are wreathed with oak, horse chestnut and mulberry, and the bowl is surmounted by an eagle-rope border. Tobacco leaf festoons, and indigenous flowers, fruits and vegetables in horns of plenty add to the ornate beauty. The motifs also include oyster shells, terrapin, canvasback ducks, wild turkey, Indian corn and swamp grass, all indigenous to the vicinity of the Chesapeake Bay region of Maryland. This is an example of nineteenth century story-telling silversmithing at its best. The silver is now in the Governor's Palace in Annapolis, Maryland.

The silver service, consisting of fifty-five pieces, presented by the State of New Jersey to the U.S. battleship *New Jersey* was made by Tiffany

& Co. in 1906. The silver is now in the Governor's Mansion in Princeton, New Jersey.

Presentation silver services continued to be made for the American Navy down to the time of the Second World War and even after the war in the late 1940's Gorham made pieces to add to some of the silver services already in use. Naturally this Navy presentation silver is not available to the collector for it belongs to the United States Government, but it is an important part of the story of American nineteenth century silversmithing. It illustrates some of the most pretentious work of the silver designers and the technical abilities of the workmen such as hammerers and engravers. There were over sixty presentation services of various sizes in use up to 1914, according to the list in *Jewelers' Circular,* November 4, 1914. The Navy has no complete list of the silver but most of the services are still in existence in storage or on display in state capitols or governor's mansions.

RIGHT. Black coffee set. Tray has engraving of ship. BELOW. Punch bowl and ladle. Bowl upheld by cast American Eagles and dolphins. *U.S.S. Delaware.* Gorham Manufacturing Co., 1910.

VIII *American Church Silver*

EARLY American church silver has been described and illustrated in *Old Silver of American Churches,* by E. Alfred Jones. Although some pieces of the nineteenth century are shown, the majority of the flagons, beakers, standing cups, chalices, and alms basins are of the seventeenth and eighteenth centuries and are the work of well-known early American silversmiths. The book includes a listing of church silver made by Paul Revere for Boston and other Massachusetts churches. These articles consist mainly of flagons, cups and baptismal basins and the majority of them were made in the last two decades of the eighteenth century.

Much of this early silver still remains in the churches for which it was made, some is in museum or private collections, while other pieces are in vaults for safe keeping. Other churches have sold their old silver and still others have remodeled their ancient plate in a style popular to a later period. Thus a chalice in Trinity Church, New York City, made by Garret Eoff in 1824, is a replica of a William & Mary piece. A silver flagon in St. Paul's Church in Baltimore was made by Samuel Kirk to match earlier standing cups and Kirk remodeled the old silver in St. Margaret's Church, Westminster Parish, and made a new paten with repoussé borders of roses and other flowers in 1825. The clergy was always interested in having up-to-date silver as evidenced in the will of the Reverend Theodore Hall of Meriden, Connecticut. "To the Church of Christ in Meriden, of which I am pastor, I give and bequeath a fashionable silver cup for their communion table to be procured at the direction of my Ex^r hereafter named." The silver procured consisted of a beaker with straight sides, flaring lip and moulded base made by Ebenezer Chittenden of New Haven (1765–1812).

Most of the silver used in the early Nonconformist churches of New England consisted of cups, beakers, and tankards which were originally designed for domestic use and were later presented to the churches. The shape and decoration of these articles followed the prevailing styles of English plate of the Charles II, William & Mary, and Queen Anne periods. There were swelling bulbous two-handled caudle cups with embossed designs of flowers and foliage, often divided into panels. The beakers used in Boston churches also followed English styles. The earliest were low and wide and were made with and without decoration or a moulded base. Later the straight sides were more slender, flared at the lip, and had a moulded base. In the late eighteenth and early nineteenth century some beakers were low, wide, and straight-sided with mouldings at the base and lip; others were bell-shaped and set on a ring foot. Some communion beakers had handles. In New York churches the beakers followed Dutch and German styles. They were tall slender cups with slightly flaring lip and were usually ornamented with all-over engraving of strap-work and panels with figures of Faith, Hope and Charity, or similar subjects.

Standing wine cups with baluster stems and domed feet and a deep bowl were of various types. The earliest is the cup in the Old South Church, Boston. It is appropriately engraved with a design of grapes and flat flutings. Other cups had plain bell-shaped bowls and taller, slenderer stems. Later the bowl was more straight-sided and was enriched with fluting. Some cups are slender with simple baluster stems and stepped

Ciborium and two covered chalices; classical urn-shaped with beading and urn-shaped finials. St. Paul's Church, Baltimore. Samuel Kirk, c. 1824. (*Samuel Kirk & Son*)

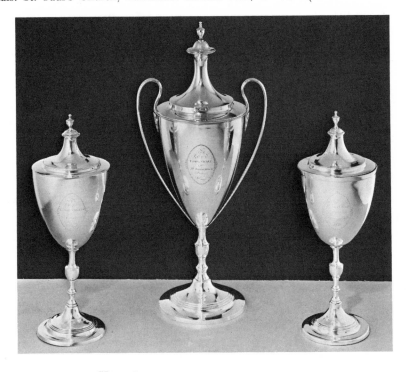

bases. Classic influences brought in the ovoid-shaped bowl with borders of reeding and a cover with slender finial. The cups made by early American silversmiths are related to these forms. The chalice proper was not used in the Nonconformist Church and was seldom made by early American silversmiths.

The chalice is used for the celebration of the Mass in the Roman Catholic Church and its form is definitely prescribed by the rubrics. In the Roman Catholic Church the chalice is used only by the priest. Therefore, it is relatively small. The chalices in early American Roman Catholic Churches were usually imported from France or other European countries, therefore there was little demand for the work of the American silversmith. Although the Anglican Church discarded the Roman chalice form, it, too, had conventions of its own governing the form of the chalice and other Eucharistic vessels. The various shapes of the chalice bowl, stem, knops, and bases have been regulated through the years by church edicts based upon ritualistic or utilitarian requirements. The circular foot was splayed from the stem to make the chalice steady, the knop was put on the stem between the foot and the bowl for easier handling, and the bowl was made deep to prevent spilling the wine.

LEFT. Chalice; hemispherical body with applied leafwork and band of chased acorn and grapevine ornament; inscription: "Property of/The Brattle Street Church/ Boston." Lewis & Smith, Boston, c. 1810. (*Collection of Philip H. Hammerslough*) RIGHT. Communion flagon with lobed body, gadroon borders and artichoke finial. Inscription: "Second Presbyterian Congregation-Albany 1816". Shepherd & Boyd. Property of Westminster Presbyterian Church, Albany. (*The Albany Institute of History and Art*)

The earliest chalices used in the early American Anglican Church were brought from England and were of the post-Reformation Elizabethan type with inverted bell-shaped cup with paten-cover, heavy short stem and circular foot. The decoration consisted of a band of interlacing strap-work filled with arabesques. Sometimes the cup was plain with only an inscription or decorated with the sacred monogram, "IHS." Later in the century the chalice was decorated with spiral fluting. A few bell-shaped chalices were made by American silversmiths in the late eighteenth century.

The paten is the dish that holds the bread or wafer. Early patens were made as covers for the chalice and the knob served as a foot for the paten when inverted and placed on the altar. The paten with the flat-knob cover that served as a foot was gradually enlarged and the foot was made to fit inside the bowl of the cup instead of serving as a handle. These flat-dish patens are the type in use today. However, there were also patens with truncated bases and one such paten was made by Bilious Ward and given to Trinity Church, Southport, Connecticut, in 1826. This type of paten was also made in a large size and used as a credence-paten. These patens were also known as salvers and sometimes served as a household utensil. English patens of this type often had a cover and were the forerunners of the ciborium which stands on a tall baluster foot.

Flagons for wine were a part of the communion plate from early times. The shapes included those with bulbous bodies and cylindrical necks and those with tall cylindrical bodies. The commonest type of flagon was one with rounded lid without any knob or finial. This was the type of flagon that came to America and influenced not only the first flagons made by American silversmiths but those for many years to come. Flagons were introduced into American communion services in the plate presented to American Anglican churches by English sovereigns. William and Mary presented a flagon and a chalice with paten cover to King's Chapel, Boston. Queen Anne presented a complete communion service which is now in St. Peter's Episcopal Church, Albany. It consists of two flagons, a chalice with paten cover, a large paten and an alms basin. Another royal service by the same English silversmiths, Francis Garthorne, was given to Trinity Church in New York City. It consists of a pair of chalices with paten covers, a pair of flagons, and an alms basin.

Flagons do not vary much in design, the most noticeable differences being the form of the lid and the divisions of the lines of moulding. Gen-

ABOVE. Communion set; two flagons, two cups, three footed patens and two alms basins. Christ Church, Savannah, Georgia. Hugh Wishart, 1816. BELOW. Flagon, chalice cups and patens. St. Paul's Church, Augusta, Georgia. J. W. Forbes. (*E. Alfred Jones,* "Old Silver of American Churches")

erally, early flagons have flat lids, but some have finials. Later, the flat-topped flagon gave place to one with domed lid with finial, tapering body, and a widely splayed foot. Some flagons are of pear or bulbous shape, and later a classic type flagon of ewer-shape was made. One made by Jesse Churchill (1773–1819) for West Church, Boston, has reeded edges and an engraved classic border of leaves and flowers, square-shaped handles and a domed cover with pineapple finial. Although straight-sided flagons continued to be made in America in the nineteenth century, the Adam-style flagon which was introduced into churches in England in the late eighteenth century was occasionally made in America from the beginning of the nineteenth century.

A great deal of new communion plate was made by American silver-smiths and silver companies in the nineteenth century. In Boston and nearby New England churches, there are communion flagons, beakers, chalices, patens, and alms basins by the following nineteenth century silversmiths of Boston: Churchill & Treadwell (1805–13); Jesse Churchill (1773–1819); Joseph Foster (1760–1839); B. C. Frobisher (1792–1862); Joseph Loring (1743–1815); Lewis Carey (1798–1834); Baldwin & Jones (1813); P. Stacy (1798–1829) and George Wells (1784–1827). Fletcher & Gardiner made cups for the Second Baptist Church of Boston and a baptismal bowl for St. Paul's Church, Boston in 1824. There is also church plate in Connecticut churches made by Connecticut silversmiths of the nineteenth century. This is discussed and illustrated in *Early Silver of Connecticut and Its Makers* by George Munson Curtis. The flagon in the First Congregational Church, Derby, Connecticut, was made by Ebenezer Chittenden (1726–1812) and chalice cups were made by Miles Gorham (1757–1847). Charles Brewer (1778–1860) made beakers for the Congregational Church of Durham; Barzillai Benjamin made beakers for the First Church, Guilford; Marcus Merriman (1762–1850) also made cups and beakers in 1825 for Center Congregational Church, Meriden, and First Congregational Church, Middletown, Connecticut, and the United Church in New Haven. Beakers made for the First Church, Northford, and Church of Christ, Durham, by Marcus Merriman & Co. are now in the Mabel Brady Garvan Collection, Yale University Art Gallery. A pair of beakers made by Bradley & Merriman in 1832 for St. Andrew's Church, Northford, is still in the church. These and other pieces of silver made for Connecticut churches were exhibited in "An Exhibition of New Haven Silver" at The New Haven Colony Historical Society in 1967.

Flagon, footed paten and alms basin. Garret Eoff, 1824. (*Collection of Trinity Church, New York, N.Y.*)

Albany church silver of the nineteenth century was made by the Albany silversmiths Isaac & G. Hutton (1767–1855) and Shepherd & Boyd (1810–1830). An alms basin made by Hutton is in St. Peter's Episcopal Church, Albany. A communion service consisting of two communion flagons, cups, and basins made by Shepherd & Boyd is in the Westminster Presbyterian Church and a communion flagon and two beakers by Shepherd & Boyd are in the First Church in Albany.

Nineteenth century silver made by the following New York silversmiths has been located in churches today. A communion set of flagon, paten cups and plates by J. W. Forbes (1808–1855) is in Christ Church, Poughkeepsie. Flagons also by J. W. Forbes are in the First Reformed Church and Trinity Church in Fishkill, New York, and cups by Forbes are in the Congregational Church in Clinton, Connecticut. The silver communion vessels formerly in Zion and St. Timothy's Church, New York City, were also made by J. W. Forbes. One of the finest early nineteenth century pieces is the delicately engraved James Duane baptismal cup made by Joel Sayre in 1802, now in Trinity Church, New York City. A communion service made by Benjamin Halsted was given to Trinity Cathedral in Newark, New Jersey, by the "Ladies of Newark" in 1806. It is still used at all services of Holy Communion.

Although American church silver of the first quarter of the nineteenth century followed older designs, the communion plate made for American churches by American silversmiths from 1820 through 1840 was influenced by Federal and Empire styles both in form and decoration. Thus we find flagons, beakers, and patens with gadrooning and reeded acanthus and classic honeysuckle borders. The flagon also became ovoid in shape and often resembled an urn-shaped ewer or pitcher set on a moulded rectangular base. Other flagons resembled the tea and coffee pots of the era and had large gadrooned lobes and acorn or pine-cone finials and were set on a pedestal with a moulded rectangular foot. Chalices also tended toward an ovoid form. A chalice with hemispherical body, flaring lip, and a flaring pedestal foot was decorated with applied leafwork and a band of classic acorn and grapevine chasing. It was made by Lewis & Smith for the Brattle Street Church, Boston, in the first decade of the nineteenth century. In 1825 Samuel Kirk made chalice cups with cup-shaped body, and melon reeding and gadrooning about the base and lip. These were similar to some made in England at this date. Communion beakers made by Shepherd & Boyd for the Reformed Protestant Dutch Church in Albany in 1817 were decorated with bands of gadrooning at the base and on the cup.

The Victorian Era brought about a drastic change in the architecture and furnishings of the Anglican Church including the communion plate.

Chalice with beaded border. J. Kitts, Louisville, Kentucky, 1851–1878. Footed paten. R. & W. Wilson, Philadelphia, 1825–1846. Dish paten. A. Osthoff, 1809–1814. (*Cincinnati Art Museum*)

The Gothic Revival movement began in England in the 1830's. This Victorian archaism, which started with a fad for sham ruins and houses which were replicas of medieval abbeys, spread to church building where it found an ally in the Oxford Movement, the Ecclesiastical Society, and the writer-designer Augustus Welby Pugin. Pugin not only sought to change the design of church architecture, but put forth definite ideas for the decoration of churches from the structural forms and furnishings down to the smallest detail of church plate. To accomplish this, Pugin published books on Gothic architecture, iron, brass, and silversmiths' work. In *Designs for Gold and Silversmiths* the second part of the book was devoted to church silver. This book was circulated in America and its archaic Gothic forms had an influence on the design of church silver from the middle of the nineteenth century on.

The Medieval Court at the Great Exhibition in London in 1851 displayed designs of Pugin which were executed by Hardman & Co. Looking at the Gothic altars, pulpits, fonts, lecterns, and church plate in the *Art Journal Illustrated Catalogue* one sees an array of medieval-looking church ornaments that were to influence church furnishings in America to the end of the nineteenth century.

The Gothic chalice of the late 14th century became the model for the chalice. The baluster stem and its center knop as well as the base had a hexagonal form. The bell-shaped cup was set in an ornamental calyx. Reflections of architecture appear in the design and the geometric quatrefoil and sexfoil forms of window tracery, arches, mouldings and pinnacles of Gothic architecture are seen in the design of the base, knop, and stem. Figures are often set within Gothic arches of the stem and the elaborate knop. There are engravings of foliage, scenes from the Passion or scenes from the lives of saints on lobes of the base. A cross or crucifix or some other symbol was placed on the center base so that the celebrant could know at what place on the lip he drank and receive ablutions at the same point. Sometimes an inscription in Old English encircled the bowl of the cup. The paten was made to fit the cup. It often had an engraved cross, lamb, fish, or pelican symbol in the center and the rim might be decorated with jewels or have a border of inscription from the Psalter. The ciborium had a cross as a finial on its cover. Flagons, alms basins, crosses and even flower vases were made in matching designs. Pugin designs show the flagon with Gothic tracery and a Gothic crocket as a finial. The candlesticks were baluster type with a heavy knop in the stem and a pricket or spike to hold the candle. The popular type cross was foliated with the symbols of the Evangelists placed in the extremities of the arms and often the figures of the Virgin and St. John were placed on arms at the base of the cross. A great deal of altar plate was ornamented with gilt and colorful enamel and precious stones.

By the mid-nineteenth century both Tiffany and Gorham were manufacturing church silver to order, as were Ball, Tompkins & Black. Cooper & Fisher of New York also made a considerable amount of church silver. In 1855 Cooper & Fisher made a communion set for Trinity Chapel consisting of two chalices, two patens, a large credence-paten on a foot and an alms basin. This was probably one of the richest communion sets ever made in America. The chalice, paten and credence-paten are now in Trinity Church, New York City. The set is of Gothic design richly decorated with chasing, parcel gilt and red and blue enamel, including symbols of the Evangelists, groups of figures and inscriptions. The chalice has a hexagonal base with a border of open-work trefoil and plaques of enameled symbols of the Evangelists. The open stem of twisted rope columns has a large hexagonal knop while the cup is ornamented with alternating oval lobes and angels in relief and has a rope border around its rim. The center of the small paten has an enameled figure of Christ with halo and is surrounded by chased grape leaves. The inscription, "Holy, Holy, Holy, Lord God of Hosts, Heaven and Earth are full of Thy Glory" is engraved in Old English and forms a border about the plate and the edge is finished

Communion silver; two flagons, two chalices, footed paten and alms basin with classical borders in relief. Grace Church, Providence, R.I. George Wells, 1832. (From E. Alfred Jones, "Old Silver of American Churches." Privately printed for the National Society of Colonial Dames of America, 1913)

Communion set, St. Andrew's Presbyterian Church. William B. Heyer, c. 1830. (*Collection of Cathedral of St. John the Divine, New York, N.Y.*)

with a heavy rope border. The credence-paten is the most elaborate piece. It has rope and pierced trefoil borders and a knop to match that of the chalice. The background surface is completely covered with engraving including borders of Old English inscriptions, and the twelve plaques of rich red, gold and blue enamel, six on the plate and six at the base, picture scenes of the Passion. The chasing was done by Segal and the engraving and enamel work was by H. B. Horlor. Cooper & Fisher also made silver for Trinity Church, including a replica of the communion silver which had been given to the church by Queen Anne.

Among the other pieces of nineteenth century silver owned by Trinity Church are a flagon, paten, alms basin, and chalice made by Garret Eoff in 1824. The chalice is a replica of the one given by William & Mary. A footed paten by Frederick Marquand is dated "New York 1827." A flagon, two chalices, and two matching patens belong to the angled late Victorian period and were made by Whiting Manufacturing Co. in 1883.

196

The communion silver made for St. Agnes' Chapel in 1892 is one of the richest sets ever made in America, according to *The Ecclesiologist.* There were two complete sets made by Gorham in Romanesque design in keeping with the church building. The pieces included two chalices, two patens, two cruets, a spoon, a ciborium, a flagon, six alms basins and a large alms basin. The stem and base of the chalices and ciborium are hexagonal, with large hexagonal knops. The base of each carries six medallions with emblems in gilt of the Agnus Dei, the Cross and the four Evangelists. The calyx supporting the bowls is embossed and richly gilt as is the lamb on top of the flagon and the cross on the ciborium. The six small alms basins have an embossed geometric pattern and each is studded

RIGHT. Chalice and footed paten with engraving and colored enamels. Church of St. John Baptist, Glenhaven, c. 1855. Cooper & Fisher (?) (*Collection of Cathedral of St. John the Divine, New York, N.Y.*) BELOW. Chalice, paten and large footed credence-paten with borders of rope and Gothic piercing, engraving, chasing and colored enamel medallions. Cooper & Fisher, c. 1855. (*Collection of Trinity Church, New York, N.Y.*)

with a large topaz. The large alms basin is the handsomest piece of the service. It is of solid silver, parcel gilt, repoussé, and is studded with two topaz and two amethysts. In the center is a symbol of St. Agnes—a lamb bearing a cross and lying on a book. The outline of a foliated Maltese cross covers the whole face of the alms basin and between the arms of the cross are embossed symbols of the Evangelists. The "fly-spoon" is made in the style of an apostle spoon, but the open-work cutting in the bowl is of grapes and leaves and the figure at the top of the handle is of St. Agnes.

In the *Jewelers' Circular,* December, 1874, the illustration of a complete silver communion service by Gorham shows foliated Neo-Gothic designs enriched with oxide and gilt and ornamented with figures of angels. This was the height of fashion in church silver at this date. By 1889 Gorham had a large ecclesiastical department and manufactured many articles for different denominations including not only communion plate but crosses, croziers, candlesticks, vases, incense boats and monstrances. A supply was kept in stock but estimates and special designs were furnished for made-to-order goods. At the Columbian Exhibition in

LEFT. Paten with engraved leaves, border of holy script and rope edges. F. W. Cooper, c. 1851. (*Collection of Cathedral of St. John the Divine, New York, N.Y.*) BELOW. Alms basin. Church of the Mediator. Whiting Manufacturing Co., before 1881. (*Collection of St. John the Divine, New York, N.Y.*)

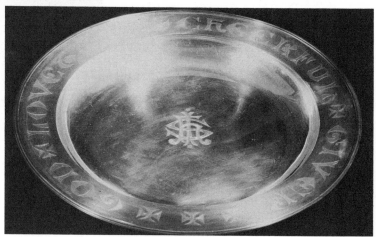

Chicago in 1893 Gorham had a large ecclesiastical exhibit which was under the direction of William J. Codman. Codman was an Englishman who had designed ecclesiastical subjects all his life. The exhibit included an elaborate gold-plated jeweled and enameled foliated altar cross with base figures of the Virgin and St. John. To go with the altar cross was a gold-plated alms basin set with crystals and gems, and a communion set.

ABOVE. Silver communion token, c. 1800. (*The Metropolitan Museum of Art, bequest of A. T. Clearwater, 1933*) RIGHT. Flagon with horizontal mouldings and engraved bands. Inscription: "St. John Baptist Church 1878". Mark P B -A B in vertical rectangle. Cross finial is a later addition. (*Collection of Cathedral of St. John the Divine*) BELOW. Part of silver communion service. St. Agnes' Church, New York. Gorham & Co., 1893. (*Collection of Trinity Church, New York, N.Y.*)

Alms basin chased by N. Heitzelman for J. & R. Lamb.
Design of passion flower and Celtic cross, 1897. (*Jewelers'
Circular*, Nov. 24, 1897)

In the center of the alms basin was a cross in the center of which was pictured the Adoration of the Magi in colored enamel, and between the arms of the cross were scenes from the life of Christ from the Annunciation to the Ascension including the Last Supper and the Resurrection. The communion set included two chalices, two patens, and two flagons, all of rich materials and exquisite workmanship.

Louis C. Tiffany designed a chapel with altar, cross and candlesticks, which was exhibited by the Tiffany Glass and Decorating Company. The cross was made of jewels and mosaic work as was a benediction candelabra which was also exhibited. An altar cross of Gothic design made by Tiffany was presented to all Angels' Church, New York City, in 1893. It was heavily plated, enriched with gold filigree, and inlaid with precious stones. A chalice and paten designed and made for a client of William H. Colson by Tiffany & Co. was made of glass and silver set with carbuncles. The knop was a crown of thorns set with rubies and carbuncles and the base was also set with stones. The paten center pictured the Crucifixion in relief. Undoubtedly Tiffany made many less elaborate chalices at this time, but research has turned up only those related to jewelry.

W. J. Feeley Co. of Providence, Rhode Island, had been manufacturing gold and silver ecclesiastical goods since 1875, and in the 1890's Theodore W. Foster & Co. of Providence, George E. Germer of Boston, and J. & R. Lamb were manufacturing ecclesiastical wares. Lamb was essentially a stained glass maker but hired the services of a silversmith to produce church silver. In 1876, Ball, Tompkins & Black had become Black, Starr & Frost, and from then on under various changes in name their ecclesiastical department was one of the most important sources of church silver in the United States. At the end of the century Cymric design derived from old Celtic manuscripts influenced the ornament of

BELOW. Chalice and paten, Celtic design studded with gems. Made for Archbishop Farley. Gorham Manufacturing Co., 1904. (*Jewelers' Circular*) RIGHT. Ciborium and chalice. Gorham Manufacturing Co. advertisement. (*Jewelers' Circular*, 1889)

church silver. An alms basin by J. & R. Lamb and chased by N. Heitzelman had a decoration of passion flowers with a Celtic cross in the center of the basin. The chalice and paten made by Gorham Manufacturing Co. in 1904 and presented to Archbishop Farley of New York by the Ancient Order of Hibernians was also ornamented with Celtic patterns.

Although it would seem that church plate was not in the realm of the collector, many Early American church pieces which are recorded are now in museum or private collections. But some church silver is still to be found in shops. Chalices, silver cups, and patens with stands that date from the first quarter of the nineteenth century are also found in shops. These are often engraved with the date and name of the donor and the church to which the piece belonged. Some of these pieces were sold by the church to raise money for a "more stylish cup." However, church silver that was presented and engraved with the donor's name is usually kept by the church even though it is no longer used. The church silver found in shops more likely came from a congregation no longer active. Many pieces have the inscriptions removed but those with inscriptions intact have more value.

Silver communion service ornamented with satin work, oxides and gold. Gorham Manufacturing Co. (*Jewelers' Circular*, 1874)

IX   *Silver Masonic Jewels and Medals*

Among the many miscellaneous articles made by American silversmiths were Masonic Jewels and Medals. Few of these small pieces were considered worthy of the silversmith's mark, but information gathered from early newspaper advertisements and records of silversmiths' workshops prove that even the important well-known silversmiths of the eighteenth and nineteenth centuries were making such articles. Also, this practice continued until the work of the individual silversmith was taken over by the silver manufacturer in the mid-nineteenth century. Although these and other Masonic emblems now abound, the adoption of such decorations was gradual. Jewels were first used in Craft lodges in 1727 when the Grand Lodge of England decreed: "Resolved that in all private lodges quarterly communications and general meetings the master and wardens do wear the jewels of Masonry hanging to a white ribbon." Each master and warden and eventually each officer of the lodge had his own jewel of office. These included the Master, Square; the Senior Warden, Level; the Junior Warden, Plumb; the crossed Keys of the Treasurer; the Crossed Pens of the Secretary; the Cornucopia of the Stewards; the Crossed Swords of the Director of Ceremony; the Sword of the Tyler; the open Bible of the Chaplain; the Baton of the Marshall; and the Lyre of the Organist.

There were Masonic Lodges in America in the early eighteenth century although the date of the founding of the first lodge is debatable. There were Provincial Lodges at the time of the following quote from Benjamin Franklin's newspaper: "There are several lodges of Free Masons erected in this Province." (*Pennsylvania Gazette* No. 108, Dec. 3 to 8, 1730). There are early records of St. John's Lodge in Philadelphia at this time.

Pastel portrait of Washington in Masonic regalia by William Williams, 1794. (*Alexandria-Washington Lodge, A. F. & A. M.*)

The Masonic Lodge was one of the most important organizations in eighteenth and nineteenth century America and membership was a status symbol sought by leading citizens of each town. Since working in silver was a most respectable craft and silversmiths were highly esteemed, had an excellent social standing, and were prominent in the affairs of their community, it is natural that they should be members of Masonic Lodges. Indeed a check of the membership lists of early lodges reveals the names of many well-known silversmiths who were active members of their lodges. Notes concerning Paul Revere and other Masonic silversmiths have appeared in Masonic publications such as the *The American Lodge of Research Transactions* of "The American Lodge of Free & Accepted Masons." However, since this data has never been published elsewhere and since it is a part of the story of American silversmithing and thus has interest value beyond Masonic circles, it deserves a wider audience. Also, the author has been able to add the names of several silversmiths who made Masonic Jewels and to provide photos of jewels never before published. These include jewels still in use in lodges today.

Boston was one of the first centers of Masonry in eighteenth century America. Early silversmiths in Boston were active members of Masonic lodges and identified as designers of Masonic Seals, Diplomas and Medals. Daniel Henchman (1730–1775) and Joseph Goldthwait (1706–1780) were members of St. John's Lodge there. Nathaniel and Benjamin Hurd were also Masons. Nathaniel Hurd designed the Masonic Seal which is now in the Museum of the Masonic Temple in Boston, and Benjamin Hurd designed a Master Mason Diploma.

Paul Revere's connection with Masonic Lodges is often quoted. Revere was a member of St. Andrew's Lodge in Boston in 1760. In 1769 he became secretary, and in the years 1770, 1777–79, and 1780–82 was Master. In 1769 the Grand Lodge records reveal that "it was voted that the Grand Lodge be provided with jewels made of any metal under silver; that the lodge accept Bro. Paul Revere's offer to make the jewels and to wait for his pay, till the Grand Lodge is in cash." These jewels do not exist today or if they do their whereabouts is not known.

From 1794 to 1797 Revere was Grand Master of the Grand Lodge of Massachusetts. During his term of office as Grand Master Revere constituted about a dozen new lodges and his custom was to make and present a set of silver jewels to each new lodge. Revere's Masonic silverwork is recorded in his two Day Books and in the records of individual lodges for which he made jewels. From 1761 through 1795 there is a great deal of Masonic work listed in the Day Books including Free Mason's Medals for Watches and sets of Masonic Jewels. The listings of items referring to sets of jewels are particularly interesting not only because the prices vary and thus indicate a difference in design and weight, but the names of the lodges for which jewels were made are recorded. The following are items which relate to Masonic silver:

1781 = July 28. Col. John Brooks	
To a sett of silver jewel for:	
Washington Lodge. Wt. 5 oz.	1–15–0
To the Making	6–15–0
1782. Jan. 9. Nat. Tracy Esq.	
To a sett of Silv. Jewel for a Lodge	3–12–0
To making Maste & Warden Jewels each	24–3–12–0
To making Sec. & Tres. 20 each	2–0–0
To mak Deac & Stewards –12/each	2–8–0
1784. June 26. Mr. Jas. Avery	
To 5 Mason's Jewels for Warren Lodge	9–0–0
1794. July 7	
S. Hadley Lodge	
To a sett of Silver Jewels	12–0–0
July 25. Mr. Sam Dana	
To a sett of Mason's Jewell	12–0–0
Sept. 5—Mr. Seth Smith Jr. of Norton	
To a sett of Mason's Jewells	12–0–0

Meridian Sun Lodge was instituted at North Brookfield, Massachusetts, in 1796 by Revere and the jewels he made and presented to this lodge are recorded in his Day Book. A set of jewels for Adams Lodge, Wellfleet, Massachusetts, is also recorded in the Day Book and in *The American Lodge of Research Transactions* page 20, vol. 5. "Paul Revere fashioned a set of jewels for Adams Lodge, chartered 1797." Despite much searching no trace can be found of these jewels.

According to Clarence E. Brigham in *Paul Revere's Engravings*, the jewels for the Tyrian Lodge, Gloucester, Massachusetts, are recorded in Revere's Day Book in the Massachusetts Historical Society. "June 15, 1773. The Tyrian Lodge Dr/to Engraving a Plate for Summons 3–0–0/ To 400 Impressions. 1–4–0/To P. Cross Keys 0–18–0/To Two Steward's Jewils 0/18–0." Revere Jr. was a member and officer of Tyrian Lodge which his father had founded.

Of the many sets of Masonic Jewels which Revere records making

Masonic Jewels made for King Solomon's Lodge, Somerville, Massachusetts, by Paul Revere in 1783. (*George G. Walker, Sec., King Solomon's Lodge*)

only a few sets are identified today. One set of Masonic Officers' Jewels is now still in use in King Solomon's Lodge at Somerville, Massachusetts. This lodge was first constituted at Charlestown, September 5, 1783. The following is an excerpt taken from the minutes of the meeting held Thursday evening, September 11, 1783. "It was then voted that the Master and

Masonic Jewel c. 1800. (*The Metropolitan Museum of Art, Rogers Fund, 1943*)

Wardens take the most effectual and speedy measures to procure the necessary tools and utensils for the lodge and it was agreed by the Master, wardens, treasurer, and secretary that they each present to the lodge a jewel suitable to their respective appointments." Revere's name appears in the minutes of the meeting of January 7, 1784, as having visited the lodge with other Grand Lodge officers to consecrate the lodge and install the officers. The jewels were probably presented at this time. Washington Lodge, Lexington, Massachusetts, also has a complete set of officers' jewels made by Paul Revere.

The custom of delegating the making of Masonic Jewels to a silversmith who was a fellow lodge member continued into the nineteenth century. In *Early Silver of Connecticut and Its Makers* by George Munson Curtis there are illustrations of the jewels owned by several Connecticut lodges. Curtis attributes those owned by St. John's Lodge, Middletown, Connecticut, to the silversmith Charles Brewer who was a member of the lodge in 1812. According to Curtis, jewels owned by St. John's Lodge, Hartford, Connecticut, were made by Samuel Rockwell and James Tiley, but according to present-day records of the lodge, the early coin silver jewels, which they own and still use, are not marked and the lodge has no record of who made them. However, James Tiley was a charter member of the lodge. Jewels owned by Mt. Olive Lodge, Essex, Connecticut, were made by about the year 1811. Also in Connecticut, Bilious Ward (1729–1777) a silversmith, was Master of the Lodge at Guilford. In New Haven, Connecticut, the silversmiths Zebul Bradley (1780–1859), Abel Buel (1742–1825), Robert Fairchild (1703–74), Hezekiah Selliman (1738–1804) and Samuel Wilmot (1777–1846) were all members of Hiram Lodge No. 1.

Old Masonic Lodges in Pennsylvania 1730–1800 by Julius F. Sachse gives the membership lists of the old lodges and a check of these lists includes the following data about silversmith members. In Philadelphia such well-known silversmiths as Philip Syng, Jr. were Masons. Syng became a member of St. John's Lodge in 1734 of which Henry Pratt had been a founder in 1730, and in 1741 he was Grand Master of the Provincial Grand Lodge. William Ball (1729–1810) was a member of Lodge No. 2. Moderns, and in 1759 he made: "2 Tryangle

Jewels and a Seal	1–7–
Engraved the seal	–16."

The minutes of the Lodge also include this item: "Bro. Ball the venerable Patriarch in Masonry was buried with Masonic honors. Joseph Richardson (1711–84) was a "Fellow in Craft" in Lodge No. 2 A.Y.M. in 1766; Thomas Shields (1765–1794) was a Past Master of Lodge No. 5 of which William Walker (1793–1816) was also a member, while John Church (1756–1806) was a Master of Lodge No. 4. and the records of the Lodge read "agreed to have a Sec. Jewel made by Bro. Church, gave him a Hard Dollar and Silver Chain of our Treasurer's Jewel to make it." Francis Shallus, who engraved the Masonic Mark Jewel in the Henry Ford Museum, was a member of Philadelphia Lodge No. 72 in 1803. In Lancaster, Pennsylvania, the silversmith Peter Getz was a member of Lodge No. 43. Getz made Masonic Medals one of which is in the Grand Lodge in Philadelphia. The obverse of the medal shows a bust of Washington and the inscription "G. Washington President, 1797." The reverse has Masonic emblems and the inscription "Amor Honor et Justitia" and "G.W.G.G.M."

Important early New York silversmiths who were Masons include Myer Myers who was Senior Warden of King David's Lodge in New York City and later moved with the lodge to Newport, Rhode Island, where he made the ritualistic silver. He also made jewels for Sir William Johnson. Louis Fourniquet was a member of Phoenix Lodge in New York in 1799. Andrew Billings was Master of Solomon Lodge in Poughkeepsie in 1801. Nathaniel Adams was Senior Warden of Apollo Lodge No. 49 in Troy, New York, and Jacob Thurston (1797–1820) was a member of Walton Lodge No. 75, Duanesburg, in 1799. In 1800 he was a Charter member of Morton Lodge No. 86, Schenectady, in which lodge he was very active until his death in 1820. He also was a member of Tyrian Mark Lodge No. 66. Thurston made jewels for Blue Lodges and Royal Arch. Thurston is also thought to have made the Mark Jewels for members of Mark Lodges in the locality of Schenectady. Mark Lodges are no longer in existence and the jewels are usually now in the possession of the descendants of the men for which they were made. Mark jewels were usually round or shield-shaped. They were suspended from the neck or worn with a ribbon in the left coat lapel. Although the ribbon was generally yellow it might be

LEFT. Silver Masonic Medal, dated April 13, 1803. RIGHT. Gold Mark Master Medal engraved by Francis Shallus, Philadelphia, July 20, 1812. (*Both, courtesy of The Henry Ford Museum, Dearborn, Michigan*)

white, red or blue. The obverse of the jewel identified the owner, his lodge or chapter, and year of advancement. The reverse contained a double circle, the inner engraved with the personal mark, the outer with the initials "HTWSSTKS," alluding to the ritual of the Mark Lodge. Various mottoes were also often included such as "Holiness to the Lord" or "Virtue shall cement us." Thurston's own Mark Jewel and that of Robert G. Dunbar, Franklin Mark Lodge No. 22, 1804, are now in St. George's Lodge No. 6., Schenectady, New York. Jacob Thurston is also thought to have made the Mark Jewels of Bro. Christopher Yates (1797); Peter D'Lamatter, Campbell's Mark Lodge (1800); also the officers' jewels of Campbell's Lodge; and the Mark Jewel of John Sherburne, Campbell's Mark Lodge No. 17. These jewels were illustrated in *Some Old Mark Jewels* by Charles H. Copestake in Part 3, Vol. III Nocalore (transactions of the North Carolina Lodge of Research 1933). The jewels for Junius Lodge No. 291, Waterloo, New York, were made by Caleb Fairchild (1830–31). These jewels are still in use in the present Lodge there, Seneca Lodge No. 113.

Silversmiths of Maryland who were Masons include Peter Galt (1777–1820); Peter Little (1775–1830) and Littleton Holland (1770–1847). There are no known references to jewels made by them. However, the records of Lodge No. 17, Queenstown, Queen Anne County, Maryland, include the following item: "Bro. James Earle Bruff's account was presented by Br. Wm. Bruff for making Maa M. Jewell, a pair of silver Compasses and a Seal at arms amt'g to 6 Currency." November 24, 1774.

The earliest mention of Masonic emblems in American newspapers was in the *New York Weekly Journal,* November 14, 1737. "Masonic Emblems—Taken out of the House of Mr. Todd, a small Silver Square, a Level, a Plumb-Rule, and Silver Pen and other Utensils belonging to the Lodge of Free Masons in New York." However, it is not known if these emblems were made by American silversmiths although American silversmiths advertised the making of Masonic Medals in the eighteenth century. Stephen Greenleaf advertised Free Mason's Jewels in the *Boston Gazette* in 1745. Such silversmiths as Christopher Hughes of Baltimore advertised in the *Maryland Journal* and *The Baltimore Advertiser,* August 20, 1773. "Christopher Hughes & Co.—Plain gold Mason brooches and medals neatly graved." John Inch, the Annapolis silversmith, was a Mason and when he died in 1763 "his funeral was solemnized in a very decent man-

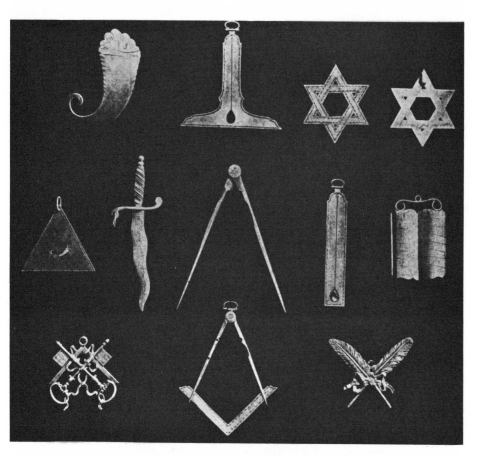

Silver Masonic Jewels of St. Taminy's Lodge made by John Potter (1813–21). (*Jewelers' Circular*, August 31, 1904)

ner, being attended by a Procession of the Brethren of the Lodge properly cloath'd.", *Maryland Gazette,* Mar. 17, 1763. Edmund Milne of Philadelphia was also a Mason and advertised the making of "Masons Medals." Duncan Beard of Appoquinimink Hundred, Delaware, was a member of the Masonic Lodge of Cantwell Bridge. The records of the lodge, March 26, 1771, read "Brother Duncan Beard was directed to make a new set of silver (Jewels)"—(J. Hall Pleasants, *Maryland Silversmiths,* p. 68).

The Albany Institute of History and Art has Masonic Jewels in its collection but none bears a maker's mark although they were undoubtedly made by Albany silversmiths. The Albany artist Ezra Ames who was a prominent Mason records the gilding and engraving of Masonic Jewels in his early Account Books. From the year of his admission into Union

Lodge in 1794, Ames had extensive employment as a painter of Masonic regalia and engraver of Masonic medals and certificates. In the Account Book—1798–1800 the following entries appear: "May 20, 1798. To engraving a War Medal $2. June 27, 1800—To gilt Masonic Meddel 1:16." In the *Albany Register,* November 25, November 29 and December 10, 1799, Ames included the following in his advertisement: "Seals M[ar]K. M[ast]r. Mason's Medals, etc. engraved neatly and elegantly." Among the Albany silversmiths who according to his Account Books, were patrons of Ames were Isaac Hutton and John W. Fryer. Either of these silversmiths or Green Hall could have made these jewels since they all did that kind of work. In the *Albany Gazette* June 1, 1821, Green Hall of Albany advertised: "Masonic breast plates and jewels. Mark Masters Medals."

Joseph Seymour (1835–1863) who worked in Syracuse, Utica and New York City advertised the making of secret society emblems. In 1850

TOP. Masonic Jewels. St. John's Lodge No. 2. A. F. & A. M. made by Charles Brewer, c. 1812. (*Alexander J. Aitken, Sec., St. John's Lodge No. 2. A. F. & A. M., Middletown, Conn.*) BOTTOM. Silver Masonic Jewels, Seneca Lodge 113. Made by Caleb Fairchild, c. 1830–1831. (*Library, Grand Lodge F. & A. Masons of the State of New York*)

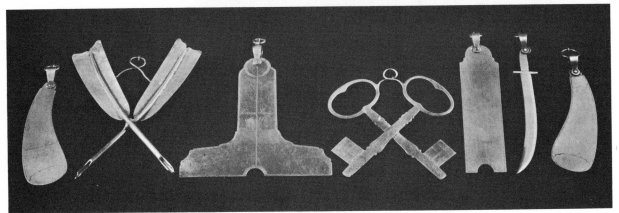

LEFT. Masonic Mark Jewel, John Sherburne, Campbell's Mark Lodge No. I., made by Jacob Thurston (?). BELOW. Masonic Mark Jewel, Henry Spencer, Felicity Mark Lodge. (*From "Some Old Mark Jewels" by Charles H. Copestake*)

the firm name was Norton & Seymour and in *The Masonic Register*, June, 1854, Norton & Seymour advertise: "Master Masons Jewels manufactured in beautiful style. Orders taken from Regalia manufacturers." The first advertisements of jewelers or dealers in Masonic Regalia had appeared in the Masonic Sentinel in 1851. In that year other dealers who advertised Masonic Jewels included Eleazor Ayers, Manufacturing Jeweler, Elias Combs, and M. J. Drummond all of New York City. In the National Freemason in June, 1863, H. O. Hood of Washington, D. C. advertised, "All kinds of Masonic Emblems manufactured to order." In 1866, The American Masonic Agency, D. B. Howell, and Harrison Pridham & Co., all of New York, and Horstman Bros. & Co. of Philadelphia were listed as

214

Masonic Jewel makers. In 1868, B. T. Hayward, C. A. Stevens, and Virgil Price were added to the list in New York City, and by 1885 an ad. of John F. Luther illustrated machine-made jewels as we know them today. However, special jewels were always made to order by silversmiths or jewelers, and makers of fine silver such as Tiffany & Co., Shreve & Co. of San Francisco, Samuel Kirk & Son and many others made individual jewels ornamented with enamel and sometimes precious stones presented by members of the lodge.

There are few old Masonic Jewels available to collectors, but since many are in the personal belongings of Masonic Brothers, the opening of an attic trunk may bring some to the market. However, the later nineteenth century jewels are colorful and although not valuable would make an interesting collection. If a jewel bears the name of a well-known person it becomes historically valuable.

Collection of Masonic Jewels. Two in top center early 19th century (see page 210 for detail). Remainder late 19th century. (*Courtesy of The Henry Ford Museum, Dearborn, Michigan*)

X *Small Silver Collectibles*

1. LATE VICTORIAN MATCH BOXES

BEFORE the days of lighters matches for cigars and cigarettes were carried in match safes—small boxes from two to three inches long with hinged lids. They were made of various materials—silver, silver plate, pewter, brass, tin, and gutta percha; a few were of wood. Most of these boxes, especially the American silver ones, date from the 1890's but many are as late as 1910. These little silver boxes offer an interesting hobby for silver collectors. Although they are not very old or rare, since thousands were made, they usually have the mark of the silver manufacturer who made them and they are intimate souvenirs of the late nineteenth century.

Match boxes are found in a great variety of shapes and designs. The style of the designs follows that of the other decorative arts of the era and because rococo, Art Nouveau, and Oriental were the influences in the late nineteenth century most of the designs on match boxes relate to one or the other of these decorative styles. There are several categories of subject matter for the collector of match boxes. In addition to rococo and Art Nouveau decorations there are boxes with subjects related to sports such as yachting, golfing, horseback riding, hunting, fishing, baseball, and football. There were also boxes with designs relating to popular indoor activities such as card playing, gambling and smoking. A coaching scene, a moose in the forest, various breeds of dogs, owls, monkeys, pigs and other animals are also to be found on match safes. There are also designs with natural-

LEFT. Three match boxes. (*Gorham Manufacturing Co., Catalogue,* 1888) BELOW. Match boxes. R. Blackinton & Co. (*Jewelers' Circular,* Oct. 5, 1904)

istic flowers and plants—roses, lilies-of-the-valley, poppies, thistles, clover, holly and leaf designs. Historical scenes and portraits of Presidents of the United States are depicted on other boxes. In the *Jewelers' Circular*, August 7, 1898, the Mauser Manufacturing Co. advertised match safes with heads of McKinley, Dewey, Sigsbee, Miles and Lee. There are also boxes that were made as souvenirs of World's Fairs including the Philadelphia Centennial in 1876, the World's Columbian Exposition at Chicago in 1893, and the St. Louis Fair in 1904. There is a match safe with a head of Columbus and a replica of the Woman's Building at the World's Columbian Exposition. This box is dated 1893. There are other dated boxes and when there is a mark of the silver company an approximate date can be determined. There are also match boxes with reproductions, of romantic paintings such as "The Storm" by Pierre Auguste Cot, and Bouguereau's "Satyr & Nymphs" and "Psyche & Love." William B. Kerr of Newark brought out a series of match boxes with these and similar paintings of nudes and cupids set in a rococo framework. The "Satyr & Nymphs" box was also made by Clarence W. Sedgwick. Sedgwick also made a box with an Art Nouveau nude in the waves. "Leda and the Swan and "Diana at the Hunt" were taken from sculpture. Boxes with signal code flags in colored enamels were also available. Match boxes made by Unger Brothers included golfer designs, smokers, the Bathers, an Art Nouveau design of a woman with peacock headdress, an Indian head, a cupid, a dragon, and daisy designs. Boxes made by R. Blackinton & Co. include a football player, a gambling scene of cards, dice, money, and a wishbone for luck, a dragon, lions, a pipe smoker, and a cigarette smoker with women's faces in the curling smoke. A unique design was a profile of a man and woman on either side of a loving cup.

There were also many match boxes with advertising. These are not made of sterling silver, but are plated or made of other materials such as

RIGHT. Match boxes, Rococo style. William B. Kerr & Co. (*Jewelers' Weekly*, vol. 10, 1895–96) BELOW. Match boxes. Clarence W. Sedgwick. (*Jewelers' Weekly*, vol. 9, 1894–95)

gutta-percha. A "free silver" match box was put out by the St. Louis Clock & Silverware Co. It is inscribed: "Westward the Star of Empire takes its Way. Free silver 16 to 1." The design is a head in a star set within a double circle. In addition to rectangular-shaped boxes there are boxes in the shapes of animals—dogs, cats, monkeys, pigs, horses' heads and elephants' heads. There is also a box in the form of an owl and still another represents a coiled snake. Other unique boxes are shaped like an old shoe, a clown's head, an Indian head, busts of famous persons, a violin, a knife, and a pair of Levis.

The most sought-after boxes at the moment are those of Art Nouveau design. The boxes that reproduce paintings and sculpture are also attractive, but the boxes of unusual shape are the most unique. Those with dates and advertising are also important and hard to find. However, good selections of match boxes are for sale at almost every antiques show. One dealer writes that he has over two hundred boxes in stock and a collector writes that his collection numbers eight hundred.

2. SILVER-HEADED CANES

WALKING canes have been in use for many centuries. They were a part of the attire of the eighteenth century gentleman and canes are pictured in many portraits by such well-known American artists as Copley and Ralph

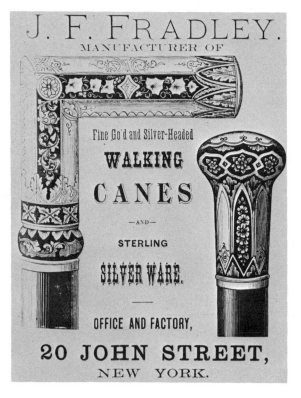

Advertisements of silver-headed walking canes. LEFT. (*Jewelers' Circular*, Oct. 1894) RIGHT. (*Jewelers' Circular*, Nov. 1895)

Earl. These canes were tall and slender and the silver, gold, or ivory head was usually of round mushroom type. However, among the advertisements of nineteenth century American silversmiths only one, Philip Syng of Philadelphia, mentions canes. "Neat chased gold cane Head." (Penna. Journal March 17, 1763) There are several advertisements of imported gilt cane heads for sale. In 1790 Benjamin Franklin willed his cane with the Figure of Liberty to Washington. But it is more than likely that the cane was made abroad. Most American men at this date were carrying swords rather than canes. By the late nineteenth century almost all American gentlemen carried canes and the silver or gilt-headed cane or walking stick became a status symbol and was found in the wardrobe of all who could afford one. Many men owned several canes which stood in the Victorian hall-rack when not in use. The popular type of walking cane still had a straight mushroom handle. It was etched, engraved, or embossed with scrolls and strapwork designs which left an oval space on top for an initial or monogram. Flowers and foliage were also placed in panels between the strapwork and often there were scenes of landscape and animals. In 1889 the Alvin Corporation advertised a staghorn cane which was decorated with silver deposit and encircled with a silver snake. The silver-mounted cane was a popular item with late nineteenth century silver companies. Although cane heads were made by many different firms, including Simons Brothers & Co. of Philadelphia; Charles Downs; Hearn

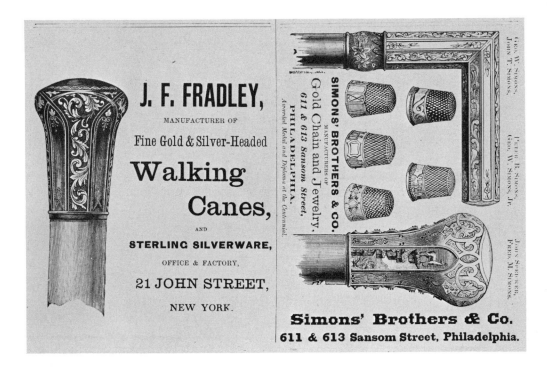

J. F. FRADLEY, MANUFACTURER OF Fine Gold & Silver-Headed Walking Canes, AND STERLING SILVERWARE, OFFICE & FACTORY, 21 JOHN STREET, NEW YORK.

SIMONS' BROTHERS & CO. MANUFACTURERS OF Gold Chain and Jewelry. 611 & 613 Sansom Street, PHILADELPHIA. Awarded Medal and Diploma at the Centennial.

GEO. W. SIMONS, JOHN T. SIMONS. PETER B. SIMONS, GEO. W. SIMONS, JR. JOHN SPENCER, FRED. M. SIMONS.

Simons' Brothers & Co.
611 & 613 Sansom Street, Philadelphia.

& Braitsch; Folmer & Clogg; L. A. Cuppia; Unger Brothers; The Sterling Company of Providence; Alvin Corporation and Rest; Fenner Smith & Co.; Otto Reichardt; Lukenburg & Hassel; the two companies that specialized in canes were J. F. Fradley and W. W. Harrison of New York City.

Fradley was established in 1869. In addition to gold and sterling silver cane and umbrella handles, the company also made dresserware, vases, desk accessories and novelties. Fradley canes were exhibited in the Paris exhibition and in the American Institute Fair of 1873. The designs included "fluted, rope, repoussé, scroll, flower and heraldic." W. W. Harrison, according to their advertisements, was established in 1876. Illustrations in their advertisements show striking designs including later Art Nouveau patterns of leaves, scrolls and flowers. Handles of their canes were also made of gold, ivory, pearl, tortoise shell, crystal, fancy wood and gun metal. Silver-mounted umbrella handles were also made by many of the same companies. Silver-mounted canes were also made by Reed & Barton, Gorham Manufacturing Company and Tiffany & Company. Tiffany canes have designs of vines and scrolls in Art Nouveau patterns and are marked "Tiffany & Co." The canes usually have a curved horizontal crook that fits the hand. Other canes have straight, curved or polo crooks.

There are several well-known collectors of silver-headed canes. The prices are not cheap, but there are some canes on the market. Two Tiffany silver-headed canes recently seen in a New York shop were priced at $75.00.

Silver-headed canes, Art Nouveau style. LEFT. Leaf and poppy designs. BELOW. Scroll design. (*Jewelers' Circular*, Oct., Nov., Dec., 1904)

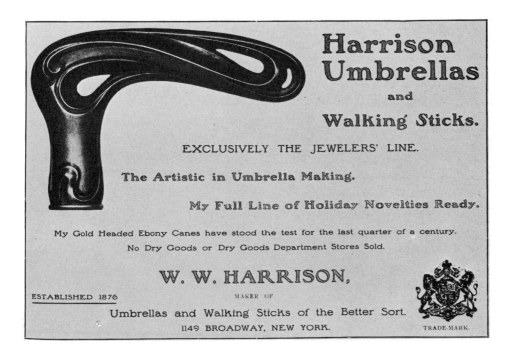

LEFT. Silver inkstand with candlestick. Obadiah Rich, c. 1830. RIGHT. Silver inkstand. Harvey Lewis, c. 1815. (*Both Yale University Art Gallery, The Mabel Brady Garvan Collection*)

3. INKSTANDS & DESK FURNISHINGS

INKSTANDS were made in America from an early date. One of the best known American inkstands is the triangular standish with three matching containers and well modelled lion feet made by John Coney which is in the Metropolitan Museum. The other famous inkstand is the standish made by Philip Syng, Jr. which was used at the signing of the Declaration of Independence. It remains in Independence Hall, Philadelphia, today. These inkstands were both made of all silver. In the late eighteenth century the canoe-shaped stand with pierced galleries stood on legs or ball feet and held cut glass ink bottles. Early in the nineteenth century the inkstand became an oblong tray with heavy gadrooned rim and wide borders. It held two matching cut glass bottles and perhaps a center taper to heat the sealing wax. The Victorian inkstand was ornamented with elaborate rococo piercing and castings. There were usually two ink bottles and styles included Grecian, beaded scroll, and pierced. The ink bottles might be melon-shaped, vase-shaped or cylindrical. They sat on florid foliaged feet.

222

Inkstands or inkwells as they were called in the late nineteenth century were often made in fanciful designs with figures of animals and humans. In 1886 one inkwell was advertised with a silver figure of a monk at prayer. There were also inkwells made in combinations of pottery and silver, ebony and silver, and glass with patterns of silver deposit. Tiffany made inkwells highly ornamented with repoussé patterns and semi-precious stones. These inkwells were thought interesting enough to be included in displays at the various World's Fairs. "Ink Sets" and "Desk Sets" were also important items in Gorham's line of Martelé silver. In the exhibition at Turin, Italy, in 1902, Gorham exhibited Martelé inkstands and desk sets.

Martelé inkwells of various designs with matching trays. (*Gorham Manufacturing Co., c. 1901–6*)

Many of the Martelé inkstands were made by Gorham for Spaulding & Co. of Chicago. Some of the ink bottles were of silver and others were of glass decorated with silver deposit or cut in a design matching the tray and silver top. There were bottles on curving leaf trays and often one or two ink bottles were combined with one or more candle sockets. These inkstands were in the various floral and sea-wave designs and sometimes they were further ornamented with nude figures of women. Other com-

Sterling silver and glass inkstands. (*Gorham Manufacturing Co., Catalogue*, c. 1900)

panies also made inkwells in Art Nouveau designs in both sterling and plated silver. Fantastic exaggerated designs were made by Pairpoint and other manufacturers of plated silver. These would make an interesting collection.

A large selection of glass ink bottles with silver tops is included in the 1895 catalogue of Whiting Manufacturing Company and between 1896 and 1915 the Wilcox Silver Plate Co. made an extensive group of cut glass inkstands of various patterns of glass with silver tops of many different designs. The glass was cut by Meriden Cut Glass Co. which was located in the same building as the Wilcox Silver Plate Co. and was actually a part of that company. The International Silver Company later absorbed the two companies. J. Straus and other cut glass companies provided the cut glass inkstands for the many silver manufacturers who made the silver tops. The glass bottles were both round and square and were sold singly or in pairs on a silver stand. There are many of these inkstands available for the present-day collector and the price is not prohibitive.

Glass inkstands with sterling silver gold-lined tops. Wilcox Silver Plate Co. (*The International Silver Co.*)

4. SNUFF BOXES AND OTHER SMALL BOXES

DURING the eighteenth century the snuff box held the position that is occupied by the cigarette case today. Snuff boxes were made of gold, silver, enamel and precious stones. They were round, oval, rectangular or heart-shaped and some were shaped like a scallop shell. Snuff boxes might be chased, engraved, or embossed and enriched with gilding. Some were decorated in high relief patterns or cast ornament. The later boxes made at the beginning of the nineteenth century were usually rectangular with rounded corners and the favorite style of ornament was bright-cut chasing of floral designs and scrolls. There was also a vogue for boxes with scenes reproducing paintings or sporting scenes cast on the box lid. Some boxes had silver lids mounted on horn or cowrie shell with an open-work design of foliage birds and flowers or scroll work.

By the middle of the nineteenth century the vogue for snuff had declined although it continued in use to the end of the century. An advertisement of Gorham Manufacturing Co. in 1881 included snuff boxes.

LEFT. Snuff box, early 19th century. Design of Hercules and Nemean Lion. RIGHT. Bottom of box with inscription. (*Both The Metropolitan Museum of Art. Bequest of A. T. Clearwater, 1933*)

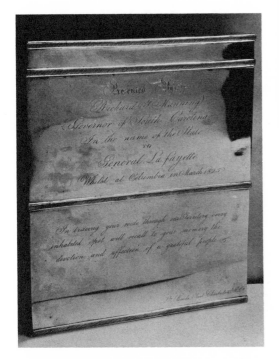

TOP LEFT. Snuff box, horn with silver top, c. 1825. (*The Metropolitan Museum of Art, bequest of A. T. Clearwater, 1933*) CENTER LEFT. Map case, L. Boudo, 1819–25. (*The Metropolitan Museum of Art, bequest of A. T. Clearwater, 1933*) CENTER RIGHT. Silver snuff box, early 19th century. (*Courtesy of The New-York Historical Society, New York City*) BOTTOM. Silver snuff boxes, engraved designs. Bramhall; Foster & Richards; A. Coles. Late 19th century. (*Cincinnnati Art Museum*)

"Presents for Gentlemen—Tobacco Boxes, Cigar Cases, Cigarette Cases, Cigar Stands, Snuff Boxes, Match Boxes, Ash Trays, Shaving Sets, Cane Heads, Scarf Rings, Scarf Pins, Suspender Buckles."

Round glove-vanity cases, soap boxes and glove stretchers. (*Reed & Barton Catalogue,* c. 1900)

Up until the mid-twentieth century the Reynolds Tobacco Company was still manufacturing snuff. Tobacco manufacturers in the South are making snuff today and snuff is for sale in grocery stores and supermarkets

Heart-shaped jewel boxes, glove and work boxes; embroidery hoops. Hand engraved, pierced and etched. (*Reed & Barton Catalogue*, c. 1900)

of the South. However, the beautiful little decorative snuff box is no longer in use. Many of the mid-nineteenth century snuff boxes made in America carried only the name of the owner and perhaps that of the donor. An interesting rectangular box in the Metropolitan Museum of Art has a

Heart-shaped and oval jewel boxes. Whiting Manufacturing Co. Catalogue 1895. (*The Metropolitan Museum of Art*)

LEFT AND ABOVE. Design for powder box and soap dish. BELOW. Design for tea bell. The Sterling Company. (*Jewelers' Weekly*, vol. 9, 1889)

die-cast design of Hercules and the Nemean Lion. It is thought to have been made by John Targee since Targee made swords with this design on the counter-guard.

In the late nineteenth century many small trinket and jewel boxes and tiny glove vanity cases were made in round, oval, rectangular and heart shapes. These are covered with engraving or embossed or pierced designs in French rococo floral and arabesque patterns. These boxes are usually marked "Sterling" and sometimes the manufacturer's trade mark is also stamped. Such boxes are inexpensive and the supply is plentiful.

5. TEA BELLS, TEA BALLS AND STRAINERS, TEA CADDIES

SMALL silver table bells have been used for centuries. In the Italian Renaissance they were made in both silver and gold and were even made by Benvenuto Cellini. Silver table bells were the usual method of summoning a domestic servant and were often a part of the equipment of the writing desk as well as the dining table. In the late eighteenth century there was a revival of the silver table bell. Bells in the early nineteenth century were chased with an all-over design of flowers or grapes and leaves and the handle was of baluster shape. Some were covered with an applied cut-work design and a heavy moulding was placed on the rim. In Victorian times

231

table bells were called tea bells. These late bells were cast. Some had all-over classical and historical designs in high relief. The handles were cast and chased, often in the form of amorini or cupids. Tea bells also followed

Gorham Catalogue, 1888.

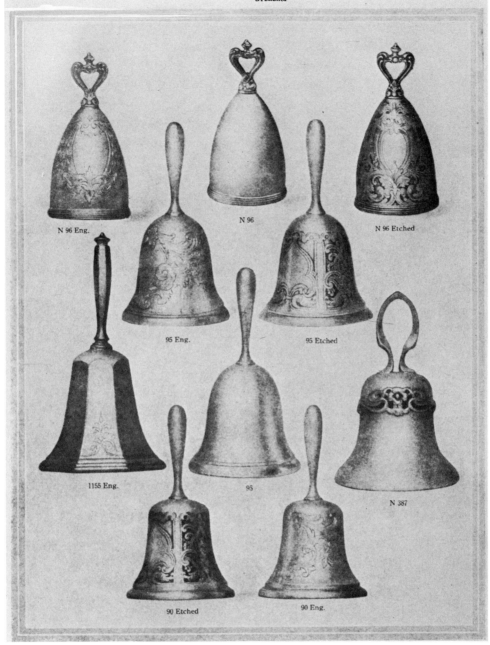

N 96 Eng.   N 96   N 96 Etched

95 Eng.   95 Etched

1155 Eng.   95   N 387

90 Etched   90 Eng.

Tea Bells. (*Reed & Barton Catalogue,* c. 1900)

the general trends of decorative ornament. Designs ranged from Renaissance with conventionalized flower and fruit swags or arabesques and masks to Oriental and Art Nouveau. Some bells were fluted with acanthus leaves or classic borders, others had naturalistic floral designs. J. H.

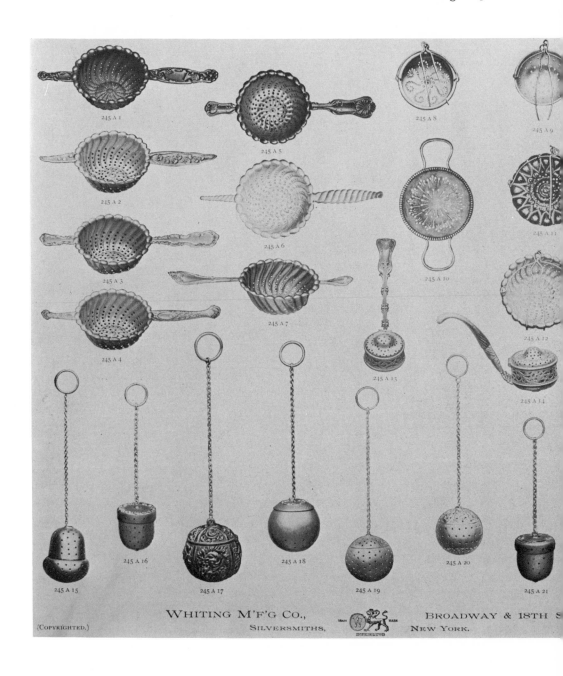

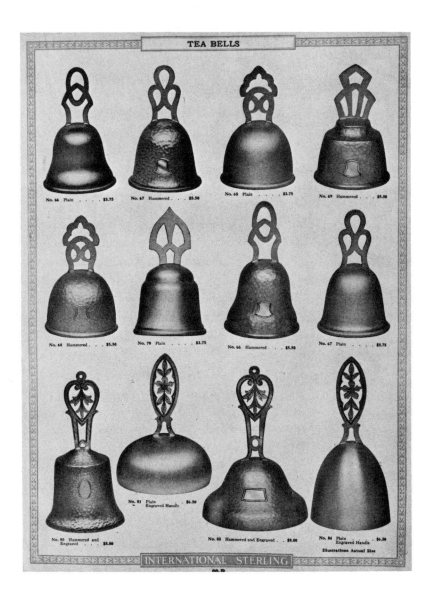

LEFT. Tea strainers and tea balls. Whiting Manufacturing Co. Catalogue, 1895. (*The Metropolitan Museum of Art*) RIGHT. Tea bells. (*International Sterling Co. Catalogue*)

Johnston of New York made bells with handles in the form of Rip Van Winkle and Peter Stuyvesant.

Tea bells were also made with handles matching the various late nineteenth century patterns of silverware such as Lily-of-the-Valley by Whiting Manufacturing Company. Many of these are marked with the manufacturer's trade mark. Tea balls and strainers of various types were also made with designs matching the patterns of late nineteenth century flatware.

Tea caddies were not in general use in England until the eighteenth century. The earliest tea caddies were in the shape of a square bottle, but probably the first type to reach America were the oval tea caddies that matched the oval teapots and sugar bowls of the Federal era. These were decorated with garlands and borders of bright-cut engraving. Tea caddies were not made by the Colonial silversmiths, but they were made by Paul Revere. The late eighteenth century tea service by Paul Revere in the Minneapolis Institute of Arts has a matching tea caddy of oval fluted form decorated with bright-cut engraving and set on a tray. There is also a matching caddy spoon. An oval tea caddy made by Andrew E. Warner in 1821 is in the collection of the Maryland Historical Society. A matching tea caddy is also included with the tea set made by Daniel Van Voorhis in 1824. Although tea caddies may have been made to match many tea sets there are few tea caddies on the market today.

LEFT. Tea Caddies. Whiting Manufacturing Catalogue, 1895. (*The Metropolitan Museum of Art*) RIGHT. Tea Caddy. Neo-classic serpentine form with flat-chased decoration. H. M. Ritterband, c. 1840. (*Gebelein Silversmiths*)

6. OPEN SALTS AND MUSTARD POTS

AT the beginning of the nineteenth century the circular bowl salt dish with three or four feet was in style. Some of these were plain with a moulded feathered or gadroon rim, shell or gadroon knees, and hoof feet. Others have a chased floral design or applied festoons with plain scroll feet but some salts had paw feet or ended in a claw and ball. Other salts were decorated with scallop shells with feet to match or hoof feet. This circular style of salt remained popular in America through the Federal Period. There were also round and oval salts with beading on their rims and bases, and salts on legs or stands with pierced designs on their bodies and blue glass liners. Some of the pierced designs were foliated scrolls and others had classic patterns with leaf or flower swags and medallions. Other designs were of circles, crescents, Gothic arches, and some were also decorated with bands of bright-cut engraving. Boat-shaped open salts which had come into style with the Adam Period in England were also made in America in the Federal Era. They were made both with and without handles. These salts usually stood on an oval or oblong base and were ornamented with bands of bright-cut engraving or beading on their rims, handles and feet. Although these were the main groups of American nineteenth century open salts there were many variations of these types.

There were small salt spoons to accompany the salt dishes. The stem pattern of the spoons followed that of larger spoons. For the collector there

Set of four oval boat-shaped salts. Beaded rim and base, leaf motif terminating in shell handles, silver gilt lining. Gerardus Boyce, New York, c. 1814. (*Collection of Philip H. Hammerslough*)

are feathered edged salt spoons made by Paul Revere, Jr. and salt spoons with tipt and thread patterns and fiddle-shaped spoons with shells, sheaf-of-wheat, and basket-of-flowers. Later salt spoons followed the various patterns of flatware. Salt spoons in Whiting Manufacturing Company's Louis XV pattern have ridged and scalloped bowls and some bowls are gilt.

Early mustard pots were round or oval with hinged lids and an accompanying spoon. Because mustard discolors silver most mustard pots were fitted with glass liners and those with pierced sides usually had liners of blue glass. On early pots the designs were hand-pierced with geometrical motifs decorated with engraving. Later designs were pierced with a hand press or machine. Tops were usually flat and tight fitting. The mustard pots of the Federal Era were oval with a domed lid and had cast or turned round or vase-shaped finials. Some of these are plain with moulded borders and some have fluted bodies, while others have pierced vertical bars, classic foliage and vases or floral designs. Mustard pots with foliaged feet ending in a classic head or lion's mask where they joined the body had

TOP. Pair of open salts. Oval with gadrooned rim, shell knees, floral chasing and three hoofed feet. Andrew E. Warner, c. 1825–1850. (*The Metropolitan Museum of Art, bequest of A. T. Clearwater, 1933*) BOTTOM. Pair of open boat-shaped salts on rectangular base. Square-topped handles, beading on rim and handles. R. & W. Wilson, c. 1830. (*Collection of Philip H. Hammerslough*)

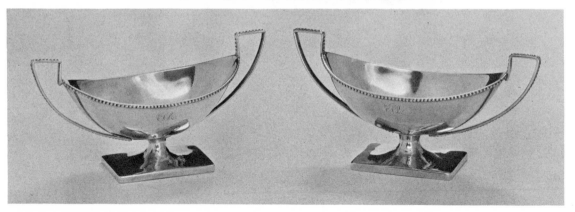

Mustard Pot. Tripod frame with leafed paw feet supporting faces crowned with grape leaves; beaded rim, grape finial. Baldwin & Co., c. 1830. (*Lent by Mr. & Mrs. Dean A. Fales, Jr., to the exhibition "Classical America", The Newark Museum*)

beaded rims and a leafage and beaded finial. These were made by silversmiths around 1830. There were also solid tankard-shaped mustard pots. One made by Joseph Lownes (1780–1816) has a border of beading. Many Victorian mustard pots are decorated with intricate scrollwork or embossing of floral designs in panels and pierced patterns of Gothic windows. All of these types of mustard pots continued to be made for many years so that the maker's mark rather than the style must be the guide of age.

7. FISH KNIVES

FISH KNIVES, slices, or fish trowels, have been in use since the mid-eighteenth century. The earliest fish knives were triangular in shape and pierced with elaborate, delicate designs of foliated scrolls. At first the pattern was in the solid silver, later the design was cut out. The pierced patterns consisted of scrolls, semicircles, flower forms, dots, and triangles. Some of these slices had engraved borders and on some the ornament was reversed with the engraving in the center and the borders pierced with a pattern of scrolls. The pierced designs were enriched with engraving. The handles were of silver or turned wood usually terminating in a shell on the surface of the blade. There were few of these early fish trowels made in America

239

and those found today were mostly made by New York silversmiths where a sophisticated society demanded the latest implements for table service. A fine rare trowel of this type was made by Myer Myers of New York (1723–1795) and one by Charles Oliver Bruff (1763–1779) has recently been on the market. A fish slice by William B. Heyer, New York (1798–1827), has an engraving of a dolphin-like fish and only a border of zigzag piercing on one edge. The handle is ivory. A little later the shape of the fish slice became asymmetrical with only one cutting edge and the blade had a curved pointed tip. The blade was engraved with a central motif resembling the ribs and backbone of a fish or with a crossed fish motif and foliated scrolls. The handles were ivory and terminated in a shell or plain

TOP. Fish slice. John W. Forbes, c. 1802. (*Collection of Philip H. Hammerslough*) BOTTOM. Fish knife and fork. Richard Smith, c. 1887. (*Miss Katherine Young, lent to the exhibition "Classical America", The Newark Museum*)

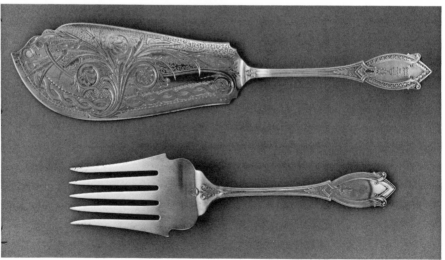

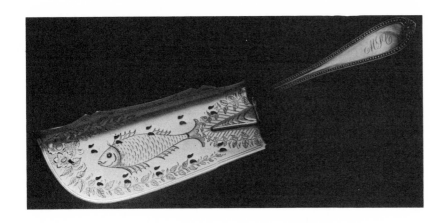

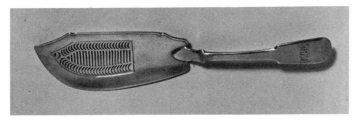

TOP. Fish server. H. P. Horton, c. 1850, Savannah, Georgia. (*Collection of James Arthur Williams*) BOTTOM. Fish slice 19th century. (*The Metropolitan Museum of Art, gift of Frederic Ashton de Peyster, 1946*) RIGHT. Fish knife, Assyrian pattern, 1847 Rogers Brothers silver plate. (*The International Silver Co.*)

triangular or oblong form at the junction of the blade. Slices of this type were made in New York in the early nineteenth century by John W. Forbes, c. 1802, Henry Longley, c. 1810, and others. Some blades were fish shaped. In 1824 Samuel Kirk made an openwork fish slice with a handle in the Kings pattern. The asymmetrical-shaped blade continued to be made throughout the nineteenth century. The factory-made silver handles usually followed the patterns of flatware. Pairs of fish servers consisting of a knife and fork with wide blades made up of four prongs were in use in the 1890's. Handles were of silver or more often mother-of-pearl. The blades of the fish knives were almost completely covered with engraving of scrolls and naturalistic fish, and late in the century might have other motifs connected with fishing such as a fish net, seaweed, or a fishing basket. There were also individual fish knives and forks. These characteristic Victorian designs on late fish servers are interesting. Similar motifs

241

elaborately engraved are also seen on other serving knives, forks, and spoons of the late nineteenth century. The early nineteenth century American fish servers are scarce and expensive, but there are many late Victorian servers at reasonable prices.

8. LADIES' CHATELAINES, BELT BUCKLES, AND HATPINS

No article was too small or insignificant for the early American silversmith and the same was true of the nineteenth century silversmith and his successor the silver manufacturer. Even such large companies as Whiting Manufacturing Company, Gorham, and Tiffany made articles of personal use such as chatelaines, belt buckles, and hatpins, but there were smaller companies that specialized in these articles. Many of these articles are now in the antique shops and available to the collector with a small pocketbook. The chatelaine has an interesting history. It was known in Roman times and was then worn by both men and women. It was made of bronze with three attached chains which held keys. Saxon chatelaines hung from a girdle. They were often made of carved ivory and held a dagger and keys. In Medieval times the chatelaine sometimes had a nutmeg grater and corkscrew as well as a key to the liquor cellar. By the eighteenth century the chatelaine had become an article of feminine attire. The chatelaine is a small flat plate attached to a flat hook which tucked into the waistband. The plate of the chatelaine was round or oval and sometimes had scalloped edges of various patterns. It is ornamented with bright-cut borders or

Silver chatelaine, American, c. 1790. (*Courtesy of The Henry Ford Museum, Dearborn, Michigan*)

scrollwork and usually has the monogram of the owner. The plate of the chatelaine was pierced by three or more chains to which such articles as bodkins, silver toothpicks, scissors or a silver-mounted pincushion might be attached. This type of chatelaine was made by all early American silversmiths and continued to be made by silversmiths as late as the 1840's. The chatelaine generally has the mark of the silversmith but chatelaines are seldom found with chains or articles attached. About 1840 the chatelaine became larger and the hooks were used to fasten a watch, a bottle of smelling salts or a pair of spectacles. Sometimes a small silver-mounted evening

LEFT. Queen chains for chatelaines. RIGHT. Chatelaine with five chains. The Sterling Company. (*Jewelers' Weekly*, 1888, 1889)

THE JEWELERS' WEEKLY.

·T·HE S·TERL·ING C·OMPAN·Y.

Design of Chatelaine.

No. 4920.

LEFT. Chatelaines of various designs. (*Gorham Manufacturing Co. Catalogue,* 1888) RIGHT. Chatelaine with scissors. (*The Smithsonian Institution*)

bag was attached to the chatelaine. The chatelaines of the 1850's and 1860's were pierced and engraved with rococo floral patterns or Moorish designs. The chains held not only a watch but also a small notebook with silver covers and a vinaigrette. By 1870 chatelaines were made in steel and electroplate and silver chatelaines might be ornamented with gilt or enamel. A review of the styles of silverware in a magazine of the 1890's tells of the "Chatelaine to suit the wearer." These included "sewing" chatelaines with needlebooks, scissors, pincushions and thimble case for the needlewoman; "Religious" chatelaines with missal or prayer book, censer, cross, and angel; and "Literary" chatelaine with book and pencil. A new "Easter Egg for sewing to be hung from the chatelaine" and a new "acorn emery" were advertised in 1890, also "spectacle cases of silver filigree, into which the leather case is slipped are very convenient worn as a chatelaine."

Elsie Bee who wrote a column for *Jewelers' Circular* in the 1890's entitled "A Lady's Rambles amoung the Jewelers," makes mention of chatelaines and belt buckles in style at that time. The following excerpts are from her column of August 28, 1895.

"Painted miniatures have been introduced in belt buckles, sur-

244

rounded by fine silver work with gleaming facets that sparkle like brilliants."

"A new chatelaine pin in silver is a wheel with a Mercury wing attached to each side of the hub. One in consequence proceeds from the back. This novelty is equally appropriate to the yachtsman or the cyclist."

"The latest buckle is a gold snake with his head thrust through a knot in his tail, making a suitable oval-form."

The column of August 21, 1895 is titled "Jewelry and Silver of the Yachting Season." The following quotes are from that column.

"A delightful brooch is an oval concave of silver gilt and within a yacht fully rigged with sails spread."

"Painted oceans and yachts are reproduced on match boxes, flasks and every conceivable article that can be carried in the hand, put in the pocket or attached to the person."

"Large square buckles of silver gilt, enclosed in knotted rope ornamentation, have the different yacht club pennants thrown across them diagonally. The colors and stripes are bolder and more effective than formerly. Colored enamels lead every other sort of ornamentation. The rope justifies its place in the ornamentation of nautical jewelry by the most ingenious coils and interlacings."

"The most novel object is a belt buckle, in form like the helmsman's wheel; this encloses a disk of silver gilt on which is a representation of the

RIGHT TOP. Silver glove colognes. (*Gorham Manufacturing Co. Catalogue*, 1888) CENTER. Belt buckle. BOTTOM LEFT. Garter buckle. (*Unger Brothers*) BOTTOM RIGHT. Belt buckle. William B. Kerr & Co. (*Jewelers' Circular*, 1895)

Silver belt and girdle pins. R. Blackinton & Co.,

sea and a yacht under full sail. These little paintings are things of beauty, even as pictures. There are buckles square and oblong treated in the same manner. The wheel is only the completest exposition of the yachting belt."

"There is little doubt that the thousands and thousands of people who will witness the coming races for the *America's* cup will each sport the prettiest emblem of the occasion that his or her means will allow."

The Sterling Company of Providence, Rhode Island, were makers of silver chatelaines, belts and belt buckles and other small novelties. In *Jewelers' Weekly,* August, 1889, this company advertised a new design of chatelaine with a flight of birds holding five chains. They also advertised "Queen Chains." The Queen was a chain which held a locket, tiny pencil, charm, vinaigrette, cube or ball of various designs. Queen balls were also made in blue enamel and black for mourning. The "Victoria" chain was a later trade name for the Queen chain. These chains were named after Queen Victoria and the first ones made were copied after the chain with attached vase-shaped vinaigrette which she wore. Victoria and Queen chains were advertised in a Marshall Field catalogue of 1891, together with various charms to be worn on them including a small scent bottle, basket, shell, ball, pitcher, teapot, heart, book, cross, opera glasses and

246

Art Nouveau design. (*Jewelers' Circular,* April 15, 1903)

Horn-of-Plenty. These charms were often decorated with pearls and other jewels. Small chatelaines to fit in the glove were made in poppy and hawthorn pattern repoussé and cut glass vinaigrettes with silver tops were also popular.

The list of silver articles made by the Sterling Company of Providence in 1889 included the following small articles and novelties: "ash trays, bells, belt buckles, bookmarks, brushes, chatelaines, flasks, garters, glove hooks, hat pins, inkstands, pencils, pen wipers, pin boxes, shoe horns, soap boxes, tape measures, champagne corks, etc." All of these long neglected articles can be collected today.

Nineteenth century belt buckles and belt pins have recently interested the collector. There are many belt buckles and belt pins in antique shops today. The majority of them are in rococo or Art Nouveau designs of flowers such as lilies and poppies, and women's heads with flowing tresses. In 1897, "Jeweled Buckles in silver used with silk and satin beltings 2 inches or more" were advertised in *Jewelers' Circular.* The designs included silver shells enameled in natural color and daisies with petals of silver and green enameled foliage. There were also silver buckles in designs for the "bicycle and athletic girl, yachting, skating, golf, horses,

247

military, dancing, and old fashioned girl." The Unger Brothers catalogue of c. 1900 illustrates belt pins with flowers and girls' heads in Art Nouveau designs. A series of children's heads illustrated the months, and there were bird and animal designs including owls, swans, ducks, eagles, bats, and horses.

In 1889 girdles and belt buckles were "the rage." They were manufactured by Herrman & Company, Reddall & Company, Battin & Company, William B. Kerr, and Unger Brothers of Newark, New Jersey; Mauser Manufacturing Company of New York City; Codding Brothers & Heilborn, and Frank M. Whiting & Co. of North Attleboro, Massachusetts; Barstow & Williams, The Alvin Corporation, Providence, Rhode Island, as well as R. Wallace & Brothers, Gorham Manufacturing Company and others including Tiffany.

In 1903 an advertisement of Unger Brothers illustrated four different designs for pins: a girl with hat and veil, a girl with bonnet and veil, a girl in a large hat wreathed with daisies and a girl's head surrounded by water lilies and lily pads. In *Jewelers' Circular,* April 15, 1903, R. Blackinton & Company of North Attleboro, Massachusetts, advertised new lines of belt pins and girdles. Five Art Nouveau designs are illus-

TOP. Lace pins. (*Gorham Manufacturing Co. Catalogue,* 1902) CENTER. Violet pin, 1895. (*Unger Brothers*) BOTTOM. Belt pins, Art Nouveau designs of womens' heads. (*Unger Brothers*)

trated but the copy states "Our line of these goods includes over 200 new and exquisite patterns in Sterling Silver." Belt buckles were popular into the twentieth century and the days of the Gibson Girl and the Floradora Girl.

The companies that made buckles and belt pins also made hatpins in some of the same designs. Alvin Corporation made brooches, belt pins and hatpins and other novelties in designs called Floradora and Runaway Girl. Unger Brothers hatpin designs included horses, ducks, stork, rabbits, fox, rams, bulldog, elephant, eagle, dolphin, and flowers and women's heads. Daniel Low of Witch Spoon fame made a hatpin with a witch design. He also made hatpins of silver deposit ware and daisy, poppy, and chrysanthemum in Art Nouveau patterns. A golf hatpin with silver head was popular in the 1880's. Silver hairpins with twisted Art Nouveau designs were made by The Sterling Company.

The above list includes many small collectibles which although not important items can nevertheless provide hours of fun for the collector. The articles are inexpensive and are found not only in antique shops but in thrift shops and other secondhand shops. The silver ones are generally marked "Sterling" and where space allows the manufacturer's mark is also included.

TOP. Scarf holders. CENTER. Lace pins. (*Gorham Manufacturing Co. Catalogue,* 1902) BOTTOM. Belt pins, womens' heads. (*Unger Brothers, 1903*)

9. COFFEE SPOONS

COFFEE SPOONS were an important item of American silverware in the last quarter of the nineteenth century. In an advertisement in *Jewelers' Circular* in 1878 Gorham devotes a separate section to coffee spoons:

COFFEE SPOONS

The attention given to this class of Spoon Work has resulted in a large and steadily increased demand. *"The Mother's"* pattern (antique in design) is perfectly adapted for the purpose, has met with a large sale, and led to an increased demand in all the regular patterns.

As this class of Spoon Work is almost invariably called for in cases, the beauty of the cases has rendered them particularly desirable for presentation purposes, while for general table use the coffee spoon is in growing demand.

The most popular combinations are

6 or 12 Coffee Spoons, either large or small
6 " 12 " " and 1 Sugar Spoon
6 " 12 " " " 1 pair Sugar Tongs
6 " 12 " " 1 Cream Ladle, 1 pair Sugar Tongs
6 " 12 " " 1 " " 1 Sugar Spoon

For such combinations, the latest novelty in style, appropriately termed *"The Harlequin,"* has become very popular. The effect of 12 differing from each other in pattern meets with general favor. This has led to the introduction of the latest novelty in this department,

Decorated Coffee Spoons

wherein each spoon, though of the same outline, but differing in ornament, is rendered particularly attractive by its novel style of decoration, engraved in colors and in endless variety of ornament.

The coffee spoons and five o'clock teaspoons of the 1890's are particularly fascinating and varied enough to be of interest to the collector. They usually came in sets of six or twelve, all different, or they could be ordered all of one pattern. Gorham were the largest producers of these spoons and they made many sets of different designs from the 1880's down into the second quarter of the twentieth century. The earliest set was the well-known "Nuremberg" spoons. These spoons illustrated the picturesque costumes and characteristic occupations of the peasants, burghers and noblemen of old Nuremberg. They had cut-out cast handles and the bowls could be ordered in sterling or gold-washed with the name or date engraved on the bowl. They were first made in the 1880's and listed in the catalogues of the 1890's and were made in three sizes, the smallest being the 4 inch coffee size. The Old Paris coffee spoons were a quaint set of amusing figures taken from old French prints. They included a wine jug twisted with a grapevine, a cupid set on clouds, a crown, a cross and crown, a knight's armor, a sailing ship, and busts of several figures, twelve different designs in all. The Alphabet coffee spoons were first made in 1885. These spoons consisted of a cut-out letter entwined with flowers or leaves with the stem wound around the handle. The bowls are fluted and scalloped and are gold-washed as are the flowers of the handles. These spoons were also made to order from special castings. In

After-dinner coffee spoons, Rusticana pattern. Ludwig, Redlich & Co. (*Jewelers' Circular,* Nov. 18, 1891)

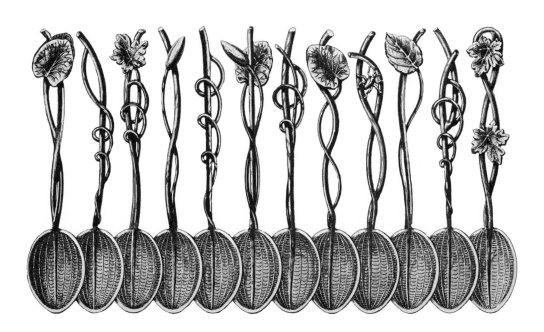

1892 Gorham brought out their set of twelve Apollo spoons. The horizontally ridged handles are topped with full-length silhouette figures in Greek dress. The bowls are fluted and gold washed. Gorham's #18 pattern of coffee spoons are of French rococo scroll or flower design but one spoon has a cornucopia of fruit, one a figure of Cupid, another a woman's head and one is a silhouette figure of a man in Roman toga. The bowls are swirl fluted and gold washed. The Victoria pattern coffee spoons have handles with various types of simple twist designs. In 1892 Gorham put out a set of Actress coffee spoons to be sold at the Actors' Fund Fair in New York's Madison Square Garden, May 2–7, 1892. Each spoon had a cut-out bust of an actress with a scroll beneath it which reproduced the subject's signature. The stems of the spoons were etched with laurel leaves, the bowl was gold washed. The actresses whose heads are on the spoons are: Sydney Armstrong, Sarah Bernhardt, Agnes Booth, Marie Burroughs, Georgia Cayvan, Rose Coghlan, Fanny Davenport, Maud Harrison, Madge Kendal, Helena Modjeska, May Robson, Annie Russell, Lillian Russell, Effie Shannon, and Rosina Vokes.

In 1892 George W. Shiebler Co. put out a set of twelve coffee spoons called Vienna Coffees. The handles were of various intricate twisted designs, each one different. They were sold in assorted designs or all of one pattern if preferred. Flower-handled spoons were especially popular in the 1890's and several companies brought out sets with floral handle designs. George W. Shiebler advertised his Flora set in 1890. These included handles with primrose, buttercup, passion-flower, narcissus, geranium, forget-me-not, wild rose, lily-of-the-valley, pond lily, pansy, pink and violet. The set of coffee spoons made by Alvin and advertised in *Jewelers' Circular*, December 13, 1893, was called Floralia. It included many favorite flowers such as lily, rose, marguerite, pansy and clover. The spoons were in flower form while the leaves made up the stem or handle. Ludwig, Redlich & Co. brought out sets of spoons called The Rusticana. The designs included stems, leaves, and flowers in twisted patterns related to Art Nouveau. They were made in berry, ice cream, jelly, and bonbon and olive spoons as well as coffee spoons. There was also a salad set and a sardine set. Also in 1892 Reed & Barton brought out a set of coffee spoons with flower handles and undoubtedly there were many more sets made by other manufacturers including Tiffany who listed Floral spoons among their souvenir spoons of 1894.

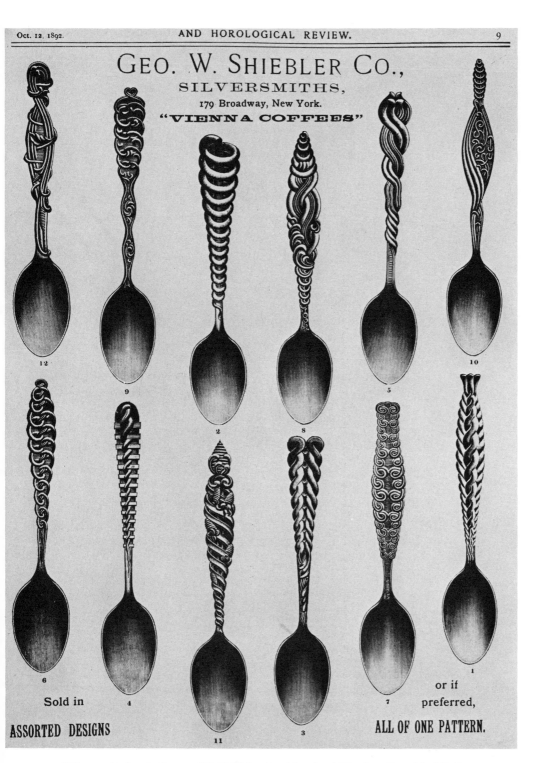

GEO. W. SHIEBLER CO.,
SILVERSMITHS,
179 Broadway, New York.
"VIENNA COFFEES"

Sold in

ASSORTED DESIGNS

or if preferred,

ALL OF ONE PATTERN.

"Vienna Coffees." George W. Shiebler Co. (*Jewelers' Circular*, Oct. 12, 1892)

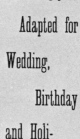

After-dinner coffee spoons, Floralia design. Alvin Manufacturing Co. (*Jewelers' Circular*, Dec. 13, 1893)

In addition to the many sets of coffee spoons, single coffee spoons were also made in most of the souvenir spoon patterns. Souvenir spoon collecting began in the 1890's when it became the custom to bring home a spoon reminiscent of the holiday abroad or of a place nearer home. It soon became a craze on which the silver manufacturers capitalized. Not only were souvenir spoons made by large companies but also by individual jewelers. The custom of souvenir spoon collecting died out in the first quarter of the twentieth century but the craze has again caught fire with antiques collectors. The vast output of souvenir spoons makes their collecting a popular inexpensive hobby within the reach of all. There are several books that give detailed information and it is not my purpose to repeat the data here. However, in addition to the many historical souvenir spoons related to cities, states, and places and persons of historic interest there were spoons of various holidays including Christmas and Easter. There were Good Luck and Honor spoons and Friendship, Love, Wedding and Silver Wedding spoons. To meet the custom of giving a spoon as an engagement present, The Sterling Silver Souvenir Company brought forth the Cupid Engagement Spoon and J. R. Tennant brought out the Cupid Spoon and Alvin, the Oracle of Love. These spoons had heart-shaped bowls and designs which included cupids, doves and orange blossoms. The majority of these spoons were made in teaspoons, coffee spoon and orange spoon sizes in sterling silver either with or without gold-washed bowls.

10. CHILDREN'S SILVER

In the eighteenth century children were fed out of spout cups. The spout cup consisted of a cup with a handle and a slender spout set at right angles to it. The cups usually had covers. The forms vary from cup to pot shape. The spout cup seems to have been an uncommon piece but one by John Edwards is in the collection of the Metropolitan Museum of Art. By the mid-eighteenth century the spout cup was superseded by the pap boat, which was a small shallow bowl with a long lip. Pap boats by Conrad Bard (c. 1825) and Bard & Lamont (c. 1841) of Philadelphia have been seen in antique shops recently. They have a moulded edge and scroll handles. The name "pap" continued in use for many years and there were pap spoons as well as pap boats in the late nineteenth century.

LEFT. Pap boat. (William I. Tenney, c. 1840) (*Courtesy of The New-York Historical Society, New York City*) RIGHT. Child's cup, beaded edge. Haddock, Lincoln & Foss, 1858–1868. (*Gebelein Silversmiths*)

Small porringers were also used by children. In the first quarter of the nineteenth century childs' cups were used and were a popular birthday gift. Many children's cups in repoussé and plain designs were made by Samuel Kirk in the 1820's and 1830's. A few years later the child's cup was referred to as a "mug." In 1847 Samuel Kirk & Son made a mug for Cadwallader Evans. It had a repoussé scene of Robinson Crusoe, his dog and hut. The mug is now in the Historical Society of Pennsylvania.

The various advertisements from the mid-nineteenth century on point up the importance of silverware as gifts for children in the nineteenth century. In 1846 Tiffany, Young & Ellis included "Childrens' Sets" in their advertising and a child's bowl in niello was exhibited by Tiffany & Company at the Paris exhibition in 1889. In 1878 Gorham Manufacturing Company included a long list of articles in their advertisement in *Jewelers' Circular:* "For Children: Cups, napkin rings, bowls, porringers, pap boats, cup sets, plates, knife, fork and spoon, Christening sets, rattles, whistles." The child's Christening Set consisted of a bowl and plate, a mug, a spoon, knife and fork, a napkin ring and often an alcohol burner for keeping food warm.

In 1888 Towle Silversmiths advertised a child's set in Pomona pattern and an A.B.C. set which also included plates and cups with "Hi Diddle Diddle," "Ring Around the Rosey," and "This Little Pig Went to Market." Reed & Barton came out with the curved-handled baby spoon which was ornamented with over forty subjects from familiar nursery rhymes and pictures including "Little Miss Muffet," "Little Jack Horner," and etchings of cat and dog subjects.

Children's pap spoons with deep rounded bowls were made in the Witch and Leif Ericson souvenir spoon designs by Daniel Low in the 1890's, and J. H. Johnston made pap spoons and a child's fork in their Knickerbocker souvenir design.

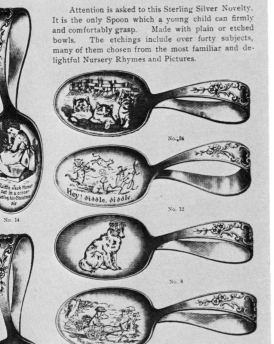

LEFT. Curved handled silver baby spoons with etched Nursery Rhymes. Reed & Barton. (*Jewelers' Circular*, vol. 26) RIGHT. Child's fork, Mayflower pattern. (Samuel Kirk & Son) BELOW. Child's knife, fork and spoon depicting Nursery Rhymes. Tiffany & Co., c. 1900. (*Courtesy of The New-York Historical Society, New York City*)

The catalogue of Whiting Manufacturing Company, 1895, included several pages of children's mugs. The designs range from plain mugs with borders of beading, gadrooning, or leaf patterns to mugs embossed with shells, delicate classical patterns, flowers, nudes and cupids. At about this

Childrens' cups. (*Whiting Manufacturing Co. Catalogue,* 1895) (*The Metropolitan Museum of Art*)

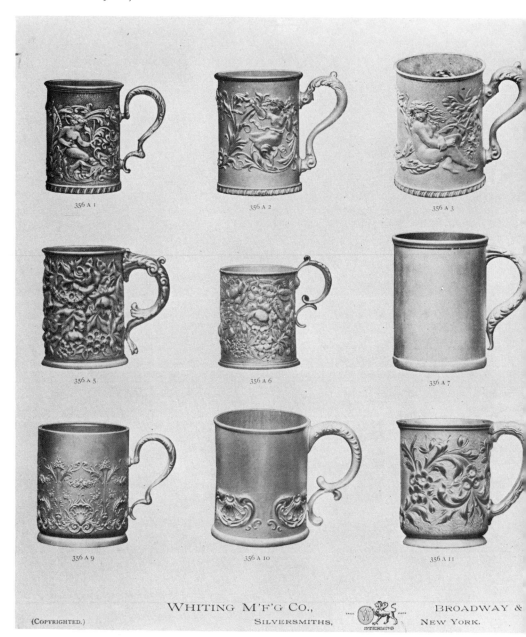

WHITING M'F'G CO.,
SILVERSMITHS,

(COPYRIGHTED.)

BROADWAY &
NEW YORK.

same date Reed & Barton made child's sets consisting of mugs, plates and bowls with borders of Kate Greenaway children, zoo animals, and one of ducks on waves. Spoon designs included Cupid, Pussy Cat and a baroque Louis XIV design. By this time all of the silver companies were

Childrens' silver rattles and whistles. (*Gorham Manufacturing Co. Catalogue*, 1888)

356 A 4

356 A 8

356 A 12

(HALF ACTUAL SIZE.)

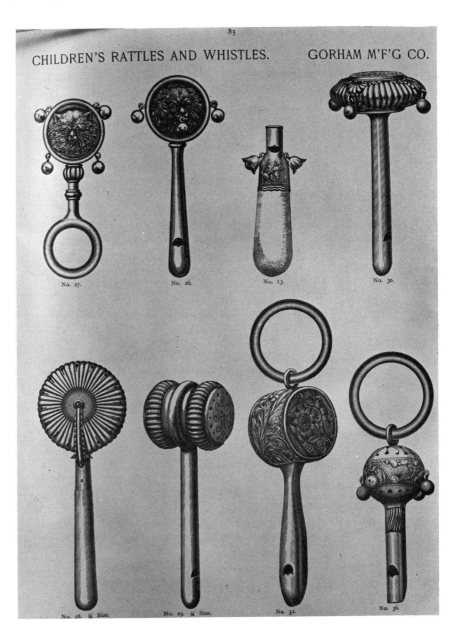

85

CHILDREN'S RATTLES AND WHISTLES.   GORHAM M'F'G CO.

No. 27.   No. 26.   No. 13.   No. 30.

No. 28. ½ Size.   No. 29. ½ Size.   No. 32.   No. 36.

ABOVE. Child's set, Nursery Rhymes, Martelé. BELOW. Child's set, Wild Roses, Martelé. (*The Gorham Manufacturing Co.*)

making children's silver and children's sets were also being made in plated ware. In 1881, according to a catalogue sent to dealers, Gorham sold children's sets of various sizes packed in special cases:

CHILDREN'S SETS

1 Child's Knife and Fork.
1 Child's Knife, Fork, and Spoon.
1 Child's Fork and Spoon.
1 Tea Knife and Fork.
1 Tea Knife, Fork, and Spoon.
1 Tea Fork and Spoon.
1 Dessert Knife and Fork.
1 Dessert Knife, Fork, and Spoon.
1 Dessert Fork and Spoon.
1 Child's Knife, Fork, Spoon, and Ring.
1 Tea Knife, Fork, Spoon, and Ring.
1 Dessert Knife, Fork, Spoon, and Ring.

Childrens' porringers and cups, Martelé. (*The Gorham Manufacturing Co.*)

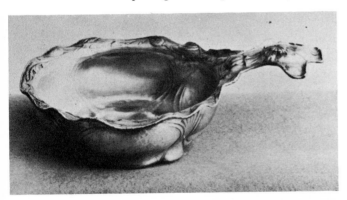

Child's christening set. (*The Gorham Manufacturing Co., 1874*)

However, of all the silverware made for children the most expensive and elaborate was Gorham's Martelé sets which were made in the 1890's and the first decade of the twentieth century. These included mugs, plates, and porringers.

Children's silverware is a field open to the beginning collector. Since many of the items are late in date and since there are few collectors the prices are reasonable.

11. SILVER THIMBLES AND SCISSORS

THE first silver thimbles used in America were imported from Europe but by the mid-eighteenth century thimbles were being made by American silversmiths. There are records of thimbles made by Paul Revere, one of which is in the Boston Museum of Art. A thimble marked "Hurd" made by Jacob Hurd is in the Mabel Brady Garvan Collection in the Yale University Art Gallery and a thimble marked "Halsted," made about 1790 when Benjamin Halsted operated a Thimble Manufactory in New York City, is in the collection of Elizabeth Galbraith Sickels. Halsted's was probably the first thimble manufactory in America although silversmiths had made thimbles as a side line along with such small articles as buttons, buckles and spoons. However, it is more than likely that most thimbles at this time were made to order, although at the beginning of the nineteenth century a few silversmiths advertised themselves as "Thimble Makers."

262

In 1824 James Peters was a maker of gold and silver thimbles in Philadelphia and in the 1830's Gorham, Webster & Price had a silver thimble manufactory at the back of their shop in Providence.

In New York George Platt set up in the business of thimble making in 1819 and later he took his two brothers into the business. This family of thimble makers of Huntington, Long Island, included the three Platt brothers, Ezra Prime, John Roshore and Edward Ketcham. Ezra Prime was a cousin of George Platt and served his apprenticeship in Platt's silver shop. In 1832 Prime left Platt and formed his own thimble manufacturing company at Huntington, Long Island, and by 1859 "Prime Thimbles"

RIGHT. Thimble advertisement, Philadelphia Directory, 1824. (*Courtesy of The New-York Historical Society, New York City*) BELOW. Silver thimbles made by Ketcham & McDougall. TOP LEFT. The Homestead, Hot Springs, Va. CENTER. Rococo embossed design. RIGHT. Design in patent papers, Sept. 20, 1881. BOTTOM LEFT. Alligator, Florida souvenir. BOTTOM CENTER. Coat of Arms, St. Augustine, Florida. BOTTOM RIGHT. Witch, Salem, Mass. (*Collection of Elizabeth G. Sickels*)

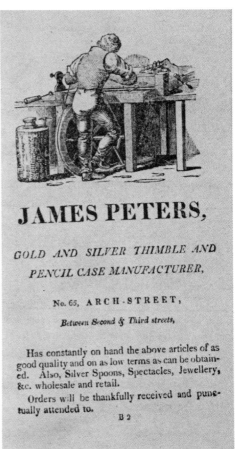

JAMES PETERS,

GOLD AND SILVER THIMBLE AND
PENCIL CASE MANUFACTURER,

No. 65, ARCH-STREET,

Between Second & Third streets,

Has constantly on hand the above articles of as good quality and on as low terms as can be obtained. Also, Silver Spoons, Spectacles, Jewellery, &c. wholesale and retail.

Orders will be thankfully received and punctually attended to.

B 2

were supplied to dealers throughout the United States and Europe. The business continued until 1890. Ketchum also started his own business and took McDougall as partner. The firm of Ketcham & McDougall became one of the largest thimble manufacturers in the United States. Another important thimble manufacturing company was Simons Brothers of Philadelphia. The company was founded by George W. Simons in 1839 or 1840 and is the only firm in America which is making gold and silver thimbles today.

In the early nineteenth century the decoration on thimbles, which consisted of flat chasing, punchwork and bright-cut engraving, was done by hand although the thimbles were usually made mechanically. Later a simple repeat border of lines, foliage or flowers was impressed by a roller. The earliest silver thimbles had pounced tops. Later an embossed scroll design decorated the tops of some thimbles and on these latter the borders were plain with an embossed edging. Trade names of late nineteenth century Ketcham & McDougall thimbles included Embossed Scroll, Embroidery Allover, Allover Embossed, and Louis XV. Other late nineteenth century thimbles had engraved borders of flowers such as pansy, lily-of-the-valley, wild rose, daisy, and autumn leaves. Other thimbles had engraved bands with scenes of houses, Dutch windmills, ships, or men with bicycles. There are also souvenir thimbles with scenes of historic places

LEFT. Silver mounted scissors and shears with leather sheath. (*Gorham Manufacturing Co. Catalogue*, 1894) BELOW LEFT. Grape scissors. (*Reed & Barton, 1895*)

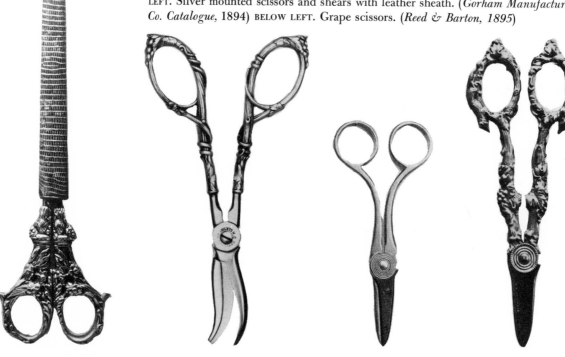

and buildings and World's Fair thimbles. Souvenir thimbles are still being made.

Early thimbles made before 1830 are rare. They are seldom marked by the maker but often are found with the name or initials of the owner. Many later thimbles are stamped with trade marks. Ketcham & McDougall thimbles are marked with their trade mark "MKD" impressed on the underside of the thimble apex. The small "c" hangs to the upper arm of the K and the "&" is in the lower enclosure. This mark was used from 1892. The Simons Brothers trademark is a shield with an old English "S" and the inscription "Established 1840" above. Prime Thimbles were not marked.

Small sewing scissors and curved blade manicure scissors offer a fertile field for the beginning collector. They were made in many designs by all of the silver manufacturing companies. The blades were usually made in Germany or England. The majority of the handles of these scissors are in rococo style with designs of "C" and "S" scrolls and flowers. However, there were a few scissors with unique handles such as the Salem Witch and the Hunter and Dog and the well-known small sewing scissors with stork handles. There are also grape scissors with handles in grape and leaf designs and there were shears with leather or silver sheaths.

TOP RIGHT. Long blade scissors. CENTER AND BOTTOM RIGHT. Pocket folding scissors. BELOW LEFT TO RIGHT. Grape scissors, grape design; grape scissors, fluted design; patent sliding blades for heavy cloth. (*Gorham Manufacturing Co. Catalogue*, 1894)

12. INDIAN PEACE MEDALS AND TRINKETS

FOR nearly three hundred years medals have been given to friendly American Indians. In colonial days the English and French had used silver Peace Medals and trinkets as a medium of exchange and friendship in trading and making treaties with the Indians. One of the earliest silversmiths to make Indian silver ornaments in the United States was Michael Letourneaux of New York as evidenced by the following advertisement: "Michael Letourneaux, Gold, Silversmith and Jeweler; He informs all merchants, traders, etc. to the interior of the United States of America, that having spent several years in Canada, he is perfectly acquainted with such ornamental manufactures in the above mentioned line as are adapted to the modern taste of the Indian native of the various tribes; not only in a style to gratify their vanity, but to advance a more important object to those concerned in the fur skin trade." (*Time Piece; and Literary Companion,* May 22, 1797)

The American Government followed the custom of making extensive gifts to Indians for friendly cooperation in the form of Peace Medals between the years 1789 and 1889. These medals were of two types: those issued by the United States Government in the name of the President, and those issued by fur trading companies or individuals. Medals given by the government were usually presented to chiefs or other influential men on the occasion of the signing of treaties or holding important conferences when federal representatives visited Indian country. These Indian Peace Medals were made by well-known eighteenth century American silversmiths including Joseph Richardson and Philip Syng of Philadelphia. The Oregon Peace Medal to the Northwest Indians was made by Paul Revere in 1787. It is in the Massachusetts Historical Society.

George Washington Peace Medals made between 1793 and 1795 were made by Joseph Richardson, with the exception of the Treaty of Greenville, and are marked with the maker's initials in a small square punch mark. Examples of these and other Peace Medals are in the American Numismatic Society, the Smithsonian Institution, the Chicago Historical Society, the Missouri Historical Society, the Pennsylvania Historical Society, and other public and private collections.

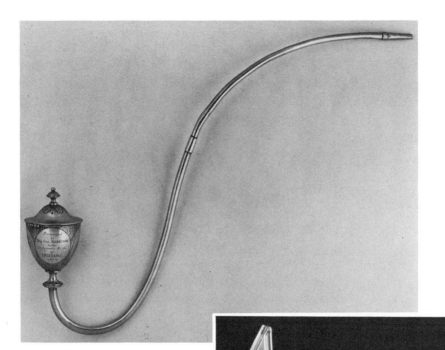

TOP. Indian Peace Pipe presented by Major General Harrison to the Delaware Tribe of Indians, 1814. (*The Smithsonian Institution*) CENTER. Silver breast ornament, Chippewa, Michigan. (*Photograph courtesy of Museum of the American Indian, Heye Foundation*) LEFT. George Washington Peace Medal, Joseph Richardson, 1792. (*Buffalo and Erie County Historical Society*)

Presidential peace medals continued to be made and distributed in 1801 by President Jefferson, and each President from James Madison down through 1889 with the exception of William Henry Harrison. The medal, made by Joseph Richardson and given to the famous Red Jacket, Chief of the Senecas, at the time of the conference of the Six Nations in Philadelphia, is now in the Buffalo and Erie County Historical Society.

Silver gorgets or crescents which were worn as breast ornaments were also made by well-known silversmiths and silver Peace Pipes were also distributed. The most valuable and ornamental Peace Pipe was that presented by General William Henry Harrison in 1814 to Indian tribes at the time of the treaty with the Northwestern Tribes of Indians. Pipes were presented to the Wyandotte, Delaware, and Shawnee Indian tribes, but the only one existing today is the Delaware pipe which is now in the

Silver brooches made by Seneca and Tuscarora Indians. (*Photograph courtesy of Museum of the American Indian, Heye Foundation*)

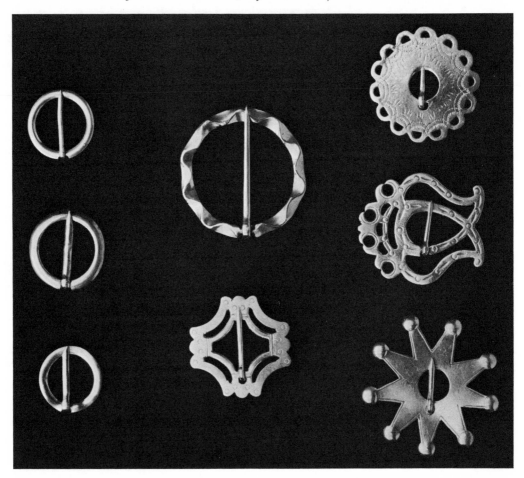

Smithsonian Institution. The pipe has an urn-shaped bowl with beading and acanthus leaf decoration in the Federal style and four oval medallions are ornamented and engraved with emblems of peace and friendship including clasped hands and a figure of an Indian and a General shaking hands and an eagle adapted from the Great Seal of the United States. The inscription in one oval reads: "Presented by Maj. Gen. Harrison to the Delaware Tribe of Indians 1814." Although the pipe is of excellent design and workmanship it bears no silversmith's mark. The complete story of the pipe is given in *Antiques* magazine, July, 1958.

Besides these important pieces there were also silver medals and ornaments of lesser value and with no special distinction, such as wrist and arm bands, hatbands, nose rings, earrings, pins and crosses. The designs of these ornaments were similar to Indian jewelry made today. Geometric piercings of hearts, triangles, circles, crescents and engraved lines, sometimes including leaves, were seen on pins and earrings of star and circle shapes whose edges were accented with silver balls. The half-bracelet and the necklace of pomegranate design were also made. Such trinkets were given by the Lewis and Clark Expedition and later by the fur traders, many of whom had Western divisions with headquarters in St. Louis, Missouri. There were silversmiths in St. Louis at this time and it is only natural that they would be called upon to make these Indian ornaments. The story of Antoine Danjen who advertised himself as a "Silversmith and Manufacturer of Indian Trinkets" in the *St. Louis Republican* throughout the year 1818, is told in the article already cited by Ruth Hunter Roach in *Antiques* magazine, July, 1958. Danjen made Indian trinkets for John Mason, Superintendent of Indian Affairs in 1810, the American Fur Company, and the Columbia Fur Company. Danjen shared the silver ornament trade with seven other silversmiths of St. Louis. There were also many other American silversmiths of the first quarter of the nineteenth century who made Indian trinkets but many of these Indian ornaments were made in Montreal by Robert Cruickshank and other Canadian silversmiths.

Indian trinkets were usually found in Indian burial mounds and there are probably many more to be dug up. Occasionally one sees a trinket in an antique shop but since similar ornaments are still being made by Indians in Arizona and New Mexico it is difficult to distinguish between the old and the new. Those made in Canada are marked "Montreal."

13 MEDALS OF SCHOLARSHIP

SMALL oval, round, and shield-shaped silver medals were made by American silversmiths and given by schools and societies in recognition of scholarship or achievement in the arts. These date from the late eighteenth century through the first quarter of the nineteenth century. Medals were cut from thin pieces of silver and the decoration seldom included more than names and other lettering and borders of bright-cut engraving although some had moulded or gadrooned borders. An examination of those in the Henry Ford Museum, the du Pont Winterthur Museum, the Bostonian Society, and the Albany Institute of Science and Art turned up few marked pieces although the small medals made by Paul Revere are often marked and thus reveal the fact that no job was too small for even this most important silversmith.

These small tokens were probably made by the local silversmith. Several have been found made by Francis Shallus, the engraver of Philadelphia (1773–1821), and are so marked. In Albany Ezra Ames engraved Masonic Medals and other small items for the silversmiths Isaac and George Hutton and John W. Fryer. Awards of merit were known to have been distributed by Mrs. Rivard's Seminary of Philadelphia and Miss Martineau's Seminary, and by the Phillips School, Mrs. Rowson's Academy and the Adams Public School of Boston. Also the Franklin School of Boston distributed medals as late as 1852. The giving of medals for scholarship was also probably the practice in other schools in the larger cities of nineteenth century America. The later medals were cast. In Columbus, Ohio, P. H. Olmstead, silversmith, advertised in 1830: "Specializes in silver seals and badges for the Sons of Temperance."

These medals although of considerable worth may be found among a tray of buttons and other small objects in a thrift or secondhand shop where they have been sent after an attic cleaning at the settling of an old estate.

TOP. Silver medals of scholarship, c. 1800. BOTTOM. Shield-shaped medal for scholarship in Painting and Geography, early 19th century. (*All The Metropolitan Museum of Art, bequest of A. T. Clearwater, 1933*)

We have seen in the course of this book that from Colonial days silver was an investment and a yardstick by which a man's wealth was judged. Gifts of plate in the form of cups, boxes, bowls and ewers were a mark of esteem. Silver was first in the service of the Church. As time progressed silver entered all walks of life and picked up the customs, reflected the times and changed with the fashions of the day. The earliest domestic plate catered to the arts of eating and drinking, but no article was too small or insignificant for the hammer of the silversmith. As the nineteenth century progressed the scope widened with the change of manners and

UPPER LEFT AND LOWER RIGHT. Obverse and reverse of gold medal won by Victorine du Pont at Mrs. Rivardi's Seminary in 1807. Francis Shallus, engraver. UPPER RIGHT AND LOWER LEFT. Obverse and reverse of Reward of Merit for writing won by H. Carey at Miss Martineau's Seminary in 1818. (*All courtesy Henry Francis du Pont Winterthur Museum*)

customs and included not only the niceties of tea, coffee and punch drinking but such refinements as fancy serving pieces and articles for the dressing table, the desk and even the bookmark and baggage label. The shift from hand-made to factory-made products not only yielded a vast quantity of silver but also a wide variety of articles. Large expensive pieces such as loving cups, candelabra and centerpieces still demanded a certain amount of handwork, but small articles could be cut and stamped out by machine and these numerous small articles broaden the field of nineteenth century silver collecting. The elite circle of silver collectors have now widened their interests to include the nineteenth century but the vast factory output has also brought silver collecting within the reach of the small collector with little money to spend. There are many collectors of spoons, but there are also neglected fields such as children's silver. Also there is happy hunting in such articles as nut picks, baggage tags, liquor corks, bottle openers, thimbles, and bookmarks, for no object was too small or trivial for the nineteenth century silver manufacturer.

LEFT TOP TO BOTTOM. Obverse and reverse of silver medals for best in class presented at Mrs. Rowson's Academy in 1819 and at Phillips School in 1833. Boston, Massachusetts. RIGHT. Franklin School Medal given to Charles C. Haven, in 1852. (*All courtesy of Bostonian Society, Old State House*)

Glossary

Amorini: Cupids or cherubs in Italian art.

Amphora: Greek vase with ovoid-shaped body, wide shoulders, short neck and loop handles.

Anthemion: Greek honeysuckle.

Arabesque: An intricate interwoven design of the Italian Renaissance.

Beading: A border ornament composed of small beadlike nodules. A popular ornament on silver in the last quarter of the eighteenth century and early nineteenth century.

Bright-cut: A form of sharp cut decoration in which the metal is removed by cutting tools to give a faceted sparkle to the surface.

Buff: To polish with a hand buff or buffing machine to smoothe the surface of the metal.

Burnishing: Rubbing the silver surface with a tool to smoothe and harden the metal and thus increase the durability.

Butler's Finish: A finish produced by a wheel of wire which makes tiny scratches giving the article a dull surface.

Cann: A lidless one-handled drinking vessel.

Cartouche: A decorative motif in the form of a shield or scroll with curled edges.

Caryatid: A statue of a woman used as a column.

Caudle Cup: A two-handled deep bowl used to serve the wine-flavored gruel called "caudle."

Chasing: A form of decoration produced by chisels and hammers. A raised ornament also called embossing.

Engraving: An ornament made by cutting lines in the silver.

Epergne: A centerpiece for the dining-table with vase and baskets for fruit, flowers and bonbons.

Etching: A surface decoration bitten-in with acid.

Feather Edge: A narrow chased edge of slanting lines.

Finial: A terminating or capping ornament on covers, varying in form from simple twistings to acorns, pineapples, flowers or animals.

Flatware: A general term for cutlery such as knives, forks and spoons.

Fluting: A type of grooving.

Fly Spoon: A spoon with a cut-out design in its bowl. It was used to remove flies or specks of dirt from the wine in the chalice.

Gadroon: A border ornament of reeds and flutes usually spiraled, sometimes called Knurling.

Geometric: An angled line design.

Guilloche: An ornamental motif consisting of interlacing circular forms usually with a conventional flower center.

Hollow ware: Articles in the form of hollow vessels such as bowls, mugs, pitchers and pots.

Husks: Festoons of seeds as in Adam Style decoration.

Matted: A dull surface made by light hammering to contrast with a burnished shiny surface.

Monteith: A large bowl with notched rim for chilling drinking glasses.

Niello: Line engraving on gold or silver which is filled in with a type of black enamel.

Oxidizing: An application of an oxide which darkens the surface of the metal. It is used in shadows to give depth.

273

Planishing: To make smooth with a planishing hammer to cover up hammer marks.

Plateau: Low long centerpiece for a dining table.

Repoussé: Relief ornament hammered from the inner side of the metal.

Rope molding: A type of border resembling a rope.

Rococo: A style of decoration characterized by curvilinear form imitative of scrolls, foliage and shellwork, asymmetrically arranged.

Satin finish: A dull appearance produced by a revolving wheel of small wires.

Scroll: A spiral or rolled decoration. S-scroll: A scroll in the form of the letter "S".

Spinning: A process of forming hollow ware by pressing the flat sheet of silver over a revolving lathe.

Strapwork: Narrow folded interlacing bands or straps.

Touch: A silversmith's mark impressed with a punch.

Bibliography

SILVER IN GENERAL

AVERY, C. LOUISE, *Early American Silver.* The Century Co., New York, 1930.

BIGELOW, FRANCIS HILL, *Historic Silver of The Colonies and Its Makers.* Tudor Publishing Company, New York, 1948.

HAMMERSLOUGH, PHILIP H., *American Silver* (3 vols., 2 supplements). Privately printed, Hartford, Conn., 1958–1967.

PHILLIPS, JOHN MARSHALL, *American Silver.* Chanticleer Press, New York, 1949.

WENHAM, EDWARD, *The Practical Book of American Silver.* J. B. Lippincott Co., Philadelphia, 1949.

BUHLER, KATHRYN C., "Silver 1640–1820", *The Concise Encyclopedia of American Antiques.* Hawthorn Books, Inc., New York

BOGER, H. BATTERSON and LOUISE ADE, *The Dictionary of Antiques and the Decorative Arts.* Charles Scribner's Sons, New York, 1957.

WYLER, SEYMOUR B., *The Book of Old Silver.* Crown Publishers, New York, 1937.

MAY, EARL CHAPIN, *A Century of Silver, 1847–1947.* Robert McBride Co., New York, 1947.

REGIONAL SILVER

BRIX, MAURICE, *List of Philadelphia Silversmiths and Allied Artificers from 1682 to 1850.*

BURTON, E. MILBY, *South Carolina Silversmiths, 1690–1860.* The Charleston Museum, Charleston, 1942.

CURTIS, GEORGE MUNSON, *Early Silver of Connecticut and Its Makers.* International Silver Co., Meriden, Conn., 1939.

FALES, MARTHA GANDY, *American Silver in The Henry Francis du Pont Winterthur Museum.* Winterthur, Delaware, 1958.

CARLISLE, LILLIAN BAKER, "Vermont Silver". *Spinning Wheel,* September 1966.

CUTTEN, GEORGE BARTON, *Silversmiths of Georgia.* Pigeonhole Press, Savannah, Ga., 1958.

WILLIAMS, JAMES A., "Savannah Silver and Silversmiths". *Antiques* Magazine, March 1967.

CUTTEN, GEORGE BARTON, *Silversmiths of Northampton, Massachusetts, and Vicinity to 1850.* Pamphlet. No date.

CUTTEN, GEORGE BARTON, *Silversmiths of North Carolina,* State Department of

Archives & History, Raleigh, N.C., 1948.

CUTTEN, GEORGE BARTON and MINNIE WARREN, *Silversmiths of Utica.* Hamilton, N.Y., 1936.

CUTTEN, GEORGE BARTON, *Silversmiths, Watchmakers and Jewelers of the State of New York Outside New York City.* Hamilton, N.Y., 1939.

CUTTEN, GEORGE BARTON, *Silversmiths of Virginia.* The Dietz Press, Richmond, Va., 1952.

HARRINGTON, JESSE, *Silversmiths of Delaware, 1700–1850.* Delaware National Society of Colonial Dames. 1939.

HIATT, NOBLE W. and LUCY F., *The Silversmiths of Kentucky.* The Standard Printing Co., 1954. Louisville, Ky.

HOITMA, MURIEL CUTTEN, *Early Cleveland Silversmiths.* Gates Publishing Co., Cleveland, Ohio, 1953.

KNITTLE, RHEA MANSFIELD, *Early Ohio Silversmiths and Pewterers, 1787–1847.* Ohio Frontier Series. Calvert-Hatch Co., Cleveland, 1943.

MILLER, V. ISABELLE, *Silver by New York Makers; Late 17th Century to 1900.* Museum of the City of New York. 1938.

New York State Silversmiths. Darling Foundation, Eggertsville, N.Y., 1965.

SABINE, JULIA, "Silversmiths of New Jersey, 1623–1800". Proceedings of the New Jersey Historical Society, LXI, No. 3, July, 1943 & No. 4, Oct. 1943.

ROACH, RUTH HUNTER, *St. Louis Silversmiths.* Eden Publishing House, St. Louis, 1967.

SCHILD, JOAN LYNN, *Silversmiths of Rochester, N.Y.* Rochester Museum of Arts and Sciences, 1944.

WILLIAMS, CARL M., *Silversmiths of New Jersey, 1700–1823.* George S. MacManus Co., Philadelphia, 1949.

VICTORIAN

HARDT, ANTON, *Souvenir Spoons of The 90's.* Privately Printed, N.Y.

MC CLINTON, KATHARINE MORRISON, *Collecting American Victorian Antiques.* Charles Scribner's Sons, Inc., New York, 1966.

MC CLINTON, KATHARINE MORRISON, *Complete Book of Small Antiques Collecting.* Coward-McCann, 1965.

SCHMIDT, GERTRUDE, "Gorham Spoons in Sets". *Spinning Wheel,* March, 1967.

SCHWARTZ, MARVIN, *Victoriana, An Exhibition of the Arts of the Victorian Era in America.* The Brooklyn Museum. 1960.

PRESENTATION SILVER

HILL, H. W., *Maryland Silver Service.* Waverly Press Inc., Baltimore, Md. 1962.

HOLLOWAY, H. MAXON, "American Presentation Silver". The New-York Historical Society Quarterly, Vol. XXX, Oct. 1946, No. 4.

KLAPTHOR, MARGARET BROWN, *Presentation Pieces in the Museum of History and Technology.* Smithsonian Institution, Washington, D.C. 1965.

MC CLINTON, KATHARINE MORRISON, "American Presentation Silver of the Seventeenth and Eighteenth Centuries". Part I, December, 1967. Part 11, January, 1968. "American Nineteenth Century Presentation Silver". March, 1968. *The Connoisseur,* London, England.

SWORDS

ALTMAYER, JAY P., *American Presentation Swords.* The Rankin Press, Mobile, Alabama, 1958.

PETERSON, HAROLD L., *The American Sword 1775–1945.* Ray Riling Press, Philadelphia.

INDIAN MEDALS, TRINKETS AND PEACE PIPES

BELDEN, BAUMAN H., *Indian Peace Medals Issued in the United States, 1789–1889.*

N. Flayderman & Co., New Milford, Conn., 1966.

LINDSAY, G. CARROLL, "The Treaty Pipe of the Delawares". *Antiques* Magazine, July, 1958.

ROACH, RUTH HUNTER, "Midwestern Silversmiths in the Trinket Trade". *Antiques* Magazine, July, 1958.

CHURCH SILVER

ANSON, PETER, *Fashions in Church Furnishings, 1840-1940*. The Faith Press, London, 1960.

JONES, E. ALFRED, *Old Silver of American Churches*. Privately printed for the National Society of Colonial Dames of America. 1913.

OMAN, CHARLES, *English Church Plate 1597-1830*. Oxford University Press, New York, 1957.

MARKS

ENSKO, ROBERT, *American Silversmiths and Their Marks, I, II, III*, 1927, 1937, 1948. Privately Printed, New York.

RAINWATER, DOROTHY, *American Silver Manufacturers*. Everybody's Press, Hanover, Pennsylvania, 1966.

KOVEL, RALPH M. and TERRY H., *A Directory of American Silver, Pewter, and Silverplate*. Crown Publishers, New York, 1961.

GLEANINGS FROM OLD NEWSPAPERS

DOW, GEORGE FRANCIS, "The Arts & Crafts in New England, 1704-1775". The Wayside Press, Topsfield, Massachusetts, 1927.

GOTTSMAN, RITA, "The Arts and Crafts in New York, 1726-1762". "The Arts and Crafts in New York, 1777-1779". "The Arts and Crafts in New York, 1800-1804". The New-York Historical Society, New York. 1965.

PRIME, ALFRED COXE, "Arts and Crafts in Philadelphia, Maryland and South Carolina, 1786-1800". Walpole Society, 1933.

CATALOGUES

Chicago Historical Society. "Samuel Kirk and Son: American Silver Craftsmen Since 1815". Catalogue, 1966.

"Kirk in U.S. Museums". Samuel Kirk and Son, Baltimore.

"Pelletreau, Elias, Long Island Silversmith and His Sources of Design". The Brooklyn Museum, 1959.

The Newark Museum. "Classical America 1815-1845". Exhibition Catalogue, 1963.

JOHNSON, J. STEWART, "Silver in Newark", A Newark 300th Aniversary Study. The Museum, New Series, Vol. 18. Nos. 3 & 4. Summer-Fall 1966. The Newark Museum.

RICE, NORMAN S., "Albany Silver 1652-1825". Albany Institute of History & Art, 1964.

The New Haven Colony Historical Society, "An Exhibition of New Haven Silver". 1967.

The Gorham Manufacturing Company. Catalogues, 1880's-1890's.

Unger Brothers, Newark, N.J., Catalogue 1900.

Whiting Manufacturing Company, New York, Catalogue, 1895. The Metropolitan Museum of Art.

MAGAZINES

Antiques Journal
Antiques Magazine
Apollo, London, England
Art Journal, 1875, 1876
The Connoisseur, London, England
Jewelers' Circular 1869-1968
Spinning Wheel
Western Collector

Index